T4-ATW-196

HAULING UP THE MORNING

Edited by

Tim Blunk
Raymond Luc Levasseur

and the editors of

Jacobin Books

THE RED SEA PRESS
Publishers & Distributors of Third World Books
15 Industry Court
Trenton, NJ 08638

The Red Sea Press, Inc.
15 Industry Court
Trenton, New Jersey 08638

Cover art by Tim Blunk
Cover graphics and design by Beth Ruck

Electronic typesetting by Malcolm Litchfield

Library of Congress Catalog Card Number: 90-61145

ISBN: 0-932415-59-8   Cloth
           0-932415-60-1   Paper

Contents

Chapter 1   HARD TIME

Chapter 2 ROOTS IN THE PEOPLE

Chapter 3 LOVE AND OTHER MYSTERIES

Chapter 4 TEACH THE CHILDREN

CONTENTS

Chapter 5 IDEAS ARE WEAPONS

Chapter 6 DREAMS ARE STRUGGLE TOO

Chapter 7 *REMEMBER THE FIGHTERS*

MIKE McCOY

THOMAS MANNING

CHIM TRANG

List of Color Illustrations
Between pages 200 and 201

Acknowledgements

Cover Design and Graphics: Beth Ruck
Cover Art: Tim Blunk
Art Editor: Beth Ruck
Art Photography: Fred Moore

Special thanks to Soffiyah Elijah, Judy Jensen, Betsy Mickel, Mary O'Melveny, Chris Ryan, Sandy Simpson, *compañeros* of the MLN— and all those whose concrete revolutionary solidarity (that is, work) made this book possible.

The title of this book is from *Poems*, Roque Dalton, translated by Richard Schaaf, Curbstone Press, Willimantic, Connecticut, 1984.

Dalou Asahi's work is reprinted from *Fighting Back!* Attica Memorial Book, 1974; with permission of Attica Brothers Legal Defense.

Some of the biographical information in this book comes from *Can't Jail the Spirit*, Editorial El Coqui, Chicago, 1989.

Ethel Rosenberg's "If We Die" is from *The Rosenbergs: Collected Visions of Artists and Writers*, Rob Okun, ed., Universe Books, 1988. It is reprinted here with the permission of her sons, Robert and Michael Meeropol.

"who killed mcduffie" from POW Journal #6 is reprinted with the permission of Spear & Shield, Chicago IL.

William Kunstler

Preface

These are the voices of political dissenters held in United States prisons. It is vitally important that they be heard, because those who have deprived them of their liberty miss no opportunity to deny vociferously that this country incarcerates people because of their political beliefs. Only one Supreme Court Justice— the late William O. Douglas— has ever publicly admitted that we have political trials on these shores, but everyone close to the legal process well understands that we do, even though few have the temerity to admit it publicly.

The selections in this volume are extremely varied, reflecting the diverse background and life experiences of their creators. What unifies them all, however, is the fact that they originate from men and women who know that they have been singled out for medieval treatment by a government that both hates and fears them. They must be listened to, if only to expose the hypocrisy of a nation that so easily and so often points an accusing finger at other countries for allegedly doing the same thing— that is, using their legal and penal systems to deter or inhibit political dissent.

Yet, there is so much more to be gained from these selections. They prove that the human spirit is indomitable, that penitentiary walls, no matter how high or how impenetrable, cannot still the tongues of those they imprison, and that art exists in the unlikeliest of places. This eloquent collection more than deserves the widest audience possible.

William Kunstler is an attorney who has long been active in support of human rights and revolutionary struggles.

xvii

The Editors

An Introductory Note

This book was born of a desire to fight a lie: the US government's incredible assertion that it holds no political prisoners. Herein we have collected the writings and artwork of some 65 political prisoners and anti-colonial prisoners of war formerly or currently held in U.S. federal and state prisons. To tell the truth about the U.S. political prisoners is to reclaim our history— the real history of the progressive social movements of the past 25 years. While the Civil Rights movement is celebrated, sanitized and rendered safe for high school textbooks and TV docudramas, some of the most dedicated fighters for Black liberation are approaching their 20th year behind the walls. George Bush mouths hollow rhetoric about Puerto Rico's self-determination while the US holds over 20 *independentistas* as prisoners of war and political prisoners.

To maintain the fiction of social peace, the US ruling class cultivates social amnesia. The penitentiaries are essential to this project. Branded "criminals" or "terrorists," social activists and militants are removed from our movements, communities and families and exiled to human warehouses. We are *disappeared* from the American consciousness, along with our histories. Our identities are denied; our very humanity is thrown into contention. Acts of rebellion, civil disobedience, and armed resistance are erased. The seams of a fictionalized past and a pacified future are drawn together around us and stapled with iron bars. But as in so many struggles around the world, we will not be denied. We organize. We fight. We dream. We create.

As editors we did not solicit or select materials based upon any political criteria. This is what the prisoners chose to contribute;

this is who we are. Struggle is clearly what is on our minds. The architects of prison repression would strip our lives of any context, any reference points that might affirm our choices. Our sacrifice should have no meaning (just as our movements should learn to stay within the bounds of powerlessness). Instead, we create a political context around us. Through writing and the creation of art we are learning to fight the lie and fight to love. It is the simple dignity of human labor that is *our own*, that we give to our struggles.

Particularly in the isolation units, where increasing numbers of us are held, words and images form the substance of life beyond the walls. They are the lifelines that connect us to those we love; they connect our movements to their own history. The pages of this book are filled with the works of those who now must discover new ways to communicate our transforming love for this world and its struggling peoples.

It bears mentioning that contrary to popular belief, prison is far from the ideal environment for the creative process. Prisoners who have nothing but idle time to fill are rare. Most prisoners work at least 40-hour weeks, often under sweatshop conditions for pitiful wages. Like most artists we must buy our own materials, and access to them is subject to arbitrary security regulations and administrative whim. Noise and overcrowded living quarters are much more the rule than the popularly imagined monastic cell. The mental peace needed to write is very hard to come by. There is no privacy; solitude is uncommon except in its numbing excesses within the control units. Then, too, there are few situations in the street where one's studio or workspace is subject to searches and destruction on a routine basis. These conditions hold for all prison writers and artists. When it comes to political prisoners, the more-or-less random abuses to which all are subject become systematic. This was the case with at least one of the contributors here, Puerto Rican POW Elizam Escobar, whose extraordinary artwork was exhibited on an international tour entitled "Art as an Act of Liberation." As the tour began in the US, Elizam found himself suddenly transferred to a federal prison where he was denied materials and space to paint.

When art becomes more than a "secure" prison pastime, when it becomes a threat to the lie, it will be suppressed.

It is not the purpose of this book to promote a particular definition of "political prisoner." While the majority of those prisoners whose works are presented here would meet almost any criteria based upon international law and custom, we have also included work by social prisoners who have become politically conscious and active in prison. To do otherwise would be to deny the reality of the US, where the criminal justice system and its prisons are principal tools of colonial as well as class oppression. Malcolm X and George Jackson are but the best-known examples of "common criminals" who were transformed in prison and became leaders of their people. We are proud to include here the works of comrades whose politics and practice were forged under the most difficult conditions imaginable, where the penalties are most severe.

We did not set out, nor do we claim, to represent all of the political prisoners in the US. There are many others, some known and some unknown to us, who have not contributed to this book, but none were consciously excluded by us.

Some of the prisoners have contributed under pseudonyms. There are many comrades we know who were arrested in the course of clandestine political work and have chosen to keep their heads down inside. This book is but one of the ways they continue to participate in the life of their movements while awaiting better days.

It is said that for every person behind the walls, a family does time. We have included some materials from the families of political prisoners. We regret not having more, because it is a sad reality that prison distorts the lives of many others beyond the individual prisoner—especially of children.

This collection is bilingual. Unless otherwise noted, English translations were provided by the authors. Some writers did not want their works translated; these appear in the original Spanish.

A final note about the title: *Hauling Up the Morning/Izando la Mañana* comes from a poem written in the form of a letter from prison, from the Salvadoran revolutionary poet Roque Dalton to Turkish poet/political prisoner Nazim Hikmet. An excerpt from the poem:

according to the news
other comrades have been arrested.
I enclose some poems from these last days,
where friends speak from their cells,
    only some of them, there are three hundred and twenty of us.

Will you give my regards to Memet? And you
take good care of your heart . . .
So long. May we keep on
hauling up the morning.

from "Letter to Nazim Hikmet," POEMS, Roque Dalton; translation:
      Richard Schaaf; Willimantic, CT, Curbstone Press, 1984.

    The translator Richard Schaaf tells us that *izar* in this context is
a rather "un-poetic" word, dockworkers' slang used by Dalton to
evoke the common feel of daily labor.
    Strong hands are needed to greet the dawn.

                        —TIM BLUNK, FROM A FEDERAL
                        PRISON, FOR THE EDITORS

This book is dedicated to Yuri Kochiyama
Steadfast on the outside
for those who stand fast
on the inside

Assata Shakur

Introduction

No One Can Stop the Rain

Watch, the grass is growing.
Watch, but don't make it obvious.
Let your eyes roam casually, but watch!
In any prison yard, you can see it, — growing.
In the cracks, in the crevices, between the steel and the concrete,
    out of the dead grey dust, the bravest blades
    of grass shoot up, bold and full of life.
Watch, the grass is growing. It is growing through the cracks.
The guards say grass is against the law.
Grass is contraband in prison.
The guards say that the grass is insolent.
It is uppity grass, radical grass, runaway grass, militant
    grass, terrorist grass, they call it weeds.
Nasty weeds, nigga weeds, dirty spic, savage indian, wetback,
    pinko, commie weeds, — subversive!
And so the guards try to wipe out the grass.
They yank it from its roots.
They poison it with drugs.
They maul it.
They rake it.
Blades of grass have been found hanging in cells, covered
    with bruises, "apparent suicides."
The guards say that the "GRASS IS UNAUTHORIZED."
"DO NOT LET THE GRASS GROW."

We say, "DO NOT STEP ON THE GRASS."
You can spy on the grass.
You can lock up the grass.
You can mow it down, temporarily,
but you will never keep it from growing.
Watch, the grass is beautiful.
The guards try to mow it down, but it keeps on growing.
The grass grows into a poem.
The grass grows into a song.
The grass paints itself across the canvas of life.
And the picture is clear, and the lyrics are true,
   and haunting voices sing so sweet and strong,
   that the people hear the grass from far away.
And the people start to dance, and the people start to sing,
   and the song is freedom.
Watch! the grass is growing.

As of January, 1989, there were 627,402 men and women in U.S. prisons. In other words, there are more people locked in U.S. prisons than the entire populations of Grenada, Dominica, St. Lucia, St. Vincent, St. Croix and the Falkland Islands combined. Since 1970, the prison population has increased by almost 150%. The U.S. prison population is growing at the alarming rate of more than 170 persons a day. The statistics are frightening but the reality is even more frightening. As the rich get richer and poor get poorer, the country becomes more and more a police state, a prison state. It is not a question of law and order. The rich make the laws and the poor are forced to take the orders. Amerika is a country that has gone from fugitive slave laws, to Jim Crow laws, to sedition laws, to McCarthyite laws, to the so-called anti-terrorist laws, without the slightest semblance of justice. Justice has meant "just-us" rich white folks, and injustice for the oppressed African, Asian, Latino, indigenous people and poor whites who live in the united states. The law is used as a weapon. The law is used as a political weapon.

Since way before the time of Jesus, the law has been used to imprison or crucify those who would run the money changers out of

2

the temple or fight for the meek and hungry. And with the rise of capitalism, and the rise of imperialism, and the rise of racist exploitation, we have seen the rise of liberation movements. More and more, prisons have been used as instruments of torture, instruments of control. As people all over the world have cried out for freedom, freedom-fighters all over the world have found themselves in chains. Leaders like Ho Chi Minh in Viet Nam, Fidel Castro in Cuba, Kwame Nkrumah in Ghana, and Agostinho Neto in Angola all became political prisoners, and somehow all survived to become heads of their countries, and lead their countries to independence. They carried the songs within them, they carried the poems within them, they carried the spirit within them, that indomitable spirit of struggle.

Prison Diary

> your body is locked behind bars,
> but your spirit remains free
> to soar as high as the stars,
> confident of what will be.
>
> — Ho Chi Minh

It couldn't be stopped, it couldn't be ignored, it couldn't be imprisoned, it couldn't be killed. Freedom was a pregnant poem, waiting to give birth, waiting to be real. In a farewell poem to his mother, thirty years before Angola was liberated, Agostinho Neto wrote:

> My mother
> (all black mothers whose sons have gone)
> You taught me to wait and hope
> As you hoped in difficult hours
> But life killed in me that mystic hope
> I do not wait now
> I am he who is awaited
> It is I my mother

3

Hope is us
Your children
Gone for a faith that sustains life.

No mysticism, just work and struggle and sacrifice. Whatever the consequences, the struggle had to go on, the struggle had to triumph. Prison was not a place for defeat, it was a place for study, for preparation. Fidel Castro wrote while in prison:

What a tremendous school this prison is! Here I have rounded out my view of the world and determined the meaning of my life. I don't know if it will be long or short, fruitful or in vain, but my dedication to sacrifice and struggle has been reaffirmed. I abhor being tied to petty trifles of comfort and self-interest.

Deep inside the U.S., in the belly of the beast, it is not easy to hear the songs and the poems of freedom. The people suffer, but their cries are drowned out by the lie machine.

Everything's good in Amerika
it's like Hollywood in Amerika

The criminals become the victims and the victims become the criminals, the cowboys are the good guys and the Indians are the bad guys, and freedom is a commodity that you can buy on the install-ment plan, but only if you have the down-payment. Democracy is painted on the minds of the people, like lipstick and mascara, while most elections are contests between rich white men who try to outdo each other in advertising wars.

Everything's fair in Amerika
you get your share in Amerika

Except if you're poor or working class, jobless or homeless, and you don't belong to the jet set. Except if you're one of the elderly who froze to death because the heat was turned off, or a 13 year old kid shot down by some racist cop.

Everything's fine in Amerika
you have a good time in Amerika

4

But in the land of the free and the brave, nothing is free and you have to be brave just to walk down the streets. Babies are dying because their parents can't pay for operations, the education system is turning out a nation of illiterates and the youth are given nothing to believe in. The lie machine tries to convince the people that a good time can be found in a crack vial, or in a syringe, in a Budweiser beer can or out riding horses in Marlboro country. While the police are selling drugs out a squad cars, the government is trying to make people believe that it is really committed to stopping the drug traffic.

The lie machine tells us that there are no political prisoners in the united states of amerika. But in a country as violent as the U.S., in a country that has intervened militarily hundreds of times, in hundreds of places, in a country that trains other countries in the techniques of torture, in a country that produced the Palmer raids, the McCarthy witch-hunts, it is absurd to believe that there are no political prisoners. The u.s. government has unleashed one of the most vicious counter-intelligence programs in history (COINTELPRO) against its own people (a program that is still being carried on today under other names), a program that "neutralized" political activists by falsely charging them with crimes, then locking them up and throwing away the key. The lie machine tells us that there are no political prisoners in the U.S. but we remember Sacco and Vanzetti, Joe Hill, Angelo Herndon and Marcus Garvey. We remember the Trenton Six, the Chicago Seven, the RNA 11 and the Panther 21. We remember the Rosenbergs, we remember Geronimo and Tetumke Witko (Crazy Horse). We remember Pedro Albizu Campos. We remember Oscar Collazo, Rafael Cancel Miranda, Irvin Flores, Andres Figueroa and Lolita Lebrón who each spent more than 25 years in prison for the crime of fighting for the independence of Puerto Rico. We remember the countless numbers of people who found themselves behind bars during the civil rights movement, during the rebellions and social upheavels of the late 1960s and early 1970s.

When you deny the political prisoners of a people, then you are in fact denying the validity of their struggle. When you deny your support to Nelson Mandela, then you are denying your support for the oppressed people of South Africa, and their struggle for liberation. Every repressive nation in history has denied the existence of political prisoners, referring to its victims as common criminals. It would

5

indeed be a crime, if we would let ourselves be duped by the preposterous denials of the U.S. government, or let ourselves be fooled by the government's hypocritical posturing around the issue of human rights. The U.S. court system has been used so relentlessly to wage war on the legitimate struggles of oppressed people, that many activists have absolutely refused to participate in the U.S. government's systemized form of legal lynching. They completely reject the government's legal, political or moral jurisdiction over their lives, accurately referring to themselves as prisoners of war.

The contributors to this anthology are political men and women. They are being held in prison because of their political beliefs and because of their political struggles. They are in prison because they struggle for liberation, because they struggle against racist oppression, because they struggle against imperialism, and against the U.S. colonization of Puerto Rico and the Virgin Islands. They are in prison because they struggle against the arms race, the rape of the environment, against nuclear waste and against the genocidal policies of the U.S. government. They are in prison because they are struggling for oppressed people's right to self-determination and for the liberation of African, Asian, Latin American and indigenous people all over the world. They are in prison because they struggle for socialism, for peace and for a new world political and economic order. Most have spent years in the movement. Some became political activists in universities, some in prison, and others in the streets. Some are Muslims, some are Christians, some are atheists, but they are united in their struggle for freedom, justice and a better world.

Because they are political prisoners, they have been subjected to the most cruel, vicious treatment that the prison system is capable of perpetrating. They are placed in maximum security control units, in solitary confinement, and subjected to all kinds of harassment, humiliation and violence. But in spite of their suffering they are strong. In spite of their suffering they make beauty. In spite of their suffering they write poems and sing songs and paint paintings. It is that spirit at work. It is that magic at work. Not the magic of pigeons in hats, but the magic of love and determination.

6

On the Road

My legs are tied with a rope, and my arms are bound
at my side,
but I smell the sweet perfume of woodland flowers
and hear the birds.
Impossible to keep these from me.
Anyhow, now the road is not so long,
And I am not alone.

— Ho Chi Minh

There exists no magic like the magic of truth and justice. There exists no beauty like the beauty of freedom.

In many places the grass is growing wild. In many places the grass is growing out of control. One day soon you will see the grass growing out of keyholes, over fences, through police barricades. You will see grass growing out of the barrels of guns and you will hear the grass sing of freedom. It is inevitable. Nothing can stop it, nothing can silence it. In the words of Agostinho Neto:

Here in prison
rage contained in my breast
I patiently wait
for the clouds to gather
blown by the wind of history
No one
Can stop the rain.

The grass is growing. Watch!

Black Panther leader Assata Shakur (also known as Joanne Chesimard) was captured in 1973 after a shootout on the New Jersey turnpike. A target of the FBI's COINTELPRO program, she was unjustly convicted of murder and sentenced to life in prison. In 1978 she escaped and was given political asylum in Cuba. Her autobiography Assata was published by Lawrence Hill Books in 1987.

Chapter One

HARD TIME

We are men, we are not beasts,
and we do not intend to be
beaten or driven as such.

—L. D. BARKLEY

Dalou Asahi

The Bangs in Prison

Bang, quiet & listen! Stay in single file.
One bang means line up and keep quiet; two bangs
means stop or go— understand? and any more bangs—
then it's on your head . . .
OK, turn around— strip and take everything off! pause—
pass your fingers through your hair, let's see your palms,
the other side, raise your arms, lift your balls, turn
around— spread your cheeks, lift your feet— now the
other one . . .
OK, Bang! Step up one— give your name, charge, bit—
and remember the number you'll be given— at all times—
Ready, move it! Pause . . .
OK, Bang! You'll be assigned a cell ... at 8 pm the bell
rings— that means no talking, at 11 pm the lights go out—
that means you'll be asleep, in the morning 3 bells, get up,
2 bells means be dressed and 1 bell means line up for chow—
chow is at 6:30 A.M. No talking in the halls! you'll come
back to your cell, and at 12:00— chow! The same
thing . . . at 4:00 chow! The same thing . . .
You'll receive one shower, once a week . . . state shaves,
once a week . . . change of clothes once a week . . . and
haircuts, toilet paper and state wages ($5 if you work)
once a month . . .
Your cell will contain 1 bed, 1 mattress, 1 (cold
water) sink, 1 toilet bowl, 1 light, 2 blankets, 2 sheets,
1 pillow and pillowcase— all in a 6 by 8 ft. cell . . .
Do what you're told and don't ask questions— then

you'll find out it's not all that bad . . .
Privileges— earphones, library books (crime and cowboy
books), commissary, and (2 hour) yard— notice, for any
infraction you receive, you'll automatically lose one
of your privileges or all of them . . .
Ready, pause . . . Bang-Bang-Bang-
to your
cells!!!

Kuwasi Balagoon

Why isn't the whole world dancin?

The first time i experienced terror and was able to keep my wits enough to examine it, i was in the notorious Vroom building, watching the goon squad proceed with a shakedown and waiting for them to get to my cell, which was the last, on the opposite end of the tier from where they had started.

As soon as i saw them in their bloused boots, overalls, helmets with plexi-glass visors, flak jackets and extra long clubs, i was frightened and curious as to what all they were up to. i as well as the brother who locked next to me, got up to see just what was to happen. "What's all this shit, look at those punks . . . it takes thirty of those motherfuckers to deal with one man?"

It didn't take long to see just what they were up to as the first man was ordered to strip, place his hands behind his head "Vietnam style" and back out of his cell. The brother next to me said something, but i said nothing, being intent on seeing what was happening, so as to have some idea what to expect. Next, the guy being searched was told to run his fingers through his hair, open his mouth, lift his balls, slowly turn around, lift his left foot, his right foot, and bend over and spread his cheeks. The brother next to me said something else, to which i replied that he should be cool.

More instructions followed: "Walk to the wall, and sit on the floor, cross legged, without taking your hands from your head." This is a pretty involved maneuver and if you don't believe me, try it. As i'd been placed in the Incorrigible Unit of the Vroom building for interrupting a funeral, pistol whipping a "corrections officer," shooting at another and aiding an escape, it became clearer that something extra could be in store for me. After five or so renditions

13

Laura Whitehorn
Untitled, 1989
crayon & ink on paper, 9″ x 9″

14

of the routine described above, without them actually vamping on anyone, i began to feel a bit at ease— but at the same time felt they might be "saving the best for last."

It was too much to think about, so I went and sat on my bed. Only to watch a pig named S——— come down to the cell next to mine and spray mace on the brother, after he had stepped from the door and laid down on his bunk. "Punk mutherfucker!" he shouted through the bars. "Don't get yourself fucked up now," S——— replied. The expedition was getting closer and i tried to decide whether to come out with my clothes on or just start swinging, stay in the cell and mess up as many as i could as they entered (after of course being soaked in mace) or coming out like everybody else and hardly being in any position to fight.

As i sat on the bed, looking out, they arrived at [my neighbor's] cell and began repeating: "strip, put your hands behind your head, back out your cell . . ." etc. as the door opened. He did as he was told. "Open your mouth," a pig instructed. When he did, the pig slapped him, causing him to stumble off to one side, as another pig punched him, saying, "Stand still!" They had tasted blood now and started getting better grips on their clubs, as one pig hit him on the arm with a stick. By now i was thoroughly terrorized; there was no fight in the brother, and the joking about "the german army," who they referred to themselves as, and good ol' boy laughs, just entangled in a massive knot inside my head. i began to look at the faces. There was this Italian jailer who had caught a few good shots some time ago by the look on his face, who never gave me any trouble personally, but had been assigned to escort me, standing at the ready. He was one of the guys they counted on. Another jailer who was running the show and had initiated knocking the brother around, told a rooky cop, "what do you expect?" There was a couple of black pigs in the gang as well, which never fails to strike me strange.

My door opened. i'd decided to come out naked and follow instructions unless i got hit, in which case I would go on at least one of them who had something exposed, as the ninety degree heat had coaxed a couple of visors up. It was a puny resolve as i felt that an attack would spell the end, Fear is a great source of power and the issue was decided as much as it could be. "Run your

15

fingers through your hair, open you mouth, lift your balls, turn around, lift your left foot, your right foot, spread your cheeks, turn around to your right, walk to the wall, sit down cross legged without moving your hands."

Somehow i assumed the position and listened to the fascist chatter behind me. "That's H———'s partner," i heard S——— instigate. i'd heard that they had vamped on H——— already. The pig who was actually in charge of the goon squad tapped the bandage on my back with his club. "Shouldn't pistol whip correctional officers— " i heard a couple of other remarks about "getting more practice at the range." i couldn't help but picture one of those creeps hitting me in the head while i was sitting in that ridiculous position. i thought for an instant that the tap was a signal to get up and i started to, but decided to wait until told, while listening to stuff being thrown around in my cell. Then finally i heard, "Ok, get up and back into your cell." The squad had begun leaving.

When i got to the door a jailer named W——— , a Jewish fascist who hates "jews and niggers," and who was later charged and acquitted of beating a prisoner, jumped in front of me and struck me in the stomach, holding the stick in both hands in the vertical butt stroke taught to Infantry. But it had no effect. Although my stomach looked out of shape since i had not been able to do sit-ups for a couple of months, it was stronger than it looked as i'd done sit-ups and leg raisers for years. Plus every muscle in my body was like a spring. As the stick rebounded off my gut and i looked him in the eye i couldn't help but smile. He responded by panicking: "Turn around, face the wall of your cell!" He who rides the tiger dares not dismount.

i looked at the wall until i knew they had all left, found a cigarette and sat down to smoke before even putting on my clothes. Later when recounting this to a prisoner who went through the same thing at the same time, i could see the recognition in his eyes. So this is state terror. The most terrifying part being watching what was happening to my neighbor, hearing what could happen to me . . . not what actually did.

This was terror. Done for the purpose of producing terror, as the search was in fact a justification and had anything been found considered contraband, it indeed would have been incidental and only by chance of ridiculous proportions. Just as the "shake downs" taking place at Marion now, after that prison has been locked down for nine months, have nothing to do with finding contraband and everything to do with attempts by the state at "behavior modification." With making prisoners so fearful, for so long, that their personalities change to that of whimps who will accept whatever the state has in mind without resistance or retaliation. They are looking for hearts, and they believe their slogan: "when you got them by the balls, their hearts and minds will follow."

Bill Dunne

Sliding Into Shadow

Joe Calloway is dying. It isn't anything alarmingly immediate like bleeding to death from stab wounds or being shoved into oblivion by the shock of a bullet. Nevertheless, he is dying as inexorably and certainly as people and psychology and physiology can decree. Joe will be one of those 37s or 41s in the obituary column that make people do a double take at the low number mixed with all those 70s and 80s, and wonder fleetingly about car accidents and murder.

I first ran into Joe about seven or eight years ago when I was consigned to the American Gulag Archipelago, the part of it known as the federal prison system. Joe was then a big, comfortable man, comfortable in his size and power and his unconscious belief that the world was a friendly place, its denizens notwithstanding and maybe even included. At an inch over six feet, with his 200 or so pounds of genetic beef tuned by occasional time on the iron pile, he had that placid disposition often found in people with whom others avoid contention, and who are not themselves the victims of arduous and competitive ambitions or extremes of oppression. Joe had a broad and open face under a shock of semi-kempt hair, with eyes set deep under fortifications of heavy brows; eyes that always seemed to see something at least half-funny. The ready smile, expansive gestures, and whiskey bray frequently applied to laughter confirmed that he did, in fact, get a kick out of much of what he saw.

I don't know if it would be animal magnetism or charisma or some other quality with which bush league psychologists might explain people like Joe, but it was easy to be attracted to him. He radiated friendliness, like you were not only okay with him, but

18

cool, too, like you didn't have to worry about any silly games coming from him (and you didn't)—like you'd known him for a long time. But Joe was just a regular guy, an average fella. In a way, that was a problem. I think that the potential many people saw in him, the outside him, set them up for a disappointment in the actual person that prevented them from getting really tight with him. He couldn't give enough warmth or heat for all the moths drawn to his apparent fire. In actuality, he could be no more to anyone than the meager comfort the rest of us could be to each other in our shared adversity—adversity only rarely brightened with real comradeship, commonality, and closeness. Many people didn't want to linger too long in the chill of the shadow of something they found too small to cast it. At the time I didn't think Joe noticed or cared.

So it went with me. I ran out of regular contact as we were moved to different blocks. We hadn't shared enough of substance to buck the tide of separation, enough to make a more solid connection. I knew that he was a "good convict" and we exchanged occasional greetings and moments of idle rapp in passing. I suppose my continued awareness of Joe was a confused combination of his visibility, the intangible attraction to his external persona, counterbalanced by my inclination to the safety of anonymity, and my own craving for the real closeness the system has made so elusive for the prisoners of its iron islands. Whatever it was, that residual thread of connection was somehow tenacious enough not to have snapped like so many others. He did not fade back into the faceless mass, and I watched him through several of the concrete caverns of the gulag that bureaucratic chance led us to share.

As I said, Joe was a regular guy: regular as in typical, run-of-the-mill, average, common, and even mediocre, though not in any derogatory sense. He was just not brilliant and, like the rest of us, didn't compensate for it with driving ambition, dogged determination, animal cunning, or obsession. Accordingly, he fell in with a group of similar people who happened to be at the right place at the right time and of the right mind to pull him. He was not inclined to initiate activity, but if his friends were down for it, then so was he. Once he was into it, though, he wasn't about any half-steppin'—a sometimes two-edged sword. But that was how he dealt with who and what he was. All he needed was to get the game on something

19

and the idea that it was the right thing to do and some support for the rightness of it from the people he was around.

Among the people he ran with, the modus operandi was to accept the slings and arrows of outrageous fortune and live as well as possible within the circumstances and try for as many laughs as possible along the way. Joe seemed as well adapted as anyone to doing just that. What could best be described as an instinctively collectivist attitude demonstrated his liking for people. The social fix he derived from sharing the slim pickings of prison hustle and being gregarious meant at least as much to him as the material aspect. Though I'm sure he didn't recognize it as such, he had the benefit/burden of a natural empathy for people.

Given the proper encouragement and some incentive, Joe might have been down for school, even though he'd never been more than a marginal student. But that was not happening. Anyway, school has a bad rap among many prisoners, and Joe couldn't discern the utility in the scant educational offerings available. He probably would have gone for a trade like auto or diesel or some other mechanics, given his inclinations, but none such were available to him. Even if they had been, he likely would have felt he had too much prison time ahead of him to learn something he'd only forget before he could use it. However, Joe appeared to have found his people, as much as anyone can in these places; though I was not privy to their relationships more than peripherally, he appeared to be tight with them. It looked as if they did as close to what they wanted as possible, considering the circumstances, and enjoyed it as much as they were capable. And Joe always did the Right Things by them, even if those things weren't always too smart.

It wasn't until a few years ago, however, that I really *met* him; that we went past the shallow—but sometimes infinitely hard—shells that everyone who walks these cages wears. He had been in the hole for five months on one of those conspiracies that live only in the minds of prison bureaucrats when I was put in the same cell on an insolence charge. He didn't look like the same Joe I'd last seen, but the friendly bear was still there. It was obvious that he hadn't been doing much exercize and had gained some weight. A lot of his robust color had drained away and he was having trouble with his teeth.

Over the next two weeks, we kicked it alot. There ain't a whole lot else to do in a cell in which you have to spend all but four or five hours a week, and Joe'd already been in it long enough for reading to wear thin. Since he'd already finished his disciplinary segregation time, he had some of his property, including a fat envelope of pictures and a bunch of those legal papers people cling to in the vain hope that they may somehow, sometime give up a technicality more potent than a hacksaw blade. Woven around and through our conversations, those things provided illustration and verification and resurrected flashes of the animation and openness that had instilled such promise into people's perceptions of Joe.

In Joe's neighborhood, growing up culminated in leaving high school and hustling a "good job" or whatever else might give one a shot at getting by as well as the preceding generation. "Good Jobs" being scarce for the largely untrained and ordinary majority, Joe, like many of his peers, supplemented his traditional jobs with this and that on both sides of the legal line. The meanness of petty scams and the meanness of spirit they (or, for that matter, being too long bound to some assembly line) engendered in people had grated on his sensibilities and alienated him. The material return of his jobs-plus existence was generally sufficient for his proletarian tastes; but he learned, though never to the point of articulation, that man does not live by material alone. And though the conscious realization didn't dawn on him, he related to his neighbors too much to be satisfied hustling in his own community or one like it. The feeling of suffocation in his locked-in, dead-end world grew, and Joe searched for an outlet that economic and social necessity and limitation rendered him incapable of providing.

The way out came in the form of Joe's learning to rob banks. A friend hooked him up with some fellas fixing to make a score who had the plot and plan all down. Joe's share was $20,000— two years' earnings and more money than he'd ever thought of seeing at one time. Being an easy touch, having many people he counted as friends, and not being skilled in the use of money, the windfall was soon gone. So were the people who had arranged the robbery, except for his friend who was in similar straits. The friend came

21

and they went— to the bank. They weren't too good at the preparation and execution and came up with only $15,000 between them.
But they were bank robbers, even if their practice made "boo-boo
bandits" a more accurate description. It was a job far more
remunerative and satisfying than 30 years as an unskilled laborer
or sleazy rip-offs of people just like them.

For the next two or three years, Joe and his friend made similar
moves as the need arose and never fired a shot. Joe didn't have
enough guile to sustain it, however. He bought a house— a
crackerbox, but a castle by his standards— not far from where he
grew up and a flashy car and lived more or less like everyone else
in that working-class neighborhood except that he didn't work.
Though he did indulge on occasion, he was no dope fiend, and
"having the bag" conferred no particular status he wanted or
sought. Neither was he into high-rolling or living faster than he
would sometimes take his Trans Am. He was content working on
his house and car, hanging out, and partying now and then while
vaguely saving for some vaguely imagined gas-station or other small
business he eventually planned to put together. More inclined to
generosity than was good for him, the saving went slowly as he
bought all kinds of stuff for them that he figured needed it. I
realized that he subconsciously sympathized with how they felt
living on the economic margins, having been there himself. His
generosity and no visible means of support (and probably some tax
questions) brought the heat and, eventually, a lot of gumshoes and
a couple of SWAT teams and a 75-year prison sentence. Maybe
Joe's was not the most admirable lifestyle, but it was a damn sight
better than many based on conscious depredations whose practitio-
ners are not even considered criminal or are only nominally so.

Looking at his pictures, I could see that the newest was five or six
years old, judging from the cars and appliances and styles and the
little dates developers sometimes put on the backs. Since Joe didn't
get any mail in the couple of weeks I was in the cell and I didn't see
any correspondence lying around, I guessed that his hustle was as
dependent on the pittance the government gives a prisoner for his
forced labor as was mine. I also figured that he didn't have any
outside stash and that the memories of his outside people were
about as short as most. I detected a touch of pain and bitterness

at this, but Joe would rather explain and excuse the failure of his people of the past than excoriate them.

Abandonment and the failure of hope-to-die connections did, however, take their toll, I saw— as did the seeming hopelessness of a future that was an endless succession of cells. Conversation ran out or at least diminished as the new topics became less relevant to him and more likely to make him feel vicarious pain over exploitation and oppression he felt powerless to affect. The mental anaesthetic and enforced ignorance of the hole was also difficult to shake off, its inertia being toward vegetation. I could usually interest Joe in a chess game, but that can only fill so much time. He would not exercize in the cell more than to get the chow from the food slot, and never came out when we were let into one of the recreation pens. It seemed like too much effort amid the encroaching malaise and lassitude of isolation. The solace he found was in sleep, an easy drug on which to become strung out in lockdown. I tried to break the spell, but could not reach that deep.

Joe was sent to Marion prison, a lockdown joint where clubs are trump and hard time reigns and the promise the future holds is dim and distant, if it is visible at all. I would hear occasional mention of him in conversations with new arrivals, conversations much the same as those had by people in refugee camps with others just in from another side of the front. Tales of what passes for derring-do in places where Joe had been became only infrequent reminiscences of an increasingly distant past. No one had anything fresh and really not much at all to say, other than the likes of, "Lemme see, who else is there . . . Jones, Smith, Calloway . . ." or, "Did you know . . .?" or, "Yeah, he's doing all right . . ." Even people who had known Joe well couldn't say much; life in lockdown ain't much to describe, especially to people who've been there. It's tough to become or do the distinguishable amid endless repetitions of the same day. Joe's shadow was getting lighter. 45,000 or so federal prisoners is really just a small town, and the neighborhood of the 4,000 or so consigned to maximum security is much smaller. But the system is designed to create separation and dislocation and break down any bonds from which people can derive the strength that allows them to resist their oppression and makes them harder to manipulate.

The next time I saw Joe was on a different mainline, and he had become a much grayer person. That wild hair was the only part of him that didn't appear to have suffered. The color of health had gone from his complexion and he was afflicted with some skin disease that looked like spider bites all over his torso and upper arms. There wasn't a tooth in his head that was real and not at least half rotten, and he'd developed a tic in his right eye. He'd put on alot of weight and, though still a big guy, it hung on him like parasitic hound skin. He was stooped, and it looked as if he hadn't done anything more strenuous than lift a spoon in years or as if he had some kind of wasting disease. He looked 60 at 33.

The rally in his spirit that came with the relative increase in freedom of a mainline population didn't continue. Joe didn't really hang out with anyone more than daily existence and his marginal hustle required, and he didn't have much rapp. He couldn't, given his limited and rusty interests and diminished physical and psychological capacities; the stimulus of a little greater freedom of action was not enough to bridge those gaps. His main pursuit was chasing the wine bag and he was frequently in some kind of hassle with the swine that put him in the hole. Though I'm sure he didn't recognize it and would never admit it, I think he may have felt drawn to the concrete cocoon of the hole. The drugging numbness of body and mind in which reality is little more than spaces between sleep such as isolation can induce can take people away from the incessantly shabby subsistence of perpetual pettiness, restriction, and repression they are powerless to escape— or even to affect significantly.

Although Joe's former self sometimes breaks through the increasingly dense layer of psycho-insulation that overlays the mental armor in which all the embrasures have been snapped shut and chinks welded, Joe is losing Joe. The poverty of enforced relegation to semi-human shadow status has driven him away from people, from self, from reality. Perhaps as an unconscious kindness to Joe, into whose personal social program kindness was written as a habit, Joe was letting himself go.

Has this member of the walking wounded been injured so seriously or frequently that recovery is no longer possible? I don't know. In some subliminal convolution of the psychology we

24

understand so little, his body appears to recognize— or to be unable to resist— the encroaching grayness. As I write this in the two AM quiet of the hole, I can hear him coughing and hacking his life away about ten cells down the tier. And I know from the tier gossip that inevitably follows the exceedingly rare midnight trip to the hospital, after the minimum hour of pleas for assistance, that he suffers other maladies. I haven't heard the formerly stentorian voice that once inhabited the man or his braying laughter in the weeks I've been on the tier. Without having known and watched, it is likely that most people would see him as just another unhealthy slob, of which there is no shortage. No one could tell otherwise from the modicum of conversation and contact that getting by required of him. But from his response to my greetings and inquiries as to whether they're taking care of him adequately, in which he pulls the cover halfway off his face and peeps out of a barren cell with nothing in it but jail issue and a few raggedy magazines to briefly reply, a shadow, *I* know

Joe Calloway is dying. Whether he could or would respond to treatment is moot, 'cause he ain't gonna get it. How long it will take him to fade away or let go is tough to tell. He undoubtedly resists at least unconsciously his mind's subversion by the oppression and tyranny of what he doesn't understand. When readers do their double take at his 37 or 41 in the obituaries, those who think of murder will be right. Joe Calloway will have been murdered as surely as someone upon whose weaknesses a song of suicide is played or who is blasted off a fence for wanting to stay sane or who is set up for the knives of lackeys for trying to induce some human action. Joe Calloway is not superman and neither is anyone else: everyone can be reached.

Sekou Cinque T. M. Kambui

Freedom

"Boom-Boom!" Sunday morning/5:30 A.M. . . .
That was a shotgun shot;
someone is taking the bid for freedom
into their own hands; Freedom! Freedom!

It was not me— i was brought out of
my slumber by the sound of the gun's boom,
breathlessly i lay there— conjuring images of
    this brave and courageous brother, springing upward, over the
wire: Leaping down, rushing across the road to the woods,
taking his life in his own hands, looking the threat of death in the
        eye;
defying death, and surrounded by the buckshots flying from
the slave keeper's gun— stretching his arms and legs for
Freedom! Freedom!

The slave-quarters is in a noisy, boisterous, clamor:
words ground together, joining, linking together feelings/
thoughts of hope, ideas of freedom, fear of death, hope
of success, doubtful thoughts that imply that there is no way
to freedom— freedom is considered elusive, inaccessible;
yet our courageous brother has made the woods, he is
free for now— he is stretching his arms to embrace his
bid for freedom, his bid for freedom!

26

Their words make jokes to hide the hope, the fear, the
question, the wonder, the wish that it had been they
who had had the guts to make the leap, reach out to
Freedom! Freedom! the slaves are cut off from news
of their brother's plight, so they cringe and hide behind
their fear exposed, naked fear of defying death, of
choosing Freedom! Freedom!

There are the slaves who, left behind
        in captivity, pray their brother's
        success; wish the dogs set on
        his heels in the woods miss his scent;
        miss their shots of steel bearing
        death to their brother— death to
                freedom, freedom!

There are other slaves who, left behind
        in captivity, pray their brother's
        capture, wish the dogs set on his
        heels in the woods catch his scent;
        don't miss their shots of steel
        bearing death to the courageous brother— the
        brother who exposed their fears, their passive
        aquiescence in their own enslavement:— death to
                freedom, freedom!

It's 11:35 pm Sunday night . . .
        HE'S AT THE GATE! HE FAILED! HE IS CAPTURED!
        Dammit, why? Why didn't he make it— why
        did freedom remain elusive for the brave
        brother? Freedom, freedom!

Some of the slaves here are in pain; they hurt
for the brother's failure to win his bid for
    freedom, freedom!
Some of the slaves are laughing— their embarrassment,
    their exposed fears, their lack of guts to defy
    their captivity w/their own bid for freedom are
    appeased; they are comfortable again in their own
    fear to take the freedom leap; they say "I knew he
    wouldn't make it . . ." No, no, to freedom! Freedom!

Katya Komisaruk

Visitor

Lysol and
gray enameled walls
I do not speak but
hear my footsteps in
      entrance
      reception
      metal detector
      hallway
      automatic door
      automatic door
      automatic door
      hallway
      waiting area
      visiting cubicle:
            your voice
            harshened by the intercom
            your hand
            pressed against the glass

Katya Komisaruk

"After seven o'clock count tonight females may use the yard until nine P.M."

Here in these northern flatlands,
I raise my collar against the night wind
and walk purposefully
in large circles.

The fence— chainlink with six barbed strands above—
is always at my right shoulder.
It quivers only slightly in the wind.
Steady companion of my rounds,
it murmurs encouragements to me—
Aeolian whisperings from a barbwire harp.

Tonight I long to lean upon it,
hook my fingers into the links,
lay my cheek against cold wire,
and feel the wind bathe me
as it pours through.

But the lights would reveal me;
the cameras would report me;
and loudspeakers would summon me
to be interrogated.

So I do not linger,
but stride by,
foregoing metallic embraces.
And the wind fondles my hair,
thrusting it back from my forehead,
as you used to, darling.

4/4/88

Katya Komisaruk

They Are Searching

The officer puts out his hand as I leave Building C.
I give him my jacket
and he checks the pockets.

The walk to my housing unit
is one hundred yards.
I keep my back straight, my head high.
Cameras, mounted on poles and walls
relay my progress to monitoring screens in Building A.
More guards watch through the mirrored windows of Building B,
as I approach.

At the door, another cop waits to explore my jacket again.
Finishing, she gestures with one hand,
indicating that I should turn my back to her.
Now I stand with feet apart,
arms stretched horizontally.
As she explores my thighs,
I stare into the distance,
demanding that my face stay
disinterested and undisturbed.

Do they think it is so easy to find?
Do they imagine I will surrender it,
simply because they force me to spread my legs
while they investigate?

32

Fools.
I've never hidden it.
I carry it openly all the time.
And their kind attentions simply make it larger.

Oscar López-Rivera

El Caído de la Gracia del Todopoderoso Señor Dólar

Te acecho desde este antro a través de un boquete de cristal que un arquitecto alienado se atrevió llamar ventana. Ahí estás a la intemperie, tirado como una hoja marchita que cae sobre el suelo y poco a poco se va descomponiendo hasta que desaparece. Sobrevives la existencia reducida al instinto, harapiento como un guiñapo, marginado de la sociedad y desenchufado del aliento del hogar y de seres amados. Comes las bazofias que recoges de los zafacones igual que las sabandijas y los ratones. Duermes en los duros y fríos peldaños de acero de la escalera del tren elevado. Tu mundo se limita a unas setenta (70) yardas de acero en esa jungla de cemento.

Recuerdo el primer día que te ví llegar con tus motetes y tu petate de cartón, abrumado por los añicos de tus sueños rotos. Eras el retrato del hombre derrotado y rendido. El día complementaba tu apariencia. Era uno pardo y agobiador como un berriento que presagiaba tu futuro y las asechanzas del tiempo y del rigor de la intemperie. Hacía un ventebal huracanado que al no poderse escapar del laberinto de los rascacielos desataba su furia contra los peatones levantando faldas, botando sombreros y pelucas, despeinando cabezas y cegando a los que no cubrían sus rostros. Pero a tí no te afectaba. Estabas tan absorto con tus aprietos que ni una tormenta podía sacudirte.

Permaneciste inmóvil hasta tarde en la noche. Sólo cuando la quietud prevalecía y todo estaba cerrado decidiste acercarte a los zafacones. Sacaste de estos algunas brozas y algunos pedazos de pan que metiste en una bolsa de papel de estraza. Subiste hasta el último peldaño de la escalera. Te sentaste y comiste algunas brozas. Luego endiste el petate y usaste los motetes para amortiguar el duro acero.

El día siguiente descubrí para que era el pan que habías guardado la noche anterior. Te ví desmigajarlo y repartírselo a un puñado de palomas que habían aparecido de la nada. Aquél gesto hecho tuyo contrarrestaba tu apariencia de patibulario, y a la misma vez servía como advertencia a los que nos pasamos la vida juzgando el libro por su cubierta.

Para las palomas tu pan era ambrosia e imán. De un puñado se multiplicaron transformándose en una manada centenaria en cuestión de semanas. La atracción fue tan fuerte que terminaron mudándose al cordón eléctrico que colgaba sobre la acera frente al "Shanghai Chinese American Food" y el "All American Hero." Pero aquella movida trajo consigo la destrucción de la bella y armoniosa relación que tú habías creado con las palomas.

Algunos de los clientes que comían en los dos restaurantes, al pasar bajo el cordón eléctrico quedaban embarrados con el excremento que soltaban las palomas. Parece que los clientes se querellaron, y los dueños respondieron a lo que les pareció ser una amenaza a sus negocios. Los chinos fueron los primeros que salieron a atacar el problema. Con escoba en mano trataban de espantar las palomas. Estas se asustaban, volaban y al rato regresaban al cordón. Los griegos hicieron lo mismo, pero pronto notaron la futilidad de sus esfuerzos y optaron por buscar otra alternativa para solucionar el problema. Así fue como le pasaron la batuta al polizonte obeso que diariamente mataba su gula, sin pagar desde luego, comiendo en los dos restaurantes. (Este como protector del orden público que era) inmediatamente vió la severidad del problema y se movió a resolverlo. Estudió la situación y no se tardó mucho en detectar que tú eras el causante de atraer las palomas allí. Como sabía que podía extraer más beneficio para su panza si no te delataba muy pronto, se tardó unos días en informarle a los chinos y griegos la raíz del problema.

Poco después, una noche se aparecieron unos sicarios en carros y perreras con sus bombos y sirenas prendidas y con macanas, revólveres y rifles. Te arrastraron por los escalones y a son de puntapies te metieron en una de las perreras con un rótulo que decía, "Chicago's Finest-We Serve and Protect". Con aquella embestida te dejaban ver por qué eran considerados los mejores y a quién protegían y servían. Mientras los sicarios cumplían su labor, los griegos y los chinos lo vitoreaban por una tarea bien cumplida.

Te desaparecieron por una semana y al regresar ya no habían rastros de las palomas ni de tus motetes. Al no encontrarlas algo reventó dentro de tí. Era como si la última rama que te apoyaba para que no cayeras en el precipicio había sido arrancada. Te deslizabas y el abismal descenso jamás te permitiría regresar al redil. Tampoco a inclinarte hacia arriba para encontrar un astro fulgido que te brindara una chispa de esperanza. Todo estaba perdido. Tus manos buscaban otras que las asieran y las estrecharan, pero sólo encontraron el ángel de la muerte de la botella. La botella era la solución final y la abrazaste con la misma intensidad que un Samurai posee cuando empuña su espada para cometer Harakari.

Antes de la embestida por los sicarios eras inconspícuo. La retraila que día tras día pasaba por tu lado rumbo al caldero de presión (donde cambiaba su fuerza productiva por un jornal) era incapaz de notar su existencia. Para aquella masa amorfa, alucinada y robotizada por su apetencia por las chucherías, sólo eras un bagazo que merecía ser ignorado si era que su vista tropezaba contigo. Su existencia le permitía preocuparse más por tener los sobacos, el ombligo y las verijas artificialmente perfumadas que sentir una chispa de compasión por un ser humano como tú.

Después de la embestida te hiciste omnipresente. Comenzaste salirle al paso a la retraila convirtiéndote para ésta en un atróz mendigo. Algunos te tiraban una moneda, pero evitaban tener contacto contigo. Tú los acosabas y ellos respondían con su escarnio. Ante sus ojos tú eras un ser tan ominoso que te veían como un miasma capaz de impregnar sus entrañas, contagiarlos y así reproducirte. Su hostilidad hacia tí era más intensa y feróz que los violentos fríos que sufrías en la intemperie. Para la horda tú habías dejado de ser un humano. Esta detestaba y rechazaba tu forma de ser porque tu individualismo no era compatible y conciliable con el prototipo de su mitología. No era el individualismo del Llanero Solitario (*The Lone Ranger*)—hombre que abandonó su riqueza para dedicarse a proteger la propiedad privada de los grandes terratenientes del Oeste, obviando el hecho que éstos se la habían robado los Nativos. No era el individualismo recio y feroz de los apoderados, a la Ford, que conquistaron el poder de las chucherías y fueron elevados al papel de Todopoderoso Señor Dólar. El tuyo era fofo, el del ser débil de espíritu y valor y sin ninguna fortitud intestinal; por ende, reducible a un paria.

La retraila biliosa y vendada por su insensibilidad, era incapaz de apreciar que tú habías sufrido la experiencia del caldero de presión. Un día caíste de la gracia del Todopoderoso Señor Dólar porque éste te había expoliado tanto que ya no tenías nada más para expoliar. A cambio de un jornal le diste las fuerzas de tus manos, pero El quería más. Le diste la fuerza de tu mente, pero El quería más. Le produciste y reproduciste dándole los mejores años de tu vida, pero El exigió más. Mientras más le dabas más demandaba El. Tu producías su riqueza y él reciprocaba produciendo tu pobreza. Dentro y fuera del caldero de presión El te negaba y anulaba tu propia actualización. Cuando ya no tenías nada más para exprimir te botó como cualquier otro desechable. La caída de la gracia del Todopoderoso te trajo al laberinto de la jungla de cemento. Pero eso no podía ser apreciado por la horda. Esta optaba, primero por ignorarte, y luego cuando le saliste al paso, por desdeñarte. Le era más facil reducirte a un paria que atreverse mirar su reflexión en su espejo que eras tú.

Desdeñado, caído y derrotado una y otra vez, abrazaste el ángel de la muerte porque su consumación te llevaría a tu consumación. Bebías con frenético empeño y con enorme pasión como sí con el alcohol que tragabas y eliminabas las deteriosas plagas que destruían la humanidad. Cometías un acto de expiación con el que pretendías liberar a la retraila de su indiferencia y de su obediencia ciega a aquél que fingía de Todopoderoso.

El alcohol hacía estragos en lo que quedaba de tí. Tu espalda se encorvaba y la cabeza y el cuello parecían desaparecer dentro de la coraza de trapos e hilachas que llevabas puesta. Tu cuerpo se atrofiaba y entre más días pasaban más tomaba una postura fetal. Donde en un tiempo había el cuerpo de un hombre se llegó el momento cuando lo que quedaba era un mostrenco que se desaparecía y se aniquilaba en su propio pellejo.

Hoy te acecho pero no te encuentro. Anoche oí la triste y horrenda noticia que habían encontrado a un mostrenco totalmented congelado. Esta mañana la oí de nuevo, pero el muerto lo encontraron bastante lejos de aquí. Mientras te buscaba por el boquete de cristal, oí el capellán decirle a un esbiro que abriera el roto por donde me dan la comida. Me preguntó sí quería confesar y comulgar. Contemplé ignorarlo porque nunca antes había venido a hablar conmigo. Pero como era día de navidad decidí no desairarlo. Me acerqué al boquete, le dije que no deseaba confesarme o comulgar. Lo que sí me interesaba era dialogar un ratito con él siempre y cuando él deseara hacerlo. Cuando accedió, traté de explicarle algo de sus experiencias observadas por mí. Le pregunté si su iglesia estaba dispuesta albergar a personas que no tenían otro techo sobre sus cabezas mas que el cielo. Mis palabras espantaron al capellán. La cara beatífica que unos minutos antes me había preguntado si quería confesar y comulgar súbitamente comenzó a contorcionarse transformándose en un semblante severo y frío. Su boca emitió unas palabras con un tono bien condescendiente como si podía impactarlo en forma positiva, pero pasó todo lo contrario. Creí que le iba a dar un vertigo. Se encrespó, su rostro se puso tenso y rígido, con una mano hizo lo que me pareció era una señal de cruz y con la otra se apoyó de la puerta para no desplomarse. En esos instantes entró una pequeña brisa por el boquete y ello me ayudó a darme cuenta que el problema del capellán era otro. Parece que había estado celebrando en grande con la sangre de cristo. Tambaleando se despidió y pronto oí su voz y la del vecino orando juntos.

Te acecho pero no te veo. El panorama en la jungla de cemento no ha cambiado mucho. A través del boquete de cristal veo la opulencia decadente, los rascacielos tocando las nubes con sus condominios para el deleite de la clase ociosa mientras que hay pobres viviendo a la intemperie; los escaparates llenos de ropa que jamás se venderá y a personas sin un abrigo para ponerse; a los zafacones llenos de comida que se ha desperdiciado y a personas muriéndose de hambre; la retraila ambulando de un punto a otro cautivos del caldero de presión y de su indiferencia; y algunos seres como tú, con sus corazones y almas atomizadas, atrapados en el laberinto de la jungla de cemento.

(Aunque esto es un cuento, durante los 17 meses que pasé en el calabozo del MCC-Chicago, ví muchos seres humanos viviendo a la intemperie y sufriendo la hostilidad del tiempo y de otros seres humanos. A esos seres humanos le dedico estas palabras. Hay que recordar que en la Estatua de la Libertad hay una inscripción en la que esta nación le pide al mundo que le de a los que no tienen un hogar y a los condenados de la tierra, sin embargo, no le puede prover un techo a los millones de seres que han caído de la gracia del Todopoderoso Señor Dolar y están forzados a vivir en las junglas de cemento de este país.)

Standing Deer

Rehabilitation Marion Style

The fresh-fish guard sez: "We'll drag him from the shower and beat the shit out of him, but there's only five of us so I better get on the phone and call for reinforcements!" His rosy cheeks were flush with excitement and the anticipation, odd as it seems, already started the faintest hint of an erection at the thought of beating the naked prisoner into a quivering mass of jelly.

The senior guard over segregation was an old lieutenant whose only dream was to make it to pension time in order that he might wither away his few remaining years in obscurity until he could fall to the ground like an overripe persimmon and go splat-t-t.

The old lieutenant turned to the new-boy guard who had the hard-on and said, "Let's leave him alone, son." The old man's voice was as quiet as mosquitoes scampering across a field of marshmallows but it oozed and dripped with authority born of many years of stomping testicles, using clubs, tear-gas, mace and shields on the front lines of combat with the children of the poor. When he spoke, his words wore the badge of finality.

When the prisoner finished his shower the old guard handed him a clean towel in exchange for the two-week-old filthy rag the prisoner had complained about.

The new-boy guard seethed in impotent fury as he watched the prisoner's rippling muscles as he dried his naked body. Standing lithe as a jungle cat on the stone gray tier, the callouses on the sides of the prisoner's hands gleamed like cauliflowers on black velvet. Each perfectly coordinated movement seemed to insolently mock the pot-bellied new-boy guard who was ten years the prisoner's junior.

40

"Wait till that old namby-pamby son-of-a-bitch retires and we get Lt. Steele up here in the Control Unit," he thought. "It won't be much longer now . . . then I'll have some fun. I'll teach that scumbag motherfucker how to ask for a towel with r*espect*."

The prisoner cast a casual sidelong glance at the five guards until his eyes locked with the new-boy guard's. With great effort he stifled the smile that was in his heart as he thought, "Wait until ole Johnson retires next month and I can get my hands on that bastard Steele. If only I can hold out that long I think I'll eat the new-boy guard's eyeballs as I tear Steele's throat out!" The thought of it sent chills of pleasure exploding like rockets in his brain. Something for his rage to feed on. A reason to get up tomorrow and a reason to go to bed.

Back in his cage the prisoner thought about the new-boy guard. "Some people want to commit suicide," he thought, "but they don't have the balls so they need a fall partner. They hire out as mercenaries and hold the key to freedom over other people's heads. They say unconsciously by their actions, 'Please kill me . . . please put me out of my misery.' Any prisoner will do, so they play the fool to them all until they ring the right chime."

He wondered why some guards are happy just to make it through the day with life and limb intact. On Novemeber 11, 1980, five guards at Brushy Mountain, Tennessee, would have been glad if they just hadn't made it to work that day. Some folks learned from the 43 dead at Attica that the state will kill its own without a whim. Marin County Courthouse, August 7, 1970, should have shown them how little value functionaries within the apparatus have. The uprisings of McAlester (Oklahoma), New Mexico, and Idaho taught them nothing. The three dead guards at Pontiac should have told them something but it didn't. Some folks learned from the death of hanging judge John H. Woods Jr. (who gasped out the last of his stinking breath on the Texas ground after being hit in the spine by a .243 with a sniper scope mounted) that they bleed and die just like us.

Convulsions of the spine for "Maximum John" just like a dog hit by a speeding car. Prior to his date with justice he delighted in the sobriquet "Maximum John" because he always gave the maximum

41

sentence to the children of the poor unfortunate enough to come before his bench. He won't do *that* no more! It might not have changed a thing, but it did change the consciousness of "Maximum John," which all the rhetoric and correct theoreticians could not or would not do. Carlos sez: "You do things with bullets because bullets are real." Could be Carlos was onto something.

In the meantime I will sit in my cage and wonder when will the Maximum Johns and the new-boy guards of this world learn that a prisoner with 1,500 years and 5 lives to do, for some reason, just don't give a fuck.

Next month! the prisoner in our story thought with a smile. "Next month!" he answered himself out loud.

Chapter Two

ROOTS IN THE PEOPLE

*Don't be surprised when I say I
was in prison. We've all been in
prison. That's what America
means—prison.*

— Malcolm X

Salvador Agron

The Political Identity of Salvador Agron— Travel Log of 34 Years

World entered on April 24th of 1943—
Into a home divided by
Religious fanaticism, alcoholism,
Spiritualism, male chauvinism
And the broken marriage of two poor working people
Who were many times out of work.

Into *El Asilo de los Pobres*
In Mayaguez, Puerto Rico—
Nuns and shelter of the poor—
Attempts at infantile institutionalization
Resisted by bed wetting,
Food snatching, tantrums
And doubt of religious instruction.
Humiliated and abused;
Pervert performing oral stimulation
On my childish organ.

Into Arrabales, shanty houses,
Curly haired barefoot boy
With dirty hands and face
Listening to sexual ecstasy
Of father and stepmother
Through a cardboard wall;
Sleeping half awake

In an unwashed canvas hammock,
Watching candles aflame to stone idols
Sanctified by the church as saints,
Dreaming with half erected penis,
Not understanding sex.

Into a plane hitting air pockets
All the way to New York,
Frightened half to death like a runaway
From a colony become an undefined commonwealth
Or the free associated state of Puerto Rico;
And I, a Puerto Rican,
Now a "little white spic"
With a dark uncle and Indian grandmother,
Into a roach-infested apartment
In front of the Daily News building,
Watching from a window
Americans with cars and money
Passing by while bums roamed the streets.
Watching, listening, learning
A foreign language by ear and memory;
Mimicking American talk in bars,
Americans laughing at me,
Enjoying themselves, giving me nickels and dimes—
My early hustle.

Into Public School,
Sleeping in the back seat,
Trying, in moments of wakefulness,
To remember a little something—
Words like *oxygen, food, sex, money,*
Naked and *poor.*
Hungry.
Fainting and banging my head against the wall
Saying: "Estupido! Estupido!"
Making the teacher worry and the others laugh.

Into a pentecostal church
In Vigilias—
Drinking coffee and eating crackers,
Listening to gospel songs,
Looking at people jump around
Speaking in strange tongues,
Saying: "Sazy zaca suzza su foo la roo!"
Still trying to understand;
The holy and angelic tongues reminding
Of my English mimicry.
Hearing sermons on the burning hell
Of fire and brimstone
Reserved for dummies like me.
Falling asleep in a back seat
And pissing all over the floor
While Christians prayed for my cure.

Into a hospital called Bellevue
With boils all over my body
Which the Chinese doctors could not define;
Sick unto death and saved only
By my faithful praying mother
Anointing me with oil.
Then into Bellevue again
For falling from a fourth floor window
While playing superman—
Jumping from a fire escape, thinking I could fly.

In the hospital probed by psychiatrists,
Labeled "problem child,"
Refusing to eat my green peas,
Arguing with the nurse,
Flinging peas on the floor.
Bed covered with a fishing net,
Reaching out, razor blade in hand,
Cutting the net.
Going to a window,
Threatening to jump out,

47

Thinking I could fly
Like the little angels of heaven
And like superman on television.

Into the neighbor's apartment
Through the fire escape window;
Stealing a flashlight, seven dollars,
Jewelry, other things,
Leaving a cigar in his mouth
While he slept his drunkenness away.
Stripped by a fanatical preacher stepfather
And whipped with a belt till blue,
Left alone and naked.
Taken to Children's Court
And signed a way to Wiltwyck,
School for problem and troubled children,
Upstate, away from home.
Mixing, integrating, learning crime,
Watching and enjoying homosexual acts,
Beaten, abused, anglonized
In name and education.
Escaping,
A wild and runaway child,
In fear, dread, trembling,
Confused and then set loose.

Into gangs, school brawls,
Hating whitey as all spics and niggers
Are taught to do by the American way of life;
Yet having white friends,
Black and Puerto Rican brothers,
Catholics, Protestants,
Confused like me;
Trying to survive in a hostile land,
Learning to fight in order to live
In the cruel American world;
Dancing to Lord Price, Presley, The Platters, The Teenagers,
Drinking wine and smoking pot—

48

The unprescribed medicine for pain—
Jitterbugging my way to Puerto Rico again.
Into the island, into Mayaguez,
Land and town of my birth,
Living in squalor
Without feeling the pain in me;
Seeing a stepmother hang while a rope from my hammock
Squeezed her troubled soul out of this world;
Indifferent to pain and poverty,
Smiling at those Puerto Ricans who kept the watch
All night long over her dead body
Shedding their funeral tears and praying
So that her soul might rest in peace.
My father scolded me for not believing
In disembodied spirits
While he drank bottled spirits to ease his pain.

Trouble all around
My girl calling me a hoodlum,
Smacking my face in public,
And I, drunk over puppy love,
Getting into a fight,
Trying to cut another boy's neck when he threw bottles at me.

Arrested and sent away again
Into the industrial school in Mayaguez
With bars on the windows.
Forced to work, refusing, resisting,
Loving Puerto Ricans
But hating institutions,
Hating tough guys
Because I wanted to be tough and rough;
Beat up again by administrators,
Refusing helping hands,
Cursing gentle voices,
Becoming hard and strong,
Fighting off sexual advances,
Making love with some,

49

Slowly becoming a person—
Alienated from all but myself.
Escaping again and again
Till escaping at last;
Not willing to be criminalized
Nor penalized nor institutionalized,
Like a runaway slave
In flight for my life.

Into New York again,
Joining the Mau Maus at Fort Green,
Stabbing, drinking, schooling,
Fooling, rolling, desperate and angry
At something, someone,
Without direction;
Stealing a car, put on probation,
Never reporting, always on the run;
Facing the cruel world— Un Macho at last
With leather jacket, brass knuckles,
Chain, knife, gun and all;
Gangfighter, street rumbler,
Rebel in an unknown cause,
Run out of Brooklyn by white boys,
Learning to hate in generalized terms
Anglos, Blacks, Ricans
And all those who needed my hate—
Half devil, half saint, part time pimp,
Part this and part that,
With a little spice and a little nice
But never complete.

Into a playground with a gang
Bearing a knife that I never used
And wearing a cape to look sinister and cruel.
Taking the blame for what I did not do,
Wanting to strike back at a cruel society—
Losing my soul in infamy.
Fading into a bloody night away from the world of reality,

50

Seeking importance and immortality.
Trapped by a legal system which believed the story
Of a wild and crazy child;
Which sensationalized crime in newspapers, movies, TV,
Never looking at the truth,
Believing the lies of a sixteen year old
With the mind of a twelve year old child;
A system ready to kill a mentally disturbed child
In the electric chair
To take public revenge and appease public uproar.

Into a prison, a mental hospital,
Strip cells, beatings,
The caped crusader went, innocent of mind;
For eighteen years he struggled
For life, liberty, dignity;
Educating himself, rehabilitating himself,
Revolutionizing his mind and body
In spite of dehumanizing
Concrete, steel and iron penal systems;
Redirecting his hate intelligently,
Changing souls and conditions around him,
Fighting the pigs,
Struggling for life.

Have I not earned the right
To freedom and flight?

Into Fishkill the revolutionary went
With fist and book,
With pen and need to reveal,
With courage for sacrifice,
To protest those injustices that persist.
Capeman, Dracula—
Call me what you please—
I work and fight for the poor.
I must continue like this until you understand

That someday I will return
To pick up the struggle where I went wrong.

Into the streets
Better prepared and ready I come;
Ready for struggle, liberation
Through power and love.
Freedom belongs to the strong.

Written May 28, 1977
Dutchess County Jail

Joseph Doherty

Death in the Rain

On a cold, dark night, after a winter-chilled day,
   people huddled in their little ghetto homes,
   safe from the cold, wet wind that moved through
   the narrow streets like a warning for the coming
   night's slumber.
The mothers make the last cup of tea for the night,
   while fathers sit dreary-eyed, spent from their
   long days without work.
Children sleep deep in dreams, and deaf to the sounds
   of the October winds,
   cuddled together for warmth in their damp, crowded
   beds.
Hallway lights reflect the life within to the dead
   stillness that chills the strong streets outside.
   Like little lighthouses they guide passers-by
   to their homes and comfort with safety and with
   speed.
Even the ghetto dogs are quiet and listen to the wind,
   as alleycats patrol the backyard walls.
The burned-out cars and war-torn streets are forgotten
   to the sounds of the rain.
Boys and girls dream of their loved ones around, and
   dream of a future without gunfire and death,
   of a life without danger, unemployment, and
   doubt,
   Of a life without war and fear,

and with freedom and rights.
With the sound on the street,
   as the rain hits the ground,
A neighbor zig-zags the puddles,
   to keep off the rain.
His hands in his pockets to cover
   from the cold, he looks for the hall light
   to guide his way home.
A smile on his face for the night he just had,
   the music, the singing, the drinking, was fun.
Thoughts of his wife, and the way she did look,
   the sweetness and beauty not so very rare
   for Belfast girls are all alone for sharpness,
   and strength, and a beauty that's one.
For when he left the club, he went all alone,
   his wife was awaiting by the fire-side at home.
   Looking forward to her husband to be in her arms,
   and sit by the fire-side to stare at the flames,
   and forget of the misery and the days yet to come,
   for their two lovely children asleep in the bed.
But there's no future to be had in this war-raged town,
   with soldiers and tanks that patrol all around.
For Belfast town is ready for to sleep,
   to forget the brutality that walks these streets.
  Crack! Crack! Crack! One. Two. Three.
   The dogs start barking, the cats run free.
Crack! Crack! Crack! Four. Five. Six.
   The children start screaming as the bullets are
struck.
   More shots are heard, the ghetto awakes,
   and frightened people sit to await.
By the fire-side at home, all alone and afraid,
   waits a sweetheart in turmoil for her husband
   to appear.
My God, Michael, walk through the door, oh please God,
   please let him appear.

But lying in an alley wet and cold was Michael's tortured
body,
 all blood and holes.
Crack! Crack! Crack! He was shot again,
 his felled body was out to be slain.
As he lay there, not a beat in his heart,
 they stood about laughing and they spat on his wounds.
Oh these brave English soldiers, they were in the mood
 for shooting up paddys on this cold, wet night.
As quick as Michael was slain, his body was moved,
 for to cover up the evidence was the rule.
  They cleaned up the blood, and the holes in the wall,
  and issued a statement that a gunman had fallen.
But Mickey was Irish, it was his only crime,
 walking alone to the beat of the rain.
The people were shocked, on the morn that come,
 to find out a neighbor was murdered and gone.
Where are these killers, and what were their names,
 these British troops that were involved in the stain.
Where is the justice, the courts, and the laws,
 the newspapers, politicians, and Parliament and all.
Where are the jails, the camps, and the cells,
 will these men be punished and banished to hell.
But what of Michael's brother, who's behind barb-wire,
 in Long Kesh camp, with no charges or trial?
Where is the justice for the Irish man in there,
 and who would tell him that Michael was dead?
 What of his wife, two kids all alone,
 a husband and father just blown to the wind?
I can tell you now where these killers do walk,
 they walk the streets still in the wind and the rain.

Joseph Doherty

Walls of Silence

In prison cell, alone, disillusioned, afraid.
Where hope sometimes lost,
Where love somehow forgotten,
to hatred, generated by walls,
heavy white bricked walls,
covered by blood, tears of self pity,
brushed over by government issued paint.
But still it cannot cover, the blood of their victims.
Still, it cannot hide the stains of their torture,
nor the wrongs, the unjust wrongs,
of slow murder of figure within.

The walls move in, nearer,
crushing bones, tearing blooded limbs,
disfiguring faces to blood stained floors.
Gagging mouths of African fathers,
with tortured wombs of Filipino mothers.
Starving the bellies of Irish sons,
while Chilean daughters raped by many.
"Where are our loved ones?" cry the children of injustice,
who await in the ghettos of nearby towns.

The blood lines on walls,
from torn finger nails, red and broken.
Swollen sores on searching eyes.
parched skins of cut, pleading lips,

whisper for justice, through cracks in the wall.
"All we ask, is bread of dignity,
for common people," under military guns.
"FUCK YOU," laugh the armies of fortune,
their stomachs full, with blood of mankind.
But, what the silence?, from beyond the window,
the so-called democracies, who hide behind lies.

Ugly faces of stains on white-covered walls.
A police bully's image, and his torturing hawks.
A new coat of paint in the walls of Manila,
won't hide the cuts of a Marcos's claw.
"Baby Doc's" flight far off to the sun,
leaves a corpse dying, imprisoned STILL.
Santiago cry the pain of darkness,
while Thatcher's H-Blocks still smell of flesh.
The crying, moaning pleas of the forgotten,
in dungeon holes of an unjust world.

But the cracks are widening on the walls of injustice.
The crumbling of mortar, beneath the strength of a people,
pouring forward in a mass of unified suffering.
As whispers become shouts, as shouts become screams,
Revolt brings the downfall of a tyranny long past.
with downfall comes change, a revolution blossoms,
blooms to the sun,
a beautiful flower of love and equality.

Old ladies drink dark, sweet coffee
in the shade of a New York's sun.
Coffee from Chile, so dark, so strong,
with joking workers, picking coffee to midday song.
Smiles on faces in South African jungle,
black smiles, white smiles, one smile.
Children laugh to Belfast street songs,
no more tanks to drown out melodies.

Sweet whispers of love, a Filipino girl's blushes,
runs through sugar cane, dry, but not bloodied.
The crumbled remains of white wall,
are dust beneath the dancing feet of Mankind.

The flickering ray of light,
shines through the cracks of darkened cell,
life rays of hope, these are my own true dreams.
Thoughts of cherry smiles, kind family faces,
a woman's breast against my cold forgotten face.
A child's chuckle, in my inexperienced arms;
a sweetheart's tears, a father at last.
Thoughts of sweet smells, bright moving colors,
and the feel of wind through green wet grass.
These are my dreams that cling to the wall.
Some day soon, my walls will fall,
in the dust, I'll dance to the chorus of Mankind.

Metropolitan Correctional Center
New York, NY, USA

Marilyn Buck

To Women Who Work

In the winds of whirling dust
whipping new york streets
a world of women
tossed by the tangible
determining our lives
young   old

old
women sitting on stoops
stooped by lives of labor
bearing children in tenuous tenements
bent over assembly lines
cleaning washing cooking
for old women
who whirl through Bloomingdales
spending shopping searching
for chalices of youth and beauty
obsessive desperation over depreciation
and obsolescence
oblivious to value

old young women sitting on stoops
too young
babies in arms
singing strident sonatas of dreams
burdened by blues
burning in eyes mirroring expectations

lived only by miss amerikas
dancing dreams of Vogue
and princes

while old women
and young women sit on stoops
needing
slaving in sweatshops in Savannah San Juan and Seoul
spinning out the desires of
old women and young women
of class
who need nothing
and want everything.

Marilyn Buck

Remembering a 15-year-old Palestinian woman in prison, chained to the bed springs. She had refused to stop singing.

Singing songs
Chained
for singing
Clear melodic minor notes
welling from sweet young throats
and mouths
which have tasted the tightness of screaming silences
spit upon   cursed   beaten
while children are dying from Boer bullets
            israeli bombs
            and slave masters' lashes
            sounding a whining wrath

And still songs soar

Sounds sung sweetly
soaring skyward
Reeling remembering revealing
souls and spirits
Women singing songs
            lullabys lovesongs
            and blues songs
            chanting cantillating songs
            of living life
            and dying death
Searching sounds not yet noted
on bars
not yet ordered on scales
Exploring the breadth of hell
Seeking the expanses of the universe
and freedom

Summer 1988

Marilyn Buck

in celebration of the Intifada

David, son of israel
slew Goliath
Laughing that one so small
could defeat one so large

He took Goliath's house
and walked in his shoes
and ate at his table

David son of israel
became the Goliath of Palestine
greedy, grasping and merciless
Laughing at the humble people
of the olive groves and desert

    Remembering only that he had been small
He forgot.

The daughters and sons of Palestine
do not forget
that a stone is just
    a stone
lying in the rubble of their homes
until it becomes a missile
Ululating resistance
Promising a storm of fire.

December 1988

Pat Gros-Levasseur

On getting organized in Cuyahoga County Jail

I was looking at you
Sister Braiding
that ancient art
and all I could think of
was "Strange Fruit."

All that intelligence
those wise eyes
spent in card games
undeveloped.

You read about Jorge
killed in his cell
you know how it happens—
been happening
Far as you know—
    400 years
Hey—"I'm serious"
    you told me
your cousin was
Beaten and
Strangled and hung and
Buried
Quickly.

Ain't none of us suicidal—

you organized me.
Makes me think of
    "Strange Fruit."

Cleveland, April, 1985

Pat Gros-Levasseur

for Carol Saucier Manning

Looking out the prison window
on the quiet late night cold
Imagining the cold sharp air
  on my Face
Fill my lungs and count the miles
  ahead
  and between
our LIBERATION
Comrade, Sister
with the strong hands of the people
the soul of a worker
the loyalty of a sister
  the tenderness of a mother
your teachings are clear
your example, matter of fact
to pull the weeds of
Liberalism
self doubt, disunity
and plant the seeds
of Liberation
wherever the Field may be.

January 3, 1985

Pat Gros-Levasseur

Been Thinking

Been thinking of our last house
   in clandestinity
   in Freedom-
it had a big porch and in the summertime
We would stay up late on Friday night.
Mama would have some wine and sing
Rocking with her girls.
Traffic would race by
That dark highway—
We were so anonymous.
The Fireflies and the stars.
Now to capture the warm sweet caresses
Without the pain.

July 11, 1986

Pat Gros-Levasseur

Lacemakers

(for Barbara on her birthday
November 10, 1986
Framingham, MA)

They sat outside
in front of buildings grey, from weather
some with doors painted bright primary
   colors.

A fishing village.
Women with dark hair, greying or white
their gnarled hands worked the lace
intricately against colorful log shaped
   pillows.
the Lacemakers.

It must have been a hard life
when art turns to toil
to support a village
when the Fishing was down or
   a boat was lost.

They sat together
sharing their news, spiced as it was
By the times, their Families,
   superstitions

Looking across at the boats, and
    the water
Far off—
They must have thought of
Trying their luck with the catch—

Still, they leaned into their work.
How their backs must have ached—
their gnarled hands
How much work they had to do
How many hours they spent.

But they would never live to see
the lace bring the money it should
or their daughters try their luck
with the catch.

Pat Gros-Levasseur

From these deprived walls

From these deprived walls
reach back to that morning
hot and green
when we hit the pavements
of our cities
determined,
open.

Remember all we saw—
the disparity
the suffering
our aching solidarity.

From in here
it all wells up
the vision
and emotion
of the choices we have made

Imam Hakim

My Pledge for the New Year

"The World is a Ghetto!"

This is a lyric from an old popular song.
When it was written, the author never thought its truth
    would last this long,
But fate has a knack of keeping the world at bay,
So we must be careful of what we say.

If we vow to do a thing, and put a time frame to it,
We better be sure we know exactly how to do it—
for many men have made resolutions—
   at least, they made the pledge,
But whether or not they'll keep their word
   is harder done than said.

A vow is sacred, it's viewed as a binding life force;
A vow is the "Beacon Light" of the Honorable men,
   and the Guide to set their course—
A vow is the pledge to do a thing— and it's
   followed by action,
A vow without results, is nothing but mass distraction.

Knowing all that I know now, I make the following vow:

My pledge this year is to gain full
employment in the liberation of my people.
I vow to LOVE them, HONOR them,
FIGHT for them, CHASTISE them, DIE
for them, CRY for them, EDUCATE them,
SHELTER them, ELEVATE them, and
PRAY with them!

Will you join me?
Will you vow to become free?
Will you seek liberty?

Peace . . .

Imam Hakim

We Will Survive

The times are a-changing,
   or so they say.
It will soon be a brighter day.
But all I know is, it's good to be alive
   and—
      We will survive!

History has taught us many lessons, of late;
 some, we have chosen to forget.
We lose sight of our goals and we start to regret,
We start to lie, cheat and soon we take a dive,
   but—
      Still, we will survive!

It's hard being regarded as second-class;
sometimes you feel you can't go on.
Yet, you then remember, we "save the best for last,"
so you strive for success your whole life long.
   now—
   You *know* we will survive!

WE WILL SURVIVE

Poor People of this world, you should feel no shame;
Poor People, don't change your looks or your names;
Poor People, your tradition and culture mean a lot;
You People— value your homeland (though some have forgot)
    Remember—
        We will survive!

This is not a poem of sad thoughts or sad times,
This *is* a reminder to keep freedom on our minds,
This *is* a suggestion to leave negative vibes behind.
    Think only that—
        We will survive!

Well, I've said my piece and if you disagree,
that's strictly up to you.
I'll stand on what I've said— as Truth—
and then do whatever I have to do.

    I will make freedom come through,
        'cause—

    We have to Survive!

                            Peace,

                                    2-25-88

Jamal Josephs

No Distance at All

five wars
countless lynchings
ten million Cadillacs later
and we still ain't free

part of it is murder
part of it is suicide
they don't care
and we can't cope
so trivial pursuits
have become a national pastime
while monumental indifference
has become an international sin
the laws of termination
are fixed and easy
if you can't use it, lose it
after all, the end justifies the means
eliminate dead weight
initiate a new final solution
to solve some tiresome old problems
ignore the violent serpent
of home-grown white supremacy
deal with the vicious monster of apartheid
through the technique of constructive engagement
while we're at it

did you constructively engage
grandmother Eleanor Bumpurs
when you evicted her with a shotgun blast
was it constructive
when you made death wish Goetz a hero
for shooting our youth in the back
how about the engagement
of electric cattle prods
on naked Third World flesh
where was that
Johannesburg N.Y. or Queens South Afrika
Steve Biko is dead
as is Malcolm
as is George Jackson
as is any voice that dares
to speak against the emperor
Nelson Mandela
has been in prison for a generation
so that other generations might be free
yet the battle escalates
the holocaust continues
execution is in
human rights are out
protest and get gunned down in Soweto
resist and get bombed in Philadelphia
then confuse the natives
by putting the killers in black-face
Heil Hitler Field Marshal Oreo
or was it Idi Amin
or was it Papa Doc Duvalier
or was it Wilson Goode
yes part of it is murder
but part of it is suicide
you see, not all lethal injections
are given as the result
of a court order

we make daily journeys
to the land of zombies
lured by the promise
of minor escapes and false enlightenment
we destroy each other in theory and in fact
and otherwise thrill ourselves to death
in the name of chic trends and undefined necessities
all hail to the crystal peace pipe
the white powder vampire
who is draining our life force
while masquerading as the best of times
so kill on,
      sniff on,
           shoot on,
                base on,
                    die on.

and if that's not enough
the angels themselves
have left you some dust
this Afrikan people
will self destruct in 5 seconds
part of it is murder
part of it is suicide
but it all feels like death

we may be the world
but for how much longer
the earth is full of madmen
who'd rather fight than switch
our people are starving
so the rich can have more caviar
in order to fatten the few
they deny the many
they used to pay farmers

not to grow food
now they don't pay them at all
things are not getting better
no matter how many multi-colored drag queens
masturbate on stage
while singing upbeat versions
of "I did it my way"
and don't believe Babylon loves you
whether it comes from a pope
          a prince
          or a deviled damned
          rappin duke
remember you're in a place
where might makes right
and just like in the movies
the empire will strike back
beneath the glitter and the lies
it is still
the land of the greed
and the home of the slave

Afrika is Azania
     is Ethiopia
     is Grenada
     is Philadelphia
     is wherever we are
the only distance between us
is the gap
that has been placed
in our minds
abide in love
and know that you have family
everywhere
every goodbye ain't gone
we have yet to say farewell
hold fast to the sword of unity

turn away death and division
in all its parts
until the distance between us
becomes
no distance at all

Leavenworth

Carlos Alberto Torres

Graciela Esperanza

entre ruinas y despojo
de ajena pertenencia
la vegetación abatida
a sus heridas se doblega
pero ya abandonó
la creciente la ribera
y otra vez el sol
pacientemente va secando
las humedades de la tierra

— "YA ABONDONO LA CRECIENTE LA
RIBERA," poema de Rodrigo
Restrepo)

Un vehículo militar se acercó a la zanja rodeada por el grupo de mujeres y niños. Los ocupantes sin bajarse miraban la escena. Observaban las caras de los presentes. Tomaban notas y repasaban una colección de retratos.

A la llegada del vehículo, las mujeres y niños se habian alejado un poco de la orilla de la fosa. En el fondo estaban tendidos varios cadáveres desfigurados. Las mujeres buscaban un rastro familiar, una vestimenta conocida, cualquier cosa que dejara saber quienes habían sido los muertos. Los cuerpos estaban hinchados y desangrados.

De pronto cambio la dirección del viento penetrando al interior del carro militar con un hedor espeso y sofocante. El vehículo abandonó la escena.

Las mujeres y niños de nuevo rodearon la zanja. Tres de las mujeres se acercaron a los cuerpos para su reconocimiento, cruzándose en su labor a cada paso. Una de ellas se arrodilló al lado de un cadaver femenino, rezándole a la Virgen en voz alta. Las demás la siguieron en su rezo arrodilladas al lado de los desconocidos muertos. Poco después, se oía en la zanja el murmullo fúnebre del llanto de los niños, el rezo susurrante de las mujeres, y el zumbido de las moscas.

Graciela era una de las mujeres que había ido esa mañana a la zanja, en las afueras del pueblito. Era una joven delgada, de piel color canela y ojos verdosos. Su cabello negro, abundante y lustroso caía suelto sobre sus hombros. Iba con las otras mujeres cada vez que sabían de nuevos cadáveres. Intentaban identificarlos. Rezaban por ellos, conocidos o desconocidos. Graciela tenía esta costumbre desde hacía un año, cuando una vecina ya vieja le rogó que fuera a la zanja porque ella no podía, para ver si entre los cuerpos descubiertos ese día, estaba el de su nieto ausente. Tristemente, Graciela había traído noticias de su nieto, a la anciana.

Había llorado no sólo por la viejita, sino también por el joven asesinado, un muchacho callado que trabajaba junto a su marido en la hacienda cafetalera. Tenía diecisiete años y era el único pariente de la anciana. Sin él, nadie quedaba para velar por ella. Días después del entierro, la viejita se enfermó, y sin la atención y tratamiento que requería, se puso grave. Graciela hizo su parte, pero a quien la anciana necesitaba ya había muerto. Vivió unos meses más. La enterraron al lado de su nieto.

En el pueblo estaban espantados por el vil crimen. El muchacho era conocido, y no se sabía por qué o quién lo quería ver muerto. El capitán del cuartel militar, al final de su corta investigación, y siguiendo la costumbre de la política oficial, concluyó que el joven había sido víctima de los delincuentes que rodeaban la zona. Así se refería él a los guerrilleros, de quienes se oía mucho pero a quienes nadie conocía. Después de aquel día, habían empezado a aparecer más muertos en la zona. Las autoridades nunca aclaraban quienes eran las víctimas; decían no saber. Casi todos eran desconocidos.

Algunos cuerpos se encontraban decapitados, otros mutilados con horrible precisión. La mayoría mostraban tiros en la cabeza; todos tenían las manos atadas atrás. En algunos casos, los cuerpos estaban desnudos, otras veces con ropas puestas al revés. A las mujeres casi siempre les faltaba la ropa interior; casi todas mostraban evidencia de violación y, en algunos casos, tenían objetos macabramente insertados en sus órganos. Aunque la mayoría de víctimas eran jóvenes, también aparecían en el fondo de la zanja, viejos y niños.

Al año del primer entierro, Graciela, acompañada de su hijito, seguía la procesión de mujeres y niños a la zanja. Ello bajo la continua protesta de su marido Juán, ya que su patrón le había manifestado que se veía mal, y era indigno de su joven esposa, que estuviera tanto tiempo fuera de casa, o piadosos auxilios a quienes la patrulla llamaba delincuentes. Juán no sólo temía lo despidieran de su trabajo en el cafetal, también se sentía obligado a hacer caso al dueño, ya que éste, generosamente, le había extendido el plazo para el pago del solar donde había construído su pequeña casa. Graciela no ignoraba las protestas de su esposo; pero, aunque él resistía, ella lograba convencerlo de que obrar de otra manera estaría mal. También él sabía que en el pueblo no había cura. A corto tiempo de la muerte del nieto sucedió que después de la primera misa de requiem, varios tiros penetraron por la entrada principal de la iglesia, hiriendo mortalmente al cura. La iglesia permanecía abierta, pero sin cura para celebrar las misas.

Por un mes no fue necesario que Graciela fuera a la zanja. Ella cuidaba las eras que tenía detrás de su casa. Cultivaba algunas legumbres para ayudar al sustento de su familia. El trabajo era muy duro, pero no le restaba tiempo a su ternura de madre y esposa.

Aquella noche se sentía nerviosa, presentía algo mal. Su esposo no acostumbraba llegar tan tarde. En la esquina del cuarto, el hijo dormía tranquilamente. Graciela lo miraba y ponía después su vista ansiosa en el camino. Nadie se acercaba. Tuvo la idea de irse sola para ver si algo le había ocurrido a Juán en el camino, pero decidió esperar. Llegó el amanecer, y ella estaba aún sentada dormida junto a la puerta de su casa. Al abrir los ojos, se sintió asustada y desorientada por la ausencia de Juán. Entró al cuarto y vió al niño durmiendo. Su miedo crecía cada segundo. Volvió a salir asustada buscándolo en los alrededores de la casa. Nada.

Cuando los primeros rayos de luz empezaban a iluminar el interior, el niño despertó. Graciela apuradamente lo vistió y le dió de comer. Salió con él en sus brazos, siguiendo a paso rápido el camino.

Se dirigía a la casa del dueño de la hacienda. Quizás hubo mucho que hacer, pensaba, y quizás se tuvo que quedar la noche trabajando. Andando, casi corriendo, rezaba por que Juán se encontrara bien. Entró por el camino de la casa y vio al mayordomo dando órdenes a algunos de los jornaleros, todos vecinos de Graciela.

— Don José — gritó la joven — perdone Don José, ¿Pudiera hablar con mi Juán?

— ¿Cómo fue? — le contestó el mayordomo — ¿Qué me dices?

— ¿Pudiera hablar un momento con Juán?

— ¿Juán? Juán no ha llegado todavía — le contestó bruscamente — me imaginaba que tampoco iba a trabajar hoy.

— ¿Qué? ¿Tampoco? Juán nunca ha faltado Don — Con palabras cortantes el mayordomo interrumpió:

— Y dígale a su esposo que si sigue faltando lo echaré de aquí. ya sabe que el dueño, Don Fernando, ha tenido mucha paciencia con Juán y con la deuda que tiene.

— Pero, él nunca ha faltado al trabajo — contestó Graciela.

— Mira, yo no tengo tiempo para estar chismeando contigo — la increpó el mayordomo — váyase de aquí, y búsqueme a Juán. Que se deje de sus vagancias si sabe lo que es bueno. Váyase, pués -

El mayordomo siguió caminando hacia sus trabajadores, gritando órdenes y dándo indicaciones con las manos. Graciela estaba totalmente perpleja. El niño empezó a llorar asustado con los gritos del gerente.

— Calla hijo, tu mami te quiere — le decía, tratando de calmarlo.

El corazón le palpitaba veloz. Se sentía tristemente humillada. No sabía que hacer. Pensó regresar al pueblito para ir al cuartel militar.

Después de llegar al pequeño cementerio que bordeaba el pueblo, el camino para el cuartel era corto y recto. Atravesaba el pueblo de extremo a extremo. Lo caminaron de prisa Gabriela y su hijo, siempre observados por hombres y mujeres. Algunas habían sido sus compañeras en la zanja. Los saludos para ella esa mañana fueron cordiales, aunque reservados. Graciela aligeró el paso. Entró al cuartel y pidió hablar con el capitán. Sentó a su hijo en una silla al lado de la puerta, desde donde el niño escrutaba el interior del local con mirada tímida. Un sargento flaco y pálido estaba sentado detrás de una mesita. Al ver a Graciela, sacó de su bolsillo un peine y lo paso cuidadosamente por su grasoso cabello.

— Dígame, señorita, ¿qué desea? — le preguntó el sargento, levantándose de su silla y acercándose a Graciela.

— Busco a mi esposo, se llama Juán Esperanza. Anoche no llegó a casa, estoy preocupada porque algo le haya ocurrido. ¿No está aquí?

El sargento miraba con atrevimiento mostrando su dentadura manchada, y sonriéndose burlonamente al escuchar lo que para él era un asunto rutinario y ridículo.

— No, que va señorita, si aquí no hay nadie. Estoy todo solito — dijo sarcásticamente—. El capitán debe llegar en un ratito, si quieres esperarlo. Además, ese hombre tuyo se debe arrepentir si es que le calentó la cama a otra y no a tí — le dijo el sargento en son de burla.

Graciela disimuló su rabia. El la había ofendido y abochornado. Qué derecho tiene para hacerlo, pensó la joven. Sin embargo, se sentía incapaz de enfrentársele. Temblando de coraje, Graciela cargó con su hijo y salió del cuartel. A pocos pasos, Graciela miró atrás y el sargento, recostado vagamente contra el marco de la puerta, estaba aun sonriendo, mostrando sus dientes manchados. Graciela caminó de nuevo hacia su casa. Hablaría con los vecinos, quizás ellos sabrían algo. Estaba insegura de cómo proceder. ¿Qué más podría hacer? Toda la mañana sintió temor de que algo malo le hubiera sucedido a Juán. Sin embargo, salió de su casa con la esperanza de que hubiera un error y que encontraría a Juán. Esperaba encontrar simpatía por él entre la gente, pero ya veía que a pocos le importaba. No estaba ahora más cerca de conocer lo que le había pasado a su marido. Empezó a sentirse desesperada con la situación. Pero de algo estaba segura, y era de que Juán nunca había dejado de llegar a la casa en todo el tiempo que llevaban juntos. Y aunque ella quisiera encontrar una interpretación o razón más cómoda para entender la ausencia, este hecho le daba vueltas en su mente, hasta producirle escalofríos.

Para descansar los brazos, Graciela dejó caminar a su hijo, quien corría torpemente hacia adelante para esperar después que su madre lo alcanzara, y correr de nuevo para otra vez adelantarse. Graciela, pensando en Juán, borraba de su mente lo peor, pero una idea fue más poderosa que su deseo de borrarla. Hasta ahora, hasta ese momento, no se le había ocurrido lo que poco a poco se iba formando en su mente. Con esta monstruosa idea dejó de caminar. Quería sentarse pero un frío de pies a cabeza le cruzaba y no le permitía el movimiento. Lo sentía ahora como torcijones en su entraña. Lentamente se convertía en calor y sudor. Empezó a moverse, caminando despacio, un poco mas rápido después, término corriendo, casi arrastrando del brazo a su hijo. Se hablaba a sí misma en voz alta, conciente en la desesperación, camino hacia la zanja musitando repetidamente.

— Que no sea verdad, que no sea verdad.

Se arrodilló y lloró a la orilla de la zanja, mientras su hijo, que reconocía el sitio, jugaba con piedritas. Graciela, inquieta fijó su mirada en el fondo de la fosa. La satisfacción de no haber hallado ahí a Juán, junto a la desesperación que aún sentía por su ausencia, hicieron revivir su coraje y frustración por las indignidades soportadas ese día. Se secó las lágrimas, se levantó y tomando nuevamente la mano del niño, se encaminó al pueblo. Seguiré buscando. Sus pasos ahora eran lentos, ya liberados del afan de una incertidumbre.

El primer sonido fue como un trueno lejano, como temblor en la distancia. Otro le siguió, otro más, y de momento el ruido se pareciá mas al repiquetear de un gigantesco tambor. Pensó en un terremoto, pero no se sentía ondulación en el suelo. Mientras más se acercaba al pueblo, más atronadores y diferenciados los ruidos se escuchaban. Si ella no hubiera estado en el pueblo mas temprano, podría creer que se trataba de sonido de petardos y tambores. ¿Una fiesta, acaso? Todo era absurdo tras la desaparición de Juán. Acercándose a la entrada del pueblito los sonidos eran ruidosas ráfagas de rayos y relampagos.

Hombres desconocidos, unos vestidos con uniforme verde de soldados, otros en ropa civil, corrían con las armas en sus manos.

Se hallaban cerca a su casa, disparando mientras iban acercándose al pueblito. Una vez mas volvió a sonar el gigantesco tambor. Hombres armados corrían al cuartel. Graciela apuró el paso siguiendo el camino de los guerrilleros, aquellos a quienes el capitán llamaba delincuentes.

Cuando Graciela llegó a la plaza, vio que un hombre de camisa y pantalón verde oliva, con un altoparlante en sus manos hablaba a los vecinos. Se veía que no era del cuartel por sus greñas y su barba. Ella no sabía qué pensar de todo esto. Poco a poco fue acercándose. Los guerrilleros tenían con las manos en alto y desarmados al sargento con quien había hablado Graciela esa misma mañana, al capitán, al mayordomo Don José, y a otros soldados. Los rebeldes los obligaban a poner atención al discurso de su compañero. Este se secaba la sien con un pañuelo rojo y azul, como los que usaban sus compañeros, amarrados en el brazo.

Graciela notó que los vecinos estaban asustados y silenciosos. Algunos niños lloraban, algunas madres mecían a los más pequeños. Los ancianos en cambio, se veían calmados; escuchaban y miraban con ojos plácidos al orador. Mientras unos guerrilleros montaban guardia vigilando los alrededores, otros hablaban casualmente a la gente que se acercaba. Se veían cansados, algunos estaban heridos.

Graciela sentía curiosidad por lo que ellos tenían para decir. ¿Por qué hacían lo que hacían? se preguntaba. Pero lo que más le interesaba, era saber dónde encontraría a Juan. Su curiosidad la hacía sentirse culpable.

Graciela escuchó al guerrillero hablar de lo imposible que era vivir debido a la pillería de los ricos hacendados, y del abuso de los comerciantes y bancos en la ciudad. Hablaba también de cambiar el gobierno, y de los cambios que vendrían después.

Observó entre los guerrilleros algunas mujeres, jóvenes como ella. Qué raro, pensó Graciela, ver mujeres armadas. Sentía esa mezcla de admiración y de respeto, la misma acostumbrada ante quienes poseen alguna autoridad. Quería oírlas hablar, y estudiarlas como se examina lo raro y curioso. Acercándose a una de ellas, le dijo:
— Perdone señorita — y acercándose aun más — ¿le pudiera hablar por un minuto?

La guerrillera, que a cambio de uniforme vestía pantalón y blusa civil, enfundó su pistola, y en voz baja y atenta le contestó:
— Sí claro, ¿qué desea?
— Yo estoy buscando a un hombre, mi marido. Quizás lo vieron, tal vez herido por el camino, tenía una camisa azul, vendría del area de la hacienda de café. ¿No encontraron a alguien así?
— No señora, en el camino no vi a nadie así. Todos están allá por el cafetal. Sólo nos trajimos al mayordomo, y eso porque nos sacó un arma. Los demás se quedaron. Dejamos unos compañeros a cargo para hablar con los trabajadores. Si quiere puede regresar con nosotros y hablar con ellos — dijo la guerrillera.
El guerrillero del altoparlante dejó de hablar. Se dió una orden y los rebeldes empezaron a retirarse poco a poco. Por otra parte, Graciela no observó que el capitán la miraba mientras ella hablaba con la joven guerrillera.

Días después de la toma de los guerrilleros, el gobierno aseguraba que se había restituido el orden y la paz, aunque la vida en el pueblo no se había normalizado. Durante el ataque los rebeldes habían entrado al cuartel, llevándose todas las armas. Lo dinamitaron después y destruyeron todos los vehículos militares. Más soldados refuerzos habían llegado, reconstruyeron el cuartel, repusieron las armas y los materiales tomados o destruidos.
El capitán encabezaba la investigación del asunto. Ya se habían arrestado a algunos vecinos. Avanzada la noche, se oían tiros. A toda hora se veían rondando la zona, autos civiles manejados por soldados sin uniforme u hombres desconocidos a los vecinos del pueblo, que entraban o salían del cuartel, acompañados por el capitán.
Una noche, Graciela y el niño fueron despertados por reflectores y gritos de alto parlante. El niño asustado comenzó a llorar inconsolable.
— ¡Alto! ¡Rindan sus armas! — gritó una voz.
Se repitió la orden. Graciela no sabía lo que sucedia. Se levantó y poco a poco abrió la puerta.
— ¡Manos en alto y salga! — ordenó la voz.

La joven levantó las manos y temerosa salió de su casa. Los soldados entraron y rápidamente revisaron la casa. El capitán se acercó a Graciela y con voz autoritaria y despótica, empezó a interrogarla.

— ¿Qué hablaba usted a la delincuente? — dijo el militar—. Bueno, hable.

Graciela, asustada y con las manos todavía alzadas le contestó:
— Por favor, no he hecho nada. No sé de qué me habla.

El capitán, pistola en mano y con la arrogancia de guapo de barrio, miraba con rencor, despectivamente a la joven.

— Dígame — volvió a repetir éste — ¿de qué conversaron? ¿Dónde están? ¿Los está ayudando? Hay testigos que reportan haberla visto con ellos el día del ataque.

— No, sólo les pregunté si habían visto a mi marido — se defendió la joven.— Ha desaparecido, no lo he visto en varios días.

-¿Porqué le preguntó a ellos? ¿Qué saben ellos de eso? ¿Anda su marido con los delincuentes?

— No, no sé — respondió Graciela — es que no sé qué le ha pasado. Quería saber si quizas ellos lo habían visto cuando se acercaban al pueblo. Yo pregunté lo mismo al sargento, ese mismo día en el cuartel.

— El cuartel, ¿estuvo en el cuartel?

— Sí. Ese mismo día, antes que lo destruyeran — contestó la joven.

— Manténgase ahí — ordenó el capitán.

Este dejó de interrogarla para volverse hacia uno de los hombres desconocidos, en ropa civil, que observaba la escena silenciosamente. Hablaron en voz baja, la consulta duró pocos segundos. El capitán regresó.

— Manténgase en su casa, está bajo arresto — le dijo —. Mañana regresaré para llevarla a la jefatura de zona. Mientras tanto, dejaré a uno de mis hombres vigilándola.

Graciela entró a su casa advertida de que tenía que mantenerse ahí. Oyó a los soldados retirarse. Sus objetos y pertenencias estaban tirados y revueltos en el piso. El niño había permanecido silencioso, agarrado a su vestido durante todo el interrogatorio, siempre junto a ella. Graciela lo miró tristemente. Le acarició su pelo. Luego lo acostó rozando su brazo tiernamente mientras se dormía. La joven empezó a recoger las cosas arrojadas al suelo por los soldados. Veía su vida tomar un rumbo horrible y espantoso. Era inocente, pero en forma cruel la trataban como delincuente. Se había sentido pequeña y adolescente frente al interrogatorio del oficial.

Había pasado ya algún rato cuando Graciela escuchó un ruido. Al voltearse vió parados en la puerta a un soldado y el capitán. Se le acercaron. El capitán la tomó de los hombros abruptamente.

— ¡Yo sé bregar con putas como tú! — le gritó.

Luego con una mano la golpeó en el pecho. Graciela, perdiendo el balance cayó al piso. Sintió como otros golpes impactaban repetidamente en su cuerpo. Por instinto se protegía de los golpes, empujando a quienes la atacaban para sacudírselos de encima. Con cada uno de sus esfuerzos se multiplicaban los golpes que recibía. La fuerza utilizada contra ella no sólo era para poseerla y atormentarla. La reacción de Graciela era mas sensación instintiva que razonada, pero con el pensamiento fijo de que con suficiente rabia podía repeler a sus atormentadores. Mientras uno le sujetaba las manos, el otro se posesionaba de ella e intentaba ultrajarla. La cara del capitán se torcía y distorcionaba con el esfuerzo mientras una sonrisa burlona se plasmaba en sus labios. Con cada empujón le saltaban gotas de sudor. Le corrían por la sien, la mejilla, para caer sobre Graciela. Pero el sudor no bastaba para que cediera el apretón de sus manos.

— Déjame el turno a mí — dijo el soldado que la sostenía del cabello.

Empezó de nuevo el atraco. Graciela trataba de voltearse y cruzar o cerrar sus piernas, pero inútilmente. con cachetadas y puños menguaban su resistencia. A ella sólo le restaban fuerzas para llorar.

— Esto es lo único que entienden estas sinvergüenzas — dijo el capitán al soldado, y mientras éste tomaba su turno con Graciela, el capitán la manoseaba.

— ¿Verdad que tú sabes quien manda aquí, amorcito? — dijó el capitán.

Y un momento después se levantó impacientemente, dirigiéndose al soldado.

— Vamos, acaba ya que me quiero ir.

— Si, ya, ya pronto — contestó el soldado.

El capitán se ajustó el uniforme y lo sacudió con sus manos, disimulando la infamia de su acción. El otro se apartó de Graciela, y dándose cuenta que unas gotas de sangre le habían manchado el pantalón le arrojó una última patada a la joven, gritándole:
— ¡Cabrona, me cagaste el uniforme!

El capitán sonriendo condescendiente a la mala suerte de su subordinado, miró a Graciela y le dijo:
— Y tú Graciela Esperanza, mañana te quiero encontrar lista para llevarte a la jefatura. No hagas que perdamos el tiempo contigo.

Salió apurado hacia su carro.

Graciela estuvo quieta por un tiempo, casi inconciente por las golpeaduras recibidas. Tenía la sensación de estar flotando y ondulando en un océano. Todo estaba silencioso. Abrió sus ojos. Tenía su vestido alzado hasta la cintura y desgarrado en el pecho. A un lado estaba su ropa interior. Sentía la humedad de su propia sangre en los muslos. Ardía su cuerpo, estaba débil. La primera reacción fue no querer aceptar lo que su mente lógica le señalaba. Se sentía desorientada, abstraída. Intentó separarse de sí misma concientemente y racionalizar en forma despejada lo que le había sucedido. Quería conducirse como cuando estaba frente a los cadáveres de la zanja. Nunca se sintió inmune al sufrimiento pero tampoco su imaginación concibió el terror frío y real que sentía ahora. La realidad de su victimización destrozaba su siquis. Miró a su hijo sentado en el colchón, sus ojos abiertos y fijos en ella. El niño temblaba, sus manos y brazos estaban tensos. Graciela se movía de lado a lado. Trataba de estirar brazos y piernas. Hacia el esfuerzo para levantarse aunque su estómago revuelto y sus intestinos en nudo le impedían movimientos. Sentía que había sido abusada y ridiculizada, la vergüenza la consumía. El instinto le decía que su violación no sólo había sido a su cuerpo sino también a su privacidad y orgullo moral. Su impotencia para poder rechazar el vejaminoso ataque le acentuaba su vulnerabilidad.

Finalmente, la joven mujer se levantó del piso arreglando su vestido para cubrir la desnudez. Tensa y nerviosa empezó a ordenar las cosas regadas por el piso. Miraba a su alrededor buscando borrar cualquier recuerdo del atraco. Sus pasos eran lentos como el de una condenada, conciente de que cada movida suya era observada por el verdugo. Se culpaba por la ignorancia al

91

no haber podido anticipar la llegada de los soldados. Por su falta de fuerza en rechazar la violación. Horribles pensamientos culpaban su inhabilidad de no haber podido proteger a su hijo para que no fuera testigo de su vejación. Con agua y un paño restregaba en su piel la mancha del despojo. Luego, al atender el niño y expresarle su cariño le ayudó a reorientarse e ignorar un tanto su dolor. Su voluntad bloqueaba el llanto de rabia e indignación. Por un momento pensó que ya había sucedido lo peor. Pero recordó las palabras del capitán. Su mente comenzó a visualizar lo que le sucedería en la jefatura el dia siguiente. Esta preocupación le instigó un nuevo miedo, diferente a lo que había sentido antes. Temía no solo los hechos sucedidos, sino, los que vendrían; lo que podría ocurrirle. Graciela caminó hacia la entrada de su casita con su vista dirigida hacia la opaca lejanía.

Ella era un conjunto de inusitados cambios emocionales. El odio y la venganza en esos momentos tejían fantasías. Se le veía una mirada de coraje, pero también de indecisión. Recordó la ausencia de su esposo. Pensó que necesitaría actuar, moverse, y no permitir que sus atormentadores lastimaran otra vez a ella y a su hijo. Jamás se repetiría, se lo prometió. No tenía otro remedio, tendría que escapar de este sitio.

Cada paso dado con el objeto de guiarse, aumentaba su valor. Se movía con más rapidez ahora, porque en su mente se formaba un plan. Dejaría sus angustias para otro momento. De nuevo se volvió a asomar por la entrada. Los soldados se habían ido. Con rapidez recogió y amontonó lo mas importante para ella y el niño. Tomando al hijo en sus brazos empezó a caminar calladamente hacia la carretera. Llevaba unos pesos, su tesoro acumulado por largo tiempo. Con este dinero podía llegar hasta la capital.

Graciela entregó todo su dinero al chofer del autobús. La llevaría un pueblo a corta distancia de la capital. De ahí continuaría a pié o como fuese posible. Después de llegar al lugar, dejó el bus y continuó caminando con su hijito por la carretera a la ciudad. Esa misma noche llegaron. Atravesaban un barrio de casas caídas y calles fangosas. Había muchos perros que ladraban al acercarse. Las calles estaban vacías. Al lado opuesto, al extremo del barrio, había un pequeño puente. Era la salida del barrio, y la entrada a la ciudad. Cerca, había un rancho con techo de lata y cartón. El niño lloraba de hambre y sueño. Su llanto llenaba el aire espeso y rancio. Graciela paró frente al rancho y llamó. Un perro ladraba desde adentro.

¿Qué quiere, quién es? decía una voz débil y femenina.

Necesito agua, contestó la joven.

El kiosko está cerrado, respondió sarcásticamente la voz anciana.

El perro seguía ladrando. La anciana volvió a hablar:

Usa la pluma pública, ¿no la ves? Más adelante está.

Graciela trataba de calmar al niño. Anduvo algunos pasos y encontró la pluma. Los primeros sorbos la calmaron un poco. Más allá notó que había un cajón tirado. Lo recogió para sentarse en él, mientras mecía cariñosa, pero nerviosamente al niño entre sus brazos.

Oiga, llamó la misma voz desde el ranchito.

Oiga, volvió a repetir.

Graciela miró al ranchito. Por la rendija abierta de la puerta salía la baja iluminación de una vela. Veía una mano extendida que le hacía señas de que se acercara. Lentamente, Graciela se acercó sospechosa hasta el ranchito.

Tenga, para el niño, decía la voz.

La extremidad de los arrugados dedos ofrecía un trozo de naranja. Con sorpresa y agradecimiento Graciela se acercó y tomó la fruta.

Y para tí niña, de nuevo salió la mano por la rendija de la puerta con otra porción de naranja. Graciela extendió la mano. El perro seguía sus ladridos.

¿Qué haces en la calle a esta hora?, preguntó la anciana.

Acabo de llegar de mi pueblo, respondió, no conozco este sitio.

La conversación entre las dos mujeres continuó. Al rato la puerta se abrió del todo y la joven pudo entrar al rancho. En el silencio de la noche se escuchaba el mumullo de las dos mujeres conversando y a intervalos, el ladrido del perro.

El piso de la choza era de tierra. Las paredes eran de tablas rajadas y de cartón. Algunos cajones se usaban como asientos. El colchón de trapos viejos servía como cama y asiento. No tenía más muebles la solitaria anciana. No durmieron mucho. En la madrugada la anciana despertó a Graciela y con tono preocupado dijo:

93

Mira niña, tenemos que apurarnos si queremos llegar antes que los otros. Podemos dejar al niño con la vecina. Yo hablo con ella, añadió la vieja.

Luego los tres salieron de la choza.

Le daremos de lo que consigamos. Todo saldrá bien, ya verás, habló la viejita, vente, apúrate Graciela.

Las dos mujeres fueron a la casa vecina.

Buenos días, Julita, llamó la anciana.

¿Qué tiene de bueno, Doña Amada? contestó la vecina.

Amada le habló animadamente a la vecina, haciendo arreglos para el cuido del niño de Graciela.

Bueno está todo en orden, le dijo la anciana a Graciela. Iremos al sitio que tengo en mente, muy bueno. Además te enseñaré otro lugar donde a veces dan trabajo. Sería temporario, pero algo es algo, le explicó Amada.

Con pasos apurados, las dos mujeres se dirigieron al área comercial de la ciudad. Era temprano, no había mucho tráfico. Acercándose a su destino, las calles angostas desembocaban en ámplias y largas vías. De los callejones y estrechas calles salían hombres y mujeres de otros barrios, que llenarían las cocinas y lavandería de los hoteles, algunos serían meseros y lavaplatos de los restaurantes. Otros componían la multitud de desempleados que se dedicaban a pedir limosna, alimentados de las sobras y el desperdicio. La procesión era solemne y patética. Era una marcha, como una caminata luctuosa. El ejército de miserables uniformados con las telas de trapería, descendían a la metrópoli con determinación de vivir; aunque con hambre en sus estómagos. Amada había sido miembro de ese ejército. Desde que enviudó años y años atrás, no conocía otra vida. Su edad no cambiaba esa única jerarquía existente, determinada en proporción al hambre y la desesperación.

Ayer echaron a Julita del trabajo, dijo Amada. Puedes pedir su trabajo, si es que ya no se lo han dado a otra.

Doblaron dos calles hacia abajo y allí encontraron el sitio que buscaban.

No puedo entrar al hotel, ya me conocen allí, le dijo la anciana con una mueca de picardía. Pero, entra tú y háblale al gerente. A él le gustan las muchachas jóvenes, dijó sardónicamente. Si no consigues nada, vete caminando y busca en los otros hoteles. Todos tienen el mismo jale.

Graciela entró y buscó al gerente. Este la apartó para hablarle en un pasillo obscuro. Era un hombre bajo y gordo. Tenía una manera nerviosa y apurada de actuar. No le gustaba que sus empleados se le acercaran mucho a menos que no fuesen hembras y bonitas. A todos sus empleados les hablaba en voz muy alta y siempre en tono mandón y abusador. Eso lo hacía sentir muy guapo y varonil. Hasta sus subalternos más rudos aceptaban callados cuanto él dijera para no ser despedidos, lo cual afianzaba más su sentido de poder.

La última que tuvo este trabajo se aprovechó de mi bondad, le dijo el gerente en forma brusca. Si vas a trabajar aquí no hagas lo mismo; trabajarás por días cuando te necesitemos. No te acerques a los clientes. Aquí es para estar trabajando, no quiero vagos, agregó el jefe.

El gerente llevó a Graciela un cuartito donde lavaban la ropa de los clientes. La joven pasó toda la mañana lavando ropa ajena. Trataba de apurarse. Había decidido ir a la oficina del periódico a buscar ayuda para encontrar a Juán, como le aconsejó Amada. Luego regresaría a encontrarse con la anciana detrás del hotel.

Cuando salió del trabajo, ya estaba obscureciendo. Las calles se vaciaban rápidamente. Las luces de las tiendas y edificios creaban una ilusión que contradecía la desolación y el vacío de interés humano. La joven siguió las instrucciones de Amada para llegar al edificio. Entró y vió al portero limpiando ceniceros en la sala de recibo. Se acercó a él y le habló. Este le indicó una oficina con el letrero pintado en la puerta: VENTAS DE ANUNCIOS. Al entrar observó que los escritorios estaban todos desocupados. Sólo había una mujer que pasaba un paño a los muebles, y recogía en un recipiente el contenido de pequeños basureros. El salón estaba ordenado, aseado y muy iluminado. Se le ocurrió a Graciela pensar que hasta a los canastos de desperdicios les hacía falta manchas o mugre. Sólo allí estaba la señora de la limpieza con quien hablar. Graciela salió del edificio desilucionada. No prestaban ayuda. Sólo se vendían letras grabadas. Buscaría a Amada.

Detrás del hotel encontró a la anciana rebuscando los basureros. Estaba echando sobras en la bolsa que llevaba. Cogía, escudriñaba, seleccionaba lo que dejaría caer en su bolsa. Graciela la observaba con enfado. Se acercó diciendo:

¿Doña Amada?

Dime niña, ¿cómo te fue?, respondió la anciana.

¿Qué hace, Doña Amada?

Ya empezó la hora de cenar en el hotel. Vén, ayúdame. Tenemos que llevarle también a Julita.

Amada continuaba sacando comida del recipiente.

Vamos a comer como ricos y de ricos, hoy; ya verás, dijo Amada.

Graciela vaciló inicialmente, pero el hambre que sentía y la despreocupación de su bienechora alejaron sus dudas. Se unió a ella en su labor.

¿Qué hizo hoy, Doña Amada? preguntó Graciela.

Ay hija, me la pasé frente a una tienda, respondió, y sin suspender por un instante su trabajo, la anciana coninuó:

Ese es un buen sitio. Pero la gente es mas bondadosa cuando entra que cuando sale. Así que uno necesita ser muy insistente si no quiere fracasar, dijo.

Después de cumplir su cometido, se dirigieron hacia el barrio.

Tenemos que pasar por uno de mis rinconcitos, le informó Amada a Graciela, dejé una bolsa escondida, no quiero que los perros me la encuentren.

La caminata de regreso fue rápida. Esa noche en el ranchito, Graciela explicó a la anciana lo que deseaba hacer. Quería seguir buscando a su marido. Le habló de sus diligencias, días atrás, y del obstáculo con la amenaza de ser arrestada, la cual la hacía sentir más limitada. No sabía cómo hacer lo más apropiado para encontrar a Juán.

Lo importante es tomar las cosas día a día, Graciela, dijo Amada. Mañana entra a la iglesia grande que te enseñaré. Quizás encontarás a alguien ahí que te ayude.

¿Un cura? preguntó Graciela. ¿Conoces a un cura que me puede ayudar?

No niña, no conozco al cura. Sólo sé donde está la iglesia.

La anciana calló y con la mirada fija en la llama azulada de la vela, dijó en tono bajo y melancólico:

El último cura que conocí fue el que ofició en el entierro de mi joven esposo, casi medio siglo atrás. Era el padre Luis y había sido también mi confesor. Murió también hace muchos años. Los acompañaron a su tumba mis sueños y fantasías de joven mujer, dijo Amada tristemente. Que raro, la primera vez que me sentí verdaderamente sola fue, no cuando murió mi esposo, sino, cuando enterraron al padre Luis. Estoy ya muy vieja para entretener a un cura con mi imaginación, y además dudo de sus absoluciones, dijo la anciana.

Al siguiente día las dos mujeres volvieron a la ciudad siguiendo la ruta acostumbrada. El gerente le dijo a Graciela que sólo la necesitaba por medio día. Ella decidió que caminaría observando las calles de día, e iría a la iglesia en busca de ayuda. Esa tarde la joven anduvo por las calles del centro comercial. Observaba lo limpio y planchado de mucha gente y las preciosidades de las vitrinas. Veía policías por todas partes. Jamás había visto tantos uniformes en tan corto tiempo. Por otra parte, las calles también estaban llenas de pobres, niños, hombres y mujeres. Había cojos, ciegos, enfermos y sanos, desarropados. Unos pedían limosna, otros vendían lotería, periódicos, cigarrillos o cajitas de chicle. Graciela sabía que estaba viendo el mismo ejército de la madrugada.

Aquella tarde, explorando, al fin llegó a la iglesia. Estaba cansada. En su caminata, su mente había repasado los acontecimientos de los último días. La tristeza atribulaba su alma; pero por la anciana había olvidado un poco lo peor de sus tormentos. Se sentía vacía. La frustración le acompañaba y el miedo le perseguía. Había creído entender lo que era el mundo. Pero era una ilusión y se iba evaporando a cada encuentro. Merecía acaso lo que le estaba sucediendo, pensó. Aquella forma de pensar pertenecía a su viejo reino de otro mundo.

Los recuerdos y nostalgias la llenaron de pena. El ataque en su casa por el capitán, la habían despertado de un sueño. Por primera vez se sintió conciente de su impotencia. Antes, en medio de su pobreza, y aun con hambre, sentía la certeza de ser capaz de hallar remedio. Creía en un balance todopoderoso pero desde el atraco, se vió por primera vez como víctima. Por primera vez el balance se desquiciaba. Esperaba que el péndulo regresara al centro y le devolviera su precioso balance. Pero no regresaba.

Subió, lentamente, los largos escalones de la iglesia enorme. Hablaría con el cura. El la ayudaría. También rezaría, tal como rezaba por las víctimas de la zanja. Rezaría porque siempre había hallado consuelo en la oración. Era su gancho al balance. Lo que la unía a todo ser. La reafirmación de su fé en esa justicia resultante del balance. Su fé en un árbitro superior, en una justicia infinita. Frente a ese árbitro no había distinción entre los hombres. Ante él formábamos una masa. Graciela se concebía como un pedazo de esa aglutinada masa. Los conflictos en la tierra eran entonces irrelevantes y frívolos.

El templo estaba vacío. La semioscuridad ensombrecía el abovedado y cavernoso interior. Graciela se persignó y postrándose de rodillas, rezó. Pidió tranquilidad. Humildemente pidió a Dios que por ese balance supremo pudiera ella encontrar a Juán. Era la única justicia que deseaba y esperaba. Rezó por su hijo, por Amada, y Julita. Se abandonó a ese péndulo ideal, rezó por ella misma para que terminara su persecución. Dios le respondía. Lentamente sentía el peso desaparecer. Sentía la tranquilidad crecer en ella. Se sentía confiada en que Dios decidiera por ella. El tormento desaparecía. Un buen rato estuvo allí, después se levantó y se persignó nuevamente. No había nadie a su alrededor.

Había anochecido cuando Graciela salió de la iglesia. Afuera, al fondo de los escalones, estaban sentadas y reclinadas varias personas. Bebían una botella que pasaban de mano en mano. Graciela pasó a su lado y sintió pena por ellos viéndolos abandonados. No se detuvo. Siguió de prisa su camino.

Se dirigía hacia al ranchito de Amada. En el camino pensó lo que debería hacer para encontrar a Juán. Tomó la misma ruta, el camino se le hacía largo. Al fin se acercó al barrio, reconocía la entrada. Cruzaría el puente y llegaría a ver su hijo. Empezó a llover y Graciela apuró el paso. La lluvia y el cansancio la distraían. No vió el auto con luces apagadas, estacionado cerca del puente, ni a sus ocupantes vigilando la entrada del barrio. Graciela ya estaba casi ahí, lo percibió tardíamente, cuando los rayos de luz cortaron la obscuridad. Ella seguía su paso mientras el vehículo se acercó con rapidez. Graciela sintió un apretón de brazos que la halaba hacia atrás. No tuvo tiempo para gritar. Una mano le tapó la boca. Tuvo la sensación de una fuerza invisible que se tragaba. Sintió una mantilla por encima de la cabeza, del cuerpo. Todo estaba opaco. Un peso en la espalda la contenía aplastada contra el frío metálico del piso. No oía voces, sólo el temblor y ronquido del motor. Trató de incorporarse pero el peso la comprimía. Trató de mover las manos pero no podía. El pánico la paralizaba. Movió los labios, estaba muda. Sintió un golpe sobre la cabeza y perdió el conocimiento.

Despertó a Graciela el roce de la suela en el piso de concreto. Los pasos resonaban más al acercarse. Se detuvieron. Luego un ruido de llaves y el chillido de la puerta. Graciela estaba bocabajo en el piso húmedo. Trataba de razonar y de entender lo que le había sucedido. Dónde estaba. Pensó que soñaba.

Levántese, le ordenó una voz.

Graciela comprendió que no soñaba.

Apure, levántese, repitió la voz.

Graciela volvió lentamente la cara hacia la voz. El dolor la atormentaba. Era como un cuchillo clavado en su cabeza. Tenía la vista empañada.

Tome la silla, volvió a ordenar la voz.

Poco a poco Graciela se fue levantando. Sus manos estaban encadenadas. Estaba descalza, sentía frío y calambres en las piernas. Abruptamente un brazo la agarró y empujó hacia una silla.

¿Por qué se fugó? ¿Qué sabe de los delincuentes de su pueblo?, una silueta borrosa la interrogaba.

Graciela no reconocía la voz.

¿Creyó que se nos escaparía, que no la encontraríamos? interrogaba arrogantemente la figura. Bueno, dígame por qué se escapó? ¿No sabe que la pena es fuerte para quienes no respetan la ley? luego, continuó dígame lo que sabe de esos delincuentes.

No sé nada de lo que me pregunta, respondió Graciela. Sólo busco a mi marido. Déjenme ir, no he hecho nada. Por favor, déjenme ir, rogó la joven.

El reporte dice que usted fue observada hablándole a los delincuentes, añadió el teniente que la interrogaba.

Como en otras veces, Graciela inútilmente trató de explicar al oficial su situación.

Ya le dije al oficial en mi pueblo, mi marido desapareció, yo lo buscaba. Le pregunté a los guerrilleros si lo habían visto en el camino.

Los guerrilleros, dice usted. ¿Simpatiza con ellos.?

Sólo quiero encontar a mi esposo, explicó temblorosamente.

Lo lamento, pero al juez no le va a gustar mucho su falta de cooperación. ¿No entiende el peligro que corre protegiendo a los delincuentes? dijo el teniente, amenzante.

He dicho la verdad, dijo Graciela con suplicante énfasis.

No nos obligue a cambiar de métodos. Existe un cargo contra usted por escapar al arresto. Además está bajo sospecha de colaboración con los delincuentes. La ley es clara y exacta al prohibir la ayuda de cualquier forma a esa gente, dijo el funcionario.

No sé nada, yo no sé nada, repetía la joven desesperadamente.

El oficial se levantó y caminó hacia la puerta.

Lástima, mujer estúpida, no sabes lo que te espera.

Con esta amenaza se retiró el teniente.

La anciana Amada se quedó esperando a Graciela. Ya había ido donde la vecina a recoger al niño. Estaba preocupada por Graciela. Alguien tocó la puerta. Era un muchacho del barrio.

Doña Amada, dijo, unos hombres se llevaron a la señorita que andaba con usted.

¿Quiénes eran?, preguntó la anciana.

No sé, creo eran los mismos. Ya sabe.

Amada sabía a quién se refería el muchacho. Sabía que nadie en el barrio acostumbraba a salir tarde por miedo a esos hombres. Si habían encontrado a Graciela, regresarían más tarde por el niño. La anciana hacía años que se había dejado de ilusiones.

Un guardia arrastró a Graciela por el piso de un pasillo. La joven abrió los ojos, el conocimiento le regresaba lentamente. El guardia vió que estaba despierta y la hizo levantar.

Vamos, ande por su cuenta, le gritó.

Apoyándose en él, Graciela lo siguió hasta un grupo de celdas. Por las rejas se veían hombres y mujeres. Otro guardia abrió la reja para que Graciela entrara. Los hombres y mujeres la contemplaban con miradas lejanas y sonánbulas. Nadie hablaba, se escuchaban sollozos pero nadie hablaba. El teniente apareció frente a la celda de Graciela. Se acercó y le dijo:

Te han dado otra oportunidad para cooperar. ¿Qué vas a hacer?

Qué digo. Qué necesito hacer. ¿No hay entre ustedes alquien que comprenda la verdad? No sé nada, sólo busco a mi marido, dijo Graciela con frustración.

El teniente miró hacia el guardia y ordenó que la trajera. Los tres caminaron despacio por laberintos de pasillos grises y mal alumbrados. Resonaban el tintineo de las llaves del guardia y los pasos del teniente contra el piso. Graciela no decía nada, su mirada era fija y sin expresión. Llegaron a una puerta maciza de madera, la cual empujó el teniente, dejando entrar los rayos del sol que empezaban a romper el horizonte. Graciela respiró profundamente. Podía saborear el aire salino del mar, y escuchar las olas.

Amada ya se imaginaba lo que tendría que hacer, más por instinto que por experiencia.

Mira muchacho, vete cuidadosamente y averíguame si esos hombres están toavía estacionados allí afuera, le dijo la anciana al mensajero. Si no me encuentras al regresar, añadió, estaré en casa de Julita. Corre y apúrate que no hay mucho tiempo que perder, dijo.

El jovencito desapareció por la puerta corriendo hacia la entrada del barrio. Mientras tanto, Amada tomó al hijo de Graciela, y protegida por la noche, paso a casa de Julita. Esta ya sabía las noticias, como todos en el barrio pronto las sabrían.

Entre Amada, sé de qué me quieres hablar, le dijo Julita.

Las dos mujeres conversaron en tono de conspiración para decidir qué hacer con el niño.

Julita, ya sabes que vendrán a hablar con todos nosotros, decía Amada. Si ven al niño se lo llevarán, y quizás a mí también.

Ellos te creen una loca, le contestó Julita, no creo que perderán su tiempo contigo. Pero uno nunca sabe con esa gente lo que va a pasar.

De cualquier manera me iré, me desapareceré por un tiempo, dijo Amada. Estoy ya muy vieja para una larga detención, concluyó.

Escúchame Amada, estás mal preparada para hacerte cargo del niño de Graciela, dijo Julita, yo arreglo con mis amigos. Tú no los conoces, pero sabes a quién me refiero. Seguramente que ellos nos darán la mano.

Amada dió unos pasos hasta llegar a la puerta. La abrió unas pulgadas y con cautela espió los alrededores. Se volvió, y cerrando de nuevo la puerta le preguntó a Julita:

¿No crees posible que ella regrese?

La pregunta no tuvo respuesta. Las dos mujeres se miraron silenciosas. Lágrimas brotaban de los ojos cansados de la viejita al acariciarle el pelo al hijo de Graciela.

Pobrecito huérfano, le decía Amada al niño, estrechándolo contra su pecho.

Dame el nene, yo me encargaré. Y lárgate tú antes de que lleguen, ordenó Julita.

Con ojos tristes y húmedos, Amada vió salir a Julita con el niño en sus brazos. Caminaba ligeramente entre las sombras de su barrio. Miraba frecuentemente hacia atrás para ver si era observada. A la distancia alguien vigilaba la entrada al barrio en un carro que rodaba lentamente.

Al salir por la maciza puerta de la jefatura, el teniente volvió a hablar a Graciela.

¿Vas a ayudarnos, o no?

Graciela se mantuvo silenciosa. Ya no encontraba cómo hacerle entender que no tenía la respuesta que él quería.

Bueno, ya pronto verás a tu esposo, dijo el oficial.

El guardia dejó escapar un gruñido burlón.

La noticia del oficial hizó sentir eufórica a Graciela. La sangre empezó a correr y el corazón a palpitar más ligero. Sus ojos se humedecían. Adelantó su paso.

¿Juan aquí?

Nadie dijo nada. Siguieron caminando. Empezaron a bajar unos escalones, que le hicieron recordar a Graciela los escalones de la iglesia. Cuando terminaron de bajar, a un lado y a poca distancia, de pie junto a una pared estaba Juan. Graciela gritó su nombre, llena de alegría. Sonreía pronunciando su nombre. Trató de correr hacia él, pero el guardia la detuvo. Le sujetó las manos.

¿Pero qué hacen? Ahí está, déjenme ir, protestaba la joven. ¡Juán!, gritaba Graciela, ¡Juán!

102

Los dos uniformados la condujeron a la pared. Graciela se safó de los guardias y corrió hacia Juán. Se apretó contra su cuerpo besándolo. Los dos lloraban. Hinchazones y verdugones deformaban la cara de Juán.

Juán, te amo. No te he dejado de buscar.

Te quiero, Graciela, decía Juán.

Los guardias trataban de separarlos, pero ellos resistían. Al fin lo lograron. Los amarraron apartados en dos postes frente a la pared.

¿Quiéres decir algo?, dijo el teniente.

Graciela sin quitar los ojos a Juán movía los labios. El teniente puso el oído cerca a los labios de Graciela, que sonreía mirando a Juán. Juán sonreía, también. Soldados con fusiles se alinearon a corta distancia de la pareja.

¡Listos!

¡Apunten!

¡Disparen!

Una joven pareja mirándose en silencio parecía hablarse con los ojos.

Tras la enredadera de matas silvestres y troncos de arboles, observaban los carros achatarrados, amontonados junto a los demás desperdicios del basurero. Aprovechaban la luz gris y sombría del amanecer para acercarse. Comunicándose con una mirada la pareja empezó a acercarse a su objetivo. Miraban a su alrededor atentos a todo ruído. En el claro oscuro silencio de la madrugada, se amplificaban los sonidos. Lentamente caminaron ente el montón de autos oxidados. El ruido que escuchaban los hizo detener. Forzaban sus ojos para poder ver lo que no eran capaces de ver. A cada paso el sumbido era más claro y definido. Podrían reconocerlo ahora claramente para acercarse con certeza.

El joven pensaba que había sido una desgracia haber sido el escogido por los guerrilleros para acompañar a Julita. El vivía en la zona y conocía los pasajes y callejones que daban al basurero. Le dijeron que Julita buscaba identificar a una joven mujer.

Con toda cautela llegaron a la repugnante nube de moscas negras que giraban sobre los cadávares hinchados de Graciela y Juán.

Con mirada impasible el teniente caminó hacia los escalones. En su mente se repetía mecánicamente la escena que había dirigido. Pensaba que siempre era igual. Los cuerpos rebotaban con el impacto de las balas. Las cabezas colgaban sobre sus pechos. La vida corría gota a gota formando a sus pies charquitos de espuma roja.

¿Qué fue lo que dijo?, preguntó el guardia.

Que tenía un hijo, respondió el teniente.

¿Eso fue todo?, dijo el otro.

Sí.

¿Y cómo se llama?

Gabriel. Gabriel Esperanza, contestó el teniente.

FIN

Kazi Toure

Like a Rock

They spoke of women's strength
silently pleading eternal wisdom
illuminating centuries of herstory
they looked like men's hands
Granma had the same (and we spoke of her)
they were calloused, not rough
proud, vibrant
labored, and tough
they looked round, felt smooth
Like a Rock
run by water since youth
i saw her spirit
all-absorbing
beneath a life-time of drudgery,
trapped dreams, of wanting
more for her children
than a koncrete penitentiary.
And it was hard to look
in those eyes—
monopoly capitals surplus value
she didn't understand the ties—
i tell you
she just understood the struggle.

8 March 89

Kazi Toure

Life Styles of the Rich & Famous

Life styles of the Rich & Famous
flaunted shamelessly in the faces
of the poor and nameless
living for the money, money, money, moooney
steppin all over you honey
let them tell it
everyone can get it—
house in florence
60 ft. yacht
summer house in Hyannis port—mercedes,
all the beautiful ladies
Life styles of the Rich & Famous
Big White Sheets/Botha
covered with blood stains of
the poor and nameless
AmeriKKKa makes the rules
movie star prez gives us the clues
talking about, "Make his Day"
carry a big stick Rambo

I'd like to "Make my Day"
do something with that Stick
for the youth of Soweto
Hollywood . . . (what'd Gil say) . . . "Hollyweird"
Ripley's believe it or not
has a spot
for "we care for you Blackman"
called, constructive engagement
pledge allegiance— to
small white sheet/ku klux & klan
Believe it— or— not.

July 86

107

Jaan Lamaan

from a Statement in Court

I am 38 years old, married to my comrade-wife Barbara Curzi-Laaman, with whom I share three beautiful children— two strong, caring and creative daughters, 12 and 11, and a bright, intense and loving son, 4. These were free children who lived underground with us.

Being involved in the revolutionary movement more than half my life and learning some of the lessons from other struggles, particularly the Vietnamese people's long fight for independence, it is apparent that the defeat of U.S. imperialism will be a protracted struggle also. This means that we have to develop a method, lifestyle, even culture of resistance that goes on from year to year. In my case, I decided to work clandestinely, but raise a family in the process. While this has risks and involves added planning and work, it certainly is possible. Some of my comrades were underground for at least a decade with the government intensely searching for them, yet ways were found to raise children while continuing to do revolutionary work. Although the government used our children to try to locate us— doing things like sending posters of our babies to schools, daycare and medical centers, putting them on TV and in magazines— they were not successful in this method. That is, our captures were not as a result of our children being traced.

My son was too young to realize he was living clandestinely but my daughters did know that their names were different at birth and that there was a reason we couldn't visit grandma and grandpa. They knew their parents were revolutionaries and the government was trying to find us because of our political work. But this did not take away from their lives, their positive accomplishments at school, many friends in the neighborhood, pajama parties, Saturday morning cartoons and trips to the zoo. In fact, while they had all this and led normal balanced lives, they also know about apartheid, about the wars in Central America, that there is injustice in this country. It gave them a certain understanding and identity with children in El Salvador or South Africa and this made them more balanced, even if less naive or innocent.

When we were captured, the government did make them suffer. They were taken into custody at gunpoint with their hands up and interrogated and held in a youth detention center for six weeks. This was done to try and gain information from them, to pressure Barbara and me and to disrupt our own legal efforts, for of course we were totally consumed with gaining their release for those six weeks.

The children are now with extended family, but split up, and the girls are back in school and doing well. Of course we all miss each other terribly and the children do have a deep loss without both of us. While this is heart-wrenching for both me and Barbara, it does not shock me, for this same amerikan empire that supports the daily savage brutality against even small school children in South Africa, that supplies the bombs that rain on the homes of Salvadoran farmers, that murdered the 15-month-old daughter of Libyan leader Moammar el-Qaddafi with a 2000 pound bomb, had no qualms about tearing apart our family. But it is just for all these reasons that I arrived at and remain committed to work for the end of this madness called U.S. imperialism.

I am an Estonian and immigrated to this country with my family when I was a small child. We lived in Roxbury, the Black community in Boston. My father was an auto mechanic and my mother worked in factories until my younger brothers and sisters began joining my older sister and me.

As so-called DPs— displaced persons— living in a very poor part of a Black neighborhood I learned first-hand about ethnic and class discrimination. While the U.S. is saturated with white supremacy and it affects everyone, I feel fortunate in having spent 6 or 7 years in a Black community and thus was not overwhelmed by the blind racism that cripples many white people. Later we moved to a blue-collar, largely Italian section of Buffalo where I lived an average life—hanging out on the corner and in alleys—more concerned about girlfriends and street life than much else. It was in Buffalo that I saw the racist attitudes of white people more glaringly and this was somewhat shocking. It struck me that for all the half-baked white supremacist concepts parroted by some kids on my block, our clothes, lunches, homes and so on were pretty similar to those of the Black kids in school. Probably most of us were marginally better, but poverty and parents out of work were familiar to us all. In those days of the late 50s and early 60s, though, this was something I just noticed and left at that.

Although school was always easy, it was boring and seemed irrelevant to my life. At an early age, it was common understanding that you would try to get a job at the Chevy plant or steel mill when they weren't laying off, and in the slow periods get by washing cars or dishes. If you were more adventurous you could survive off the street, but of course it was understood that you'd wind up in prison sooner or later. Most tried to do a little of both. I quit school at 16, got a job, and wasn't above making extra money if possible.

Working from car lots to the steel mill, I saw both the great weaknesses and strength of working people—the racism of whites and the power of the unity of workers. While working at Bethlehem Steel, which still had a residue of militant working class under-standing and input from left wing groups, our local which had a younger, more third world leadership went on a wildcat strike. Despite cops, old white union hacks from the international, and the company, we were half-way successful in our battle, but more importantly the need to cast aside racism and develop militant solidarity was very educational to me.

An underlying reason the company probably settled was so it could get back to production, because this was 1965 and the U.S. invasion of Vietnam was in its sharp upswing. This was about the time I remember the first neighborhood kid coming home in a body bag and of course the draft was scooping up young men left and right. This led me to start thinking, but my main concern was still mostly my car, parties, hanging on the corners and in bars. In early 1966 I was arrested and convicted for assault and sentenced to a 5-year Youth Act term.

110

The next 20 months was not only a real eye opener, but a time for a lot of reflection and education for me. Fighting to survive the naked brutality of N.Y. state's prison system, I finished high school, took up reading factual and progressive books and had the good fortune of meeting a couple of clear-sighted Black prisoners who patiently shared their understanding of the true economic and social nature of Amerika with me. This, coupled with my own life experience, started an understanding falling together in my mind.

As a white working class male you had the opportunity to get a second-rate schooling, including mis-education in at least history, economics and social studies, and which by and large taught you to obey instructions and accept life. From there you either hit the lower end of the working world or were pushed into the military, in which case you had the opportunity to risk your life while killing third world people far away in their own countries who were fighting for their freedom. If you didn't choose either of these options, then most likely you'd end up in prison, where if you survived you'd get your secondary education— get kicked into line to accept a life of wage labor, of working yourself into an early grave while making some boss or corporation rich. Or you could learn to break laws better, hustle and steal, but accept the fact that you'd spend most of your life in and out of prison.

As an added incentive, safety valve or perhaps just a further dehumanization, as a man you could oppress and vent your frustrations against your woman— your wife and women generally. And of course as a white man, you'd probably get a little better job a little sooner and keep it a little longer than a Black or other third world person would, and all the while you would be encouraged to hate and fear people of color.

At 18 and 19, incarcerated in a N.Y. state prison, I had achieved this level of understanding, although it was very unclear what the solution could be for me or poor and working people in general. I knew there were socialist countries and I had the proud heritage of my grandfather, who unfortunately died before I was born, who was involved in the independence struggle of Estonia against the czarist Russian empire, as a member of the Bolshevik Party; but I really did not understand socialism. My own parents, having survived the ravages and dislocations of World War II, were not socialist nor did they see it as any kind of solution.

After my release I spent the next three years at Cornell and the University of New Hampshire. I became active in anti-draft counseling and anti-war work. I joined SDS and later helped found new chapters. While I learned some things in classes, my real education came through a few close friends who were students from Ireland and Palestine and my friendship and association with Black revolutionaries and work with the Black Power movement, especially the Panthers. Anti-imperialism and the direct support of national liberation struggles were a major focus of my activity and in turn led me to develop a clearer understanding. I came to understand that Marxism was the clear tool by which to not only comprehend the problems, but develop solutions for them as well.

In 1970 I left school, returned to Buffalo and became involved in community, youth and labor organizing and struggles. Already by this time, it had become necessary for me to utilize some clandestine procedures to do effective work. Nonetheless, being on parole from my Youth Act sentence, I had my parole revoked in late 1970 for doing anti-racist youth organizing and was sent to Attica. While there I had the privilege of working with some righteous revolutionaries.

My sentence expired a few months before the historic Attica uprisings and I was released, but soon I was mourning the murders of some of my close comrades in that rebellion. I returned to full time political work, but with the government already keeping close watch on my activities, I went underground . . . .

112

Chapter Three

LOVE AND OTHER MYSTERIES

*At the risk of seeming ridicu-
lous, let me say that the true
revolutionary is guided by a
great feeling of love.*

— CHE GUEVARA

Alan Berkman

A Modest Supposal

I have been told by mutual friends
concerned with both your happiness and mine
that your self is currently secreted away
in a certain familiar well muscled, olive complected
ebony haired (turned with gray since I saw you last?)
sparkling eyed (with, perhaps, depths of sadness and a
    touch of hardness)
body
that is entombed in steel and concrete
itself layered by mayhem, madness, and pain
the only exit being through tessellated gates
controlled by a supremely indifferent key
    carrying Charon,
the price of passage being submission and selling of
    the soul.
A price you will not pay.
All of the above located on the manicured grounds
of a certain fashionable institution for women
in the bucolic blissfulness of upstate New York.

And I?
Perhaps you've heard from the above mentioned friends
that I am currently perched on the head
of a large imperial eagle that guards a
    cavernous courtroom
in which I can be seen talking to a jury
about me who is sitting at the defense table

115

rebutting charges made by dedicated servants of the system
about a me that sounds only vaguely familiar
in the ways a mummy resembles its progenitor.
And at the end of the day
at the conclusion of the pretense and play
we all regroup into the one familiar body
that is stripped of its civilized dress but not, I hope,
    of its dignity.
and, draped in shackles and chains
is herded back to the cage in a dungeon
in the city of brotherly love.

So . . .
suppose you take part of your self and I take part of mine
and suppose we send them sneaking through bars and
over fence and wall
to rendez-vous in true clandestine fashion
in a certain familiar New York apartment
where, unseen but perhaps sensed by the current occupants
we can meet, greet, rejoice, and soar
while discussing loved ones and little ones,
the pettiness and pain of prison,
the courage of the comrades in Central America,
the future as seen in the face of the children
and a million topics of mutual interest.

Suppose South Africa, suppose Nicaragua, suppose El Salvador,
suppose the Philippines, suppose New Africa, suppose Puerto Rico,
suppose Chile and Grenada and Mexico, suppose Palestine
suppose one day the dreams come true . . .

*Written while on trial in Philadelphia, Winter 1987: to an
imprisoned comrade, Judy Clark, when she was being held in a
punishment 23-hr-a-day lockdown unit for a 2 year sentence.*

Ray Luc Levasseur

mémêre (grandmother)

the blues say if you born under a bad sign you got trouble
you born in the shadow of the mills
you born near a river
and you got more trouble still

mémêre walked thru that shadow
to work at 13
to work you understand
as a child
to breathe that dust
work that machine
    & to find her husband
who'd been there since 13

an unlucky # you say?
no
french-canadian   french-speaking catholic
proud   sensitive   loving   hardworking &
exploited

1 of 11 children
who had children
who took in other children &
bro & i
when the next generation of women
went into mills & shoe factories

that alone should tell you something bout strength

she read the cards &
told the fortunes
for those with broken hearts
dismal jobs & uncertain futures

when urban renewal flattened their apt
they built a small house in the country
that was pleasant for a spell till
the mill caught up with pépère &
he'd breathe hard & shake & sometimes fall
in the chicken coop
then i'd come to lift him in my arms &
put him in the kitchen
where mémère cleaned him up &
rolled a bull durham
which she had to hold
cause his hands shook so much

she took him to the v.a.
but neither could stand the shock
of neglect
so he came home to die

the govt gave her the coffin flag &
$22 a month pension
not enuff for eye drops she'd say
then the little house was gone &
to avoid the poor house on the hill
she moved in with her daughter, my ma
who worked 2 jobs to keep the wolf
from the door

118

mémêre burned the holy candle
when i was in 'nam &
put it out with relief
when i returned only
to light it again
the day i got out of prison

she loved all her children
holding each of us
to her bosom
over decades of time
thru each sickness
celebration &
bout with the blues

her dream was that
we'd finish school
("no quittin" she'd say)
& make the great escape
from the mills
which some did & some didn't
back home where women still
hold up half the sky
but without unions
on assembly lines
that boss says is for
"soft brains and nimble fingers"
makin circuit boards 'stead a shoes
with husbands more quick to split &
where stamps help feed the kids

she died while i was underground
the fbi hangin from trees
at catholic cemetery
cause they knew i was close
to her
but i wasn't there
didn't even know she'd died
till some pig laid it on me
trying to pry out information

before death she'd been sick
with the feds at the docs
probing how much could she take
how many questions to ask
an old mill woman
of the doc
who'd received their flyer
with our kids on it
saying snitch if these kids
come to you sick

but all she said was
"I hope I see him before I die"
see— with her eyes filled with
glaucoma & cataracts & cornea trouble
damn near blind
pigs gone she'd retrieve
her magnifying glass &
look at the pictures
of underground children
i'd sent her
incl her namesake
simone eva

that she'd never met
but loved
cause we felt it
cross the shadows &
troubles
mémêre's love
helped hold us strong.

january, 1988

Ray Luc Levasseur

Bro & I

That's Bro and I in that trash heap there. We were just little shits then. Folks called us mouse and mole. We lived over a barbershop which set across the street from a shoe factory where our Ma worked. I could throw a whiffle ball from our front stoop and hit the side of the factory. It was that close.

We were happy to have the town dump as our backyard. Yeah, man, it was a playground filled with adventure and treasure. Together, we killed our first rats there. We figured the more we got scurrying around in that heap, the less we had to lay traps for in the apartment. Fact is, though, we liked killing them. I don't know why, we just did. Just like when we killed snakes and cut them up into 9 pieces to make sure they never saw the light of day again. Less than 9, we were told, and the pieces were liable to grow back together and come looking for us. We had enough problems with rats.

The dump edged right into the riverbank where Bro and I went after the fish, ripping their bellies apart with 3-hookers. That was a time when we were never seen without our bamboo poles close at hand. The fish were easy prey because they were sick and swam real slow and near the surface. Chemical waste dumped in the river by the mills and factories cast its own net over the water. The old-timers told us not to eat the fish that had black spots and weird growths on them. For a time we ate the better-looking ones but then Ma said we best leave them alone as well.

When we wanted a decent eating fish, we went up by the last mill and crossed the dam when the water was low enough, then made our way along the shoreline to the big pines that had been knocked into the water by violent northeasters. We'd carefully make our way out on those moss-covered logs and get us a mess of perch, bullheads and a few smallmouth bass. When we could get her to do it, Ma would roll them in crushed saltines and we'd eat them fried.

Some folks might think having a dump for a backyard is a bad thing, but you've got to look at the whole picture. To Bro and I it was the center of the universe. The old man was off somewhere most of the time and Ma had to work in the shoe factory and take in sewing to pay the bills. Even the guy at the barbershop was charging us full rate for haircuts. There were no organized sports in town and we had no car.

A mountain of trash was a natural attraction. Here we found comic books, magazines, old appliances and cardboard boxes. The cardboard we used to build imaginary fortresses from which we fought battles against enemy soldiers and alien invaders. One time we made a cardboard maze like we had seen at an amusement park funhouse, charging neighborhood kids a nickel to crawl through it.

We retrieved beer and soda bottles for quick cash to supplement our other income from worms, nightcrawlers and selling newspapers. Any bottle or jar that couldn't convert into cash we pitched into the river followed by a barrage of stones. There was nothing like a direct hit to propel us into the ranks of the Cisco Kids and Lash LaRues of Saturday afternoon matinees.

Bro and I felt that this was *our* world as long as we could avoid the caretaker of the dump. He told Ma he really didn't mind us playing there, it was just that he was worried we might catch something. Something insurance wouldn't cover, no doubt. He was easy enough to avoid since he didn't like the place himself and preferred shooting craps over on the south side.

The worse we suffered were occasional cuts and bruises from slipping and sliding on the rather unstable foundation a trash heap presents. The most traumatic moments came when reaching under something to give a yank and coming up with a handful of dogshit or spoiled mayonnaise. We'd run around like madmen, trying to find a rag to wipe it off with.

The only sad moments were when the caretaker thought the mountain of trash had grown too big and set a torch to it. Ashes were no fun to play in.

The grandaddy of rubbish piles was located in a neighboring town. It was where most of the serious junk pickers went with their gunny sacks. Once in a great while, Uncle Joe would take us there, on what he called a Southwestern Maine Field Trip. We were amazed to see a family living in a shack at the edge of the dump. They were the unofficial custodians of the place. There were 13 kids, and under the father's guidance they would fan out through the trash, inspecting it as if searching through the remains of a downed airliner. They always seemed to find the best stuff, and when a trash hauler arrived with a new load, they got first dibs. But there was plenty for everybody and Bro and I would always return with something to excite our fancy.

As the sun moved from east to west, the shoe factory cast a giant shadow that crept across the street right up to the barbershop door. The factory was private property that Bro and I were not allowed into, except to sell our newspapers. But with its own pile of waste in the rear of the building, it was too much of an attraction to avoid altogether. From a nearby woods, Bro and I would conduct quick strikes into that factory waste pile and run off with refrigerator-size boxes and plastic streamers.

There was always a chemical odor to the air, and pipes from the building dropped liquids directly into the river, changing the color of the water, which regurgitated it as foam along the shoreline.

The factory stood as the largest building in town. It was a wooden clapboard structure built at the turn of the century. Naturally, the owners had painted it gray to harmonize with the metal lunch buckets of the workers and the machinery that could be heard blocks away. From outside, it looked worn out with its chipped paint and gritty windows. The windows only opened inches, so we rarely saw more than a hand flicking out a cigarette butt (which if we were courageous enough, we retrieved). But we knew they were all in there: Ma, aunts and uncles; the folks we saw

124

in church and around the neighborhood; those men we saw weave in and out of the rear entrance to the Knights of Columbus hall—the only sanctified watering hole in an otherwise dry town. Most, like us, were French-Canadian. By that I mean that our people came from Quebec or their parents or grandparents did.

Our little home over the barbershop was set in the midst of several textile mills and the old shoe factory. The river gave life to the mills and the mills gave work to us. There had been better days for textiles and shoes. The mills were dying now, but not without a last gasp. Most of the unions had been broken years before. Now it was each unorganized worker for themselves. Low wages insured that we lived on the edge of someone else's dream.

Then came what they call the runaway shops. Many mills closed and ran away south to look for even cheaper wages. One of those laid off was our grandfather. He had worked for years in a woolen mill behind the catholic school we went to. Another factory built at the turn of the century by money from Massachusetts, it was several stories high and made of brick. It looked to me like a big threat in the middle of the street. After it closed, our grandfather finished off his years doing yard chores for a rich lady. Not being able to carry a lunch bucket and pick up a check every Friday left him feeling like an old pair of shoes that had been discarded.

With the mill closed and the workers laid off, the building stood like a tomb. Bro and I played baseball with the other neighborhood kids in a sandlot overlooking the east side of the mill. One warm summer night, while he was waiting his turn at bat, Alphonse Lebreque picked up a stone and sent it crashing through one of the mill windows. As if on cue, the rest of us grabbed whatever missiles we could lay our hands on. It quickly turned into a fusillade, followed by the echo of shattering glass. We threw until our small arms were weary and the entire side of the mill was pockmarked with holes. Luckily, Bro and I had moved away from the group to search for more stones when someone yelled, "The cops are coming!" On the fly, we hit the priest's flower garden then cut through the church parking lot, making our best Batman and Robin moves back to the dump. From the high ground we could see the police lights circling the mill.

When Ma got home from work the next day she brought the shop gossip with her. "You two break any windows," she said, "you're going to wind up using chamber pots at the county jail."

At that age I couldn't imagine anyone being tighter than Bro and I. We were just a year apart and some folks thought we were twins. We did everything and went everywhere together. Whatever I wanted to do, he would follow without question. If I said, "let's walk to Wyoming," he'd fall right into step figuring I already had a plan on how to deal with lunch. We shared every secret, dream and fear we had. We were more than just brothers—we were the best of friends.

Our family extended all the way to Quebec, but for Bro and I it was Ma who held things together. When my father was gone she would say to me that I would have to be the man of the house, since I was the oldest son. But I knew better. It was she who worked so hard to provide for us. She instilled in us the worth of being honest, hardworking and loving. She was a self-effacing woman, sensitive and caring. Not without much difficulty, it was her lot to get by from one paycheck to the next in a world of male bosses and an itinerant husband who berated her for being uneducated and culturally deficient. They tried to strip her of anything meaningful in being French-Canadian, worker and mother. But through the daily grind and the limited opportunities, she prevailed.

When the mills closed, she refused to die with them. The pressures of unemployment during slack times and two jobs at peak times failed to deter her. When my father showed up she'd patiently wait for the storm to pass and then get on with her life, seeing to it that her sons were properly cared for. Ma was the long distance runner, carrying her lunch to work each day as if it were the burden of Sisyphus.

A family excursion for us was a walk to Belanger's supermarket for ice cream and then back home to share the laughter of a TV comedy. "Why watch something that'll make you sad?" Ma would say with a smile.

The mills, however, were no laughing matter. They have a way of wearing out your body parts and leaving you to get by on meager social security payments in old age. Worse yet, they could easily grind your aspirations into so much dust. All our lives Bro and I were told to stay out of the mills. It was like being told to stay out of jail—easier said than done. The key to escape was supposed to be education. Get smart and wear a white collar. Stay dumb and become a slave to the shop bosses.

One late winter afternoon, Bro and I got home from sledding on Butternut Hill and found Ma crying in the kitchen. The boss, the always nameless, faceless boss, had screamed at her for not working fast enough to meet her quota. He had humiliated her in front of the other workers. This was a woman who worked for low wages with no protection that a union might offer. The shop was so cold that she often worked with her coat on. We felt helpless. Our impulse was to run across the street and confront this bossman and break his nose—all 4 feet, six inches of us. But that wasn't real. All we could do was continue to go our way, aware that something evil lurked inside the factory. We consoled each other by saying that once we were in high school we'd come looking for this guy and torture him with Killer Kowalski's claw hold.

Bro and I knew that when you're little in an unbalanced world, you get stepped on. We took our share of lickings from bigger kids in the neighborhood. Not all the time, you understand, just when the mood struck them.

A big kid called "Pepper" took particular pleasure in tormenting me. The son of the local sawmill owner, he would wait in ambush behind some tree or culvert and spring on me as I walked by. He wouldn't touch Bro but he would punch and kick me. When he was overtaken by a more vicious streak, he would shoot me with his BB gun. These confrontations always ended with me running as fast as I could for home, snot all over my face, with Bro chugging along behind me, equally terrified. Ma would clean me up and tell me there was nothing she could do—not even a basic boxing lesson. "Just try and stay away from him," she'd say. Sure, I thought to myself: it's like staying away from cigarettes when you want to quit smoking. The fuckers are everywhere.

Bro and I thought we'd found the answer in the back of one of our comic books. We sent for the Charles Atlas muscle builder course. But when little more than a bill arrived with a photo of the muscle man himself, we resigned ourselves to avoiding Pepper's turf.

Ma had always warned us that the river was dangerous, and the day came when we saw it kill. Bro and I were floating on tubes at a public swimming hole when a woman began screaming hysterically that she couldn't find her son. He had disappeared in the water. All us kids retreated to the shoreline while the older folks began a search. Moments later a man found the body of a boy my own age and carried him to shore as one would a bride. The boy's tongue protruded grotesquely from a purplish death mask. Bro and I were so scared that when we walked home we didn't even take our shortcut across the dam.

Even before Vietnam claimed its local body count, the river took lives—as did the mills. A school chum, René Levesque, was 16 when he lied about his age to go to work in one of the woolen mills. Before he finished his first year he was killed, sucked into a machine and asphyxiated. One day he had been sitting next to me in school, and the next he was fighting off a machine that had got hold of his arm and was dragging him to a violent death.

René's nickname was "chocolate" because his skin was dark. The first time I heard the word "nigger," it was as the nickname of another dark French-Canadian kid. According to a lot of people where I come from, a French-Canadian is a "frog" and the factories are populated by dumb workers with French surnames. Early on,

128

Bro and I stopped speaking French to try and sneak into American culture.

Death is not the sort of thing little kids stay preoccupied with. If the trash heap behind our apartment was the center of the universe, the river was the Milky Way. From the first time we fished its shoreline with safety pins and fatback, the river was our fascination. There was something about it that called out to us. Walking through the wooded riverbanks was like opening the pages to the wonders of nature. Lady Slippers, teaberries, snapping turtles and hedgehogs awaited our steps. There were trees to climb, dried pine needles to be smoked, "precious" stones to be found and polished. I still remember the lengthy discussion about whether a triangular stone was a real Indian arrowhead. We never walked anywhere along that river without being on the lookout.

Then there was "the rockies," scene of many a young boy's rite of passage. This was a place upstream where the river narrowed to less than 100 yards. We would sit and watch boys just a couple years older than us take the plunge from a high, rocky ledge and swim the river to the other shore. I knew it was a challenge I would have to meet someday, though I wondered where I would get the courage. For Bro, it would never be. He couldn't swim a lick.

My time came one summer when Bro and I, along with a half dozen other kids, set out to conquer our fears. At the rockies, seven of us stripped down to our shorts and left our fishing poles with Bro, who sat dejectedly under a tree. With our loudest Tarzan yells we leaped into the water and swam for dear life, never missing a stroke. When we reached the halfway mark and I didn't feel winded, I knew it was a piece of cake and I would live to see another day. Just as important was the pride that swelled in my chest as I reached the other side.

Once we were rested, we engaged in a round of backslapping. Then we climbed a big old pine and swung out over the river on a rope, doing cannonballs into the water. Our laughter echoed down the river.

129

Before the summer passed, we had made our way further up river to Indians' Last Leap— again leaving Bro behind at the rockies. The Leap was a high rock ledge split by a narrow stream that flowed into the river. This is where we demonstrated our diving skills. A precise and shallow dive was necessary to avoid hitting the rocks that lay hidden below the surface of the water. You had to know exactly where your head was going in order to avoid a trip to the hospital.

The legend that went with the Leap served to further activate our adrenaline. Seems that in colonial times, an Indian man chased by white settlers had tried to escape by jumping from one ledge to the other. He missed and fell to his death. The legend was that his bones and spirit waited in an underground tunnel at the bottom of the pool. It was rumored that more than one diver had disappeared while exploring the tunnel. We didn't think being French-Canadian exempted us from the sins of the white man, so we never stayed after dark.

These rites of passage were a turning point for Bro and I. As the years went by, I began to play organized sports while Bro stuck to the river, ever on the watch for that one big trout. I went to winter dances; he went ice fishing. I went to work in one of the mills, while he strayed into construction. When there was a showdown with economic hard times, I left town while Bro remained behind.

Then came another rite of passage: Vietnam. Neither of us knew a damn thing about the war but all the patriotic zeal of hundreds of Saturday afternoon matinees came home to roost. We felt an obligation to serve.

When we returned from 'Nam it was to a different time and we had both changed. I couldn't forget the war and neither could Bro. I hated it; he grappled to understand it.

After the war we rarely saw each other, so it was a surprise one cold February day when he called to ask me to go ice fishing at his shanty on Loon Pond. Most of the day was spent tending our traps and sipping on Blue Ribbon. We caught some good-sized pickerel and talked about the old days. Conversation on current topics revolved largely around backhoes, bulldozers and chainsaws.

As the sun began to set we made our final rounds to gather up the traps. Meeting again at the outside of the shanty, I looked at my brother and saw an uneasiness in his large gray eyes. Giving him a light tap on the shoulder I asked, "What's up, dude?"

Never the type to easily express himself, Bro turned to me and said, "You know, man, when I was about nine months into 'Nam we was up by Ben Cat one day and these two Vietnamese kids were brought in by MedEvac. I had to carry one to the hospital but when I picked her up she began to scream. The other kid was her sister and she didn't want to be separated. Mama-san was probably dead." We both stood in silence for a moment.

"So I took them both, one in each arm, and carried them to the hospital unit. I told the medic to be sure to keep those kids together, they were sisters."

He paused to light a cigarette. "But I'll never know, will I? And that still bothers me. When I saw those kids, I thought about how is it that we can hurt kids like this—kids like you and me were—and feel good about anything we're doing in 'Nam. It don't take no great mind to know that kids are innocent."

I crushed the last beer can and tossed it into the shanty. Facing each other under the first stars of a crystal clear night, both of us were fighting back tears. With the ice crackling beneath our feet, we embraced for the first time since we were kids.

"Bro," I said, "I love you."

Judy Clark

Portrait

The photograph is from a formal sitting and she is dressed for the occasion. She presents herself quite the little lady. Her hair is intricately braided and set off by three purple and pink ribbons. Yet her spontaneous seven-year-old energy breaks through the formality of the posed setting. For all her bows and frills, she greets us with an impish grin that promises scuffed knees and mischievous pranks followed by gales of laughter. Her rich, dark chocolate skin is perfectly smooth and unblemished, almost shimmery. Her chin is strong as she juts it slightly forward, lifting her face to meet the camera's eye with an expression full of youthful pride and self-confidence. She tries to hide the childish gap between her front teeth, but her smile nudges her lips open and dimples her cheeks into two rosy brown plums. She charms me with her beguiling smile that glows over her whole face, reminding me of another's charms.

Now, as always, when I look into this child's bright, cheerful face, my eyes travel to her mother's picture which is taped next to hers on my cell wall. They share the same eyes, delicate eyebrows, broad nose. But the similarity goes deeper than their features. It's their spirit. That twinkling, mischievous energy and glow. In her mother's face, innocence has given way to strength and tempestuous determination. This tender-tough woman who challenged prison walls and my own inner defenses to enter my heart. Now we nurture a love that transforms so much heartache into energy, growth and mutual affirmation.

I recall the stories my sweetheart told me of her own girlhood. Commanded to wear dresses every Sunday for church, she would sneak away to the playground where she would swing, run, leap, unmindful of— or rather in rebellion against— the constraints of her garments. She'd come home to face the consequences of her torn, dirty dress, determined to remain free of frilly impositions. She's been irrepressible every since.

As I gaze at the little girl's picture, I wonder if she feels similarly to her mother. Her face shows that her laughter and energy must be irrepressible. But the avenues she chooses and the conflicts or encouragement she encounters? These remain a mystery to me. For all I have to feed my imagination is this one photograph.

I think of her mother looking at her copy of this same photograph on her cell wall. I imagine she shares my musings about the ribbons and frills. Ah, but how many more questions run through her mind? And more, the anger and longing that swells in her heart as she looks into the eyes of her daughter she has not seen since days after she gave birth to her in prison.

A knot grows hard and hurtful inside me, lodged in that place where mother-love and woman-love come together. Just when it threatens to burst into unbearable rage and pain, I turn again to this smiling, happy child and find in her face, the hope I need to go on.

Bedford Hills, 1986

133

Judy Clark

New Year's Poem

It is not my tears that can make you understand
nor my anger, though I still claim it
It's not out of love nor concern for me,
nor guilt or that elusive self-criticism
that you will ever even try to understand
But only if you come to feel the need
on your own
for yourself
to enter the frightening chasm
explore the dark, nightmare void between us
between "free-world" and prison
between outside and in

Not that you will ever know
my world inside
much less my inside world
But to touch tentatively into your own?

Everyone has her nightmares,
her prison cells and solitary boxes
that she alone can enter,
hesitant, fearful of getting trapped
without the key to get out.

Jan. 2, 1987,
the Box

Judy Clark

Sister Says

Sister says,
"There must be a light at the end of the tunnel."
These months,
there is no tunnel,
no end,
just the glare and heat of an interminable desert.

And I
hold on
and on and on and on
consumed by the effort
to hold on.

But now, an oasis!
Painting tiny gardens of plants in large pots.
I sit close up and peer in
to catch a lizard's eye view
as each leaf
becomes a tree
and the plants form a forest
in which I lose myself

and find
   the magical interplay of light and dark
      the grey grandeur of deepening shadows
      the infinite universe of greens and browns
a lush, peaceful respite
from my desert trek.

Tucson, Arizona f.c.i., 7/88

Edwin Cortés

A Soldier of the Motherland

The motherland was always primary.
The armed struggle had paved the way.
There was plenty of Rhetoric,
there was now a need to take a step forward.
Our step was concrete action
with a cry of "Long Live the Revolution."
Although behind these prison bars
there are no reasons for regret.
With your example you can rest assured
that in our country you have planted the seeds for the future.

Dedicated to my comrade P.O.W. Alberto Rodríguez on his
birthday 4/17/87

Edwin Cortés

Un Soldado de la Patria

La Patria siempre fue primero
la lucha armada brindó el sendero
La retórica era bastante
había que dar un paso adelante
Nuestro paso era acción
con un grito alto "Viva la Revolución"
Aunque detrás de las rejas
no existe razones para quejas
Con tu ejemplo puedes estar seguro
que en nuestra patria existe el futuro.

Dedicado al compañero y PDG Alberto Rodríguez

Edwin Cortés

The Charade

The Yankees robbed our land
and we are the ones accused of Sedition.
That is why I proclaimed myself a Prisoner of War
assuming the posture of non-recognition of the
colonial jurisdiction.

Our national heroes Don Pedro Albizu Campos and Don Juan
   Antonio Corretjer
advanced the position of "Retraimiento"
refusing to recognize any institution imposed by U.S. Imperialism.
This is in conformity with my convictions
in order to project the destruction of colonialism.

The Yankees separated you from me

and have tried to defame me as a terrorist.
But I am very happy and proud
to be considered a socialist.

I was given an excessive sentence
but I hope you understand that the yankee beast created these
   circumstances.
From Puerto Rico, Chicago to Pennsylvania is a long distance
but I reaffirm my support for National Independence.

Dedicated to my son Carlos on his birthday, 11/26/86

Edwin Cortés

La Charada

Los yanquis nos quitaron la tierra
y nos acusan de sedición.
Por eso me proclamo prisionero de guerra
asumiendo la postura de la no jurisdicción.

Nuestros heroes nacionales Don Pedro y Don Juan
crearon el principio de retraimiento;
rechazaron reconocer las instituciones
impuestas por el imperialismo.
Está en conformidad con mis pensamientos,
así proyectamos la destrucción del colonialismo.

Los yanquis me separaron de tí
y trataron difamarme como terrorista.
Estoy orgulloso y bien feliz
siempre comprometido a los principios socialistas.

Me dieron una larga sentencia;
espero que entiendas que los bestias yanquis crearon estas
    circunstancias.
Desde Puerto Rico, Chicago a Pennsylvania es una larga distancia
pero afirmo mi apoyo a la independencia.

Edwin Cortés
Prisionero de Guerra
11/26/86)

Edwin Cortés

Confidence in My People

As a father sitting here in my chair, I am always thinking of you.
Although I am incarcerated in a yankee dungeon,
your upbringing burns in my heart.
We must try to forget the 600 miles that separate us.

Every passing day I imagine your growth.
I always inquire about your well-being
as well as alleviating your discomforts.
Through your letters, telephone calls and visits I recognize your
    beautiful thoughts.

I emphasize the importance of your education
the necessity to learn how to read and write
and especially to learn how to live.
Yours is a new generation.

Everything in your life is an important moment
and I want to share them with you.
We must show our enemy the strength of the family as part of a
    nation.
I hope that is how you feel about my incarceration.

When the day arrives and we are united,
which could be in five, ten or twenty years—
Until then you will always be in my thoughts.
We will one day celebrate our triumph and witness the destruction
of Yankee Imperialism.

Dedicated to my daughter Noemi on her birthday, 12/13/86

Edwin Cortés

Confianza en Mi Pueblo

Como padre siempre pienso en tí, hija, sentado en mi silla;
Aunque estoy preso en un campo de concentración,
tu crianza arde en mi corazón.
Tenemos que olvidarnos de las 600 millas.

Cada día me imagino tu crecimiento;
Siempre quiero saber de tu bienestar,
igual que aliviar tu malestar.
Detrás de las cartas, teléfono y visitas conozco tus bellos pensamientos.

Enfatizo la importancia de tu educación;
Que aprendas a leer y escribir,
y especialmente sepas vivir.
Porque tú eres parte de una nueva generación.

Todo en tu vida es un importante momento;
Quiero compartirlo contigo,
para demostrarle la fortaleza de familia a nuestro enemigo.
Espero que así pienses de mi encarcelamiento.

Cuando llegue el día en que estemos unidos;
puede ser en cinco, diez o viente,
siempre estarás presente en mi mente.
Un día celebraremos el triunfo de ver a imperialismo yanqui
   destruído.

12/13/86

Edwin Cortés

Struggle in Order to Live

To my beloved wife,
a beautiful comrade.
Since the first day that I met you,
we have shared a happy life.

During those times
we have passed difficult moments.
But as two partners
we acted to resolve them in our own manner.
Comradeship!!!

Today although physically separated from you
these barriers have not affected my Love.
By force I was taken from you
and by the armed might of our people we will be
reunited, to once again begin to live.

In Cuba, our sister nation,
we saw the elimination of oppression and exploitation.
It was a real and applicable experience
to our vulnerable and colonial reality.

We felt the Humanization
and the people's cry of "Long Live the Revolution."
It is defamed for its socialism
but today it is a phantom for U.S. Imperialism.

With our triumph
we will be reunited
to share, construct and once again begin to Live.

Dedicated to my comrade on her birthday, 1/25/85

Edwin Cortés

Luchar para Vivir

Mi querida esposa
una compañera tan hermosa.
Desde el primer día que te conocí
compartimos una vida feliz.

Durante esos tiempos
pasamos difíciles momentos.
Como una pareja
actuamos de nuestra manera.
En compañerismo.

Hoy estamos físicamente separados
pero como siempre bien enamorados.
Por la fuerza me llevaron de tí
en la victoria nos reuniremos para ser otra vez feliz.

En Cuba nuestra hermana nación
vimos que acabaron con la explotación y opresión.
Fue una experiencia real y aplicable
a nuestra realidad colonial y vulnerable.

Sentimos la humanización
y con gritos "Viva la Revolución".
La llamaban vil por su socialismo
hoy se convierte en un fantasma para el imperialismo.

Con nuestro triunfo
estaremos juntos.
Para compartir, construir y otra vez vivir.

Vincent Kay

Letter in September

(Upon release from Billerica County Prison,
Mass. 1980)

I

Almost overnight the field empties:
blood rhythms no longer
beat with fever,
and the velvet scraps of the bee
trapped between two windows
now collects silt-like pollen
beneath the thin-to-fat
parings of the moon.

Something similar remains
lodged between us—
remnants of the memory
of a place
—the quirk you had
of arriving an hour before
the time we'd planned on:
you'd wait,
slowly undress as you watched me
in the mirror
continue to dress, ready myself
for your arrival.

It was your way, not to arrive,
but appear, suddenly in semi-darkness,
half-amused, half-afraid to touch
our reflection braided between
flakes of silver
peeling away
what we could see of ourselves
in this memory of light.

II

All about the visiting room
wide angles
and shadows of angles cut
into quarters the small table
cross-hatched by metal gridwork.
You fell back into shadow,
were gradually led back to words:
spoke of a spiraling flight
between two fixed points,
how it was like a third voice
interrupting the quiet between
the two of us, old friends
who had not seen each other
for too long a time.

Bits of darkness began to drop
inside the room.
We became more transparent:
blue silhouettes mixed
with perfume, cigarettes, the sweat
as our fingers looped through
chain-link that put us
back in our separate place.

150

III

I was given a release date.
Outside, leaves circled
and cracked against the building.
We both knew days could only shorten
as we watched without words
the last leaves ripped from dry branches.
From the fields that wrapped the prison
in vertiginous distance,
a small quiet grew larger,
but lighter
until almost weightless it lifted
from the ground,
part reflex, the rest
our first honest thought together
as we imagined for the last time
crossing this field—
the wet paths of matted timothy
and clover behind us
— as we turned to each other
turning back across the field . . . no field.

IV

Afterwards we sat absorbed
in the season's first wool shirts
partly unbuttoned,
listened to late blueberries drop
like rain onto dry oak leaves.
A group of birds sat
black as paper-cuts, lifting
the rimed heads of girl-like boughs
— where we sat, you laughed,
I listened to the sound of wings
moving along the field's edge.

Barbara Curzi-Lamaan

For Susan

In a real spurring of strength
I met your Spirit
In the field, my heart danced
    with yours
as we signaled each other,
    back and forth
to the deep dismay of our enemy.

When I met your face—
    your body—
the face much smaller
than I had imagined—
The body less round—
I saw the compact unit
of a Human-Woman
Spirit-Heart-Strength
Burning though your eyes

FOR SUSAN

Your little self
made me reflect
hard
    on how
the Human mind
and soul
are the sources of power—
———
that really count
in a world where
large men
    try
to overpower others
through force—
You gave me even more
    hope
to feed my already hopeful
Revolutionary Spirit

As I see you in my mind
making great leaps
in thought and in action
So that all who look
can see—

See you
    My Sister-rade
Soar far above
any limits they impose

Psyching them out
 as you do
    my Sister Psychee

Always pushing that muscle
to bear more of the weight
So that all strengthened—
   together—
Encouraged by each other's
   persistance/Resistance
we will throw them off

To Free the World
and reconstruct
A Life where our Bodies
can dance together
  along
    with our hearts.

All as one—
  we'll bear life— into the New Day
Born of our Sweat and Blood and Love . . .

October 5, 1985

Barbara Curzi-Lamaan

Winning Battle

Seizing—   with unbindable Hope
        we take the Future
        and shower with care
        the blossoms of optimism

        Nurtured
                with unending warmth
                and brilliance
                from our Dreams
                Life bursts forth
                even from the cracks
                between the concrete blocks

Ascending—with unstoppable strength
        even within the pits
        of the enemy's barren soil:

        Determination   makes us whole
                        as we survive
                        the blows
                        and surpass the pain
                        and defeat defeat

    for with our Love for Life,
            Venceremos

Barbara Curzi-Lamaan

Look at Our Beautiful Sister

for Yvonne Melendez Carrión

As a child's
    her eyes
        are tender — full of sincerity
        always questioning
        but always with an open mind
           behind them—

Soaring — Her Spirit
    generous — never having accepted greed
    ingenious — in her creative expressions
    Audacious!
        She's fierce in the face of injustice
        as she cuts through it
        with her justness

She exudes strength to all
    she takes into her heart
        — heart open
           to all
               but those who
                 downpress

In her we see the: Sister/caring
      Mother/warmth   Child/innocence
      Lover/beauty Woman/strength
        That we love most about
           our Human-Sisters

She stands for her People/Humanity
pushing off the yoke
      of the oppressor and
         breaking it
with her strong — hands/mind/soul
     Look at Our Beautiful Sister!

12/1/85

Barbara Curzi-Lamaan

For My Parents

Like a river that flows
Creating and nurturing
Life
As it goes

Through the years
So has your
Love
Been

You bore problems
With a grin
And in times
When tears would flow

That's when clearly
Your love did grow.

Grateful are we
That you stuck it
Through

'Cause what would
We do
Without
You Two

9/2/87

Barbara Curzi-Lamaan

For My Children

Sad ones of my womb
though your mother
be in terror
under the direct
blow
   of the oppressor

Fear not
our whole fate
as the whole
will not be led
down the path of
   utter stupidity.

Believing not in the lies
of those who make up
their "truth"
for the convenience of
their pockets

Their greedy wishes
will not be fullfilled

As, in a peek ahead,
I have seen
glimpses of
what is trying to be
Where people have decided
consciously to deal
directly
with their oppressive enemy

Though many are gone
and others will go
during the process
    The Future is ours,
        Yours
                to shape, model and build.

3/3/85

Barbara Curzi-Lamaan

For My Sisters
("For Those of Us Who Dare")

For those of us who dare
to look beyond
the images they present
as real—
To see the makings
of things,
as they are:
connected—
    related—
        engaged—

To acknowledge the Truth
as the majority
of the world's reality

To see the amerikan dream
turned into a nightmare
when it costs
the lives and sacrifice
    of so many
        for so little

for the empty materialism
and material emptiness
that they try to fill
into the gaps
where
    love
        should
            be.

Untaught to Love
    Trained to compete
        to supercede
            to overpower
        to over-do
            to over-rule

    We mustn't let them
    continue over . . .

We can take our visions
    Join them—
        Blend them—
            into Reality
                Teaching
            Sharing
        Struggling
    Creating for us all
    a New Tomorrow
    For those of Us who dare . . . .

3/4/85

Alberto Rodriguez

El Compañero Combatiente

One

As the barrio woke from its collective slumber, with its customary sweet smells of Puerto Rican coffee to be enjoyed with soda crackers and white cheese (or if times were good with fried eggs and ham), while drifting out of wide open windows one could hear the nostalgic sounds of Los Panchos or Daniel Santos, the clinic was bustling with activity. Doña Maria was busy emptying a small box of medical supplies, meticulously removing labels or whatever else might identify its origins. Her husband, Rafa, was in the basement firing up the old octopus furnace as he did most mornings. Today promised to be at least as hot as yesterday but garbage and other things needed to be turned into ashes. Up front, Doctor Federico M. Cornier stood sentinel, keeping an eye out for those who waged an undeclared war against the clinic, while preparing files for those patients he hoped would be coming in today.

Like the whole Puerto Rican community, the clinic was under constant police and fbi surveillance, even more so because of the name it chose for itself: "Clínica del Pueblo Ramon Emeterio Betances." An fbi and police task force had entered the clinic once before but was forced out when confronted by a large, angry gathering of community people who had turned out in support of the clinic. Frustrated in their efforts to harass the clinic's workers into abandoning their work, scare the community away or construe something legal into illegal so as to charge the clinic with "seditious

163

conspiracy," the task force settled down into an unceasing war of nerves in which they had yet to score even a minor victory.

As Federico turned around to put his folders away, he heard a familiar voice.

"What's up, Doc?"

Federico recognized the voice and a smile came to his face unbidden; but he decided to say nothing and pretend not to have heard the voice, at the same time feeling foolish for playing such juvenile games.

Doña Maria, also hearing the voice, yelled out from one of the examining rooms, "How are you, mi Eva, up so early?" Without waiting for a response she continued to work on her labels, humming a song which for some unexplainable reason had crept into her mind.

Eva stood staring at Federico's back, beginning to question the wisdom of coming inside in the first place. She was a typical Puerto Rican, small in stature but with beautiful large expressive eyes, a smile that melted snow cones and a walk some would consider scandalous. She had an uncanny ability to change her facial appearance and look South American, Italian, Greek, Arab, Iranian and had at several times passed as Jewish. Her light skin and large nose helped in these endeavors. She had lived in the neighborhood for most of her life and had an unearned reputation for being morally loose, which was based less on real evidence than on the need of bored people to gossip. She always seemed to dress in the most flamboyant manner. This particular morning she wore spray-painted-on blue jeans which had the gossips wondering how she had gotten into them in the first place, a red silk blouse opened down past its initial intentions, mod sun glasses and the brightest of red lipsticks.

Eva stared at Federico, who continued to look over a patient's file. He felt her stare, and the usual unsettling feeling he experienced whenever she was around or her name was mentioned began to creep over him. Federico had first met Eva about eight years ago. She was 19 then and single, while he was married with one child. Now he was divorced and that marriage and that child seemed to have belonged in some other life— or maybe someone else's life. He still felt a bit confused around Eva, for she seemed to be both a part

164

of his past and his present. There was precious little in his life like that now.

Eva finally broke the silence. "So what you doing on this beautiful sunny morning?"

"Oh, just taking care of these files before my patients come in," he answered as he put the file away.

"But why so early?"

"It's always better to take care of such things early in the day."

"You work too hard, Doc. You should take a break some time. You know what they say about all work and no play—"

"Yes! I sure do!" Federico shrugged. "But right now work must take a priority over play."

"Work! work! priorities! priorities!" Eva mocked, looking annoyed while pushing back her long black hair. "That's all I hear lately."

Federico, amused by her attitude, searched for a response. "It's not that I'm some sort of a workaholic, Eva. I do miss being able to go for walks in the park or to the beach without a care in the world. You can't even imagine how long it's been since I've seen a movie or eaten in a real restaurant. I miss those things more than I care to admit." Federico moved around the corner slowly, and continued: "But these are difficult times we're living in, and everyone must do his share."

Eva stepped away from Federico, as if unsure of how to respond. After a moment of silence, she shrugged her shoulders and said, "Well, I don't know about you but I'm going downtown to see what's happening and do a little shopping." She carefully placed her bag on the counter and looked herself over in the mirror hanging from the wall.

Federico pleaded, "But Eva! you know damn well it's dangerous to go downtown. The police stop and harass all Puerto Ricans going through there. Hell! All Latinos or New Africans for that matter . . ."

"Not me," Eva said defiantly. "I go there all the time, and anyway, the police know me pretty good."

Federico could not help but demonstrate his disapproval, and in a grave voice said, "I don't think that is something to brag about around here."

"Why not!" Eva shouted angrily, taking off her sunglasses and showing the anger engulfing her. "Listen, I go wherever I please, nobody tells me what to do. Especially you!" — pointing her finger at Federico's chest. Federico felt anger and disgust as well as pity, all at the same time. In Eva, he saw many of the same attitudes that had characterized his own beliefs not so long ago. He was wondering how to respond when Doña Maria called from the rear of the clinic:

"Eva, EVA! are you still here?"

Eva stepped back and looked over some shelves, answering in a disinterested voice, "Yeah, yeah, I'm still here— though I really don't know why!"

"Well, why don't you come and give me a hand, we have lots of work to do today."

"Sorry, Doña Maria, not today. I really do have lots of things to do."

Doña Maria retorted sarcastically, "Yes, poor Eva always has a lot of things to do," and disappeared again behind some partitions. Eva turned toward the counter with her head slightly lowered, as if hoping that Federico would say something in her defense. But Federico had returned to looking over some files. In a voice barely loud enough for Federico to hear, Eva mumbled, "Anyway, pretty soon you won't have to worry about me anymore." She grabbed her bag from the counter and was out the door in what seemed like one smooth movement.

Seeing her walk out of the clinic, Federico moved slowly around the counter, not sure of what to say or do, and stepped out the front door. By the time he was outside, Eva had crossed the street and was moving quickly. For a second he stood staring at Eva's walk, which was like a dancer's. He finally shouted at the top of his lungs: "Eva! Eva!"

She turned, looking annoyed.

"Come by the clinic later so I can better explain what I was trying to say." Eva smiled and turned the corner without answering. As Federico watched her he noticed a parked car with two men in it, watching a little too attentively. Federico stepped back into the clinic wondering if Eva would indeed return and why the surveillance so early this morning.

Two

The heat of the day refused to leave, even after the sun had set and been replaced by the moon. Federico sat with Rafa and Doña Maria in the courtyard of the house they shared. The clinic was housed in an old building down the street, which was owned by Federico. He lived with Rafa and Doña Maria, though, because it was more economical— besides, they wouldn't have it any other way. Their house had been built before the city had raised the street level in order to prevent flooding, so what used to be a front yard had become a sunken courtyard, providing some privacy. It was in this courtyard that Federico, Doña Maria and Rafa spent their evenings. Few people ventured out anymore, due to the indiscriminate arrests and beatings by the police and the "anti-terrorist task force" which the community had come to hate with a passion. Those who couldn't stand the heat inside their apartments huddled on the fire escapes or back porches. Many young people still came out at night to socialize, love, set up ambushes, and stone cops.

Federico was sitting on a home-made bench with his strong athletic legs stretched out in front of him and his hands folded behind his head. Rafa and Doña Maria sat on old kitchen chairs by the basement door. Rafa was using the light from the open basement door to fix an old lamp that had been donated to the clinic. Rafa was a large dark man who had worked as a skilled mechanic until a factory accident cost him several fingers on each hand. He still had the ability to fix anything. All the shelves, partitions and counters had been built by him. Doña Maria was also using the light to read a letter in a soft, barely audible voice that only her husband could hear, gently caressing his arm while she read.

Federico sat on the other side of the courtyard, admiring the love these two people had for each other. He leaned against the wall and thought about how much his life had changed from what it had been just a little over a year ago.

Federico had been born and raised in this very community. Over the years very little had changed. Children still played on the streets since there were no playgrounds, and on every street corner there was a *bodega* selling everything from milk and bread to *bolitas* and *pitorro*. Large sections of the community had been ravaged by urban renewal via arson, but the people resisted. Real estate and insurance agents, politicians and policemen cajoled, lied, deceived, threatened and even used violence to force Puerto Ricans to leave. But it seemed that for everyone who did leave there was someone ready to take their place. Unemployment, dilapidated housing, poor health care and a decrepit educational system along with drug addiction, alcoholism, AIDS and violence afflicted the people. A corrupt and stagnant political machine held sway over the community. While over the years, selected Puerto Ricans had been integrated into this regime, its character of deprivation, scandal, common thievery, atrophy and roguery continued unabated.

In spite of all this, the community persevered, and with the influx of new immigrants from the island as well as newcomers from Mexico and Central America, it grew in numbers. It seemed the community had accepted as its motto the name of a local restaurant, *"Aqui Me Quedo."*

El Barrio was where on any given day in a *bodega*, restaurant or any street corner you could hear the old folks talking about politics with the same fervor that others spoke of religion, cockfights, baseball games or collectively dreaming of returning to *"la isla del encanto."* Walking down the streets, one's senses were bombarded by the relentless beats and beautiful rhythms of Latin music, and the smells of *alcapurria, rellenos de papa* and *morcillas* penetrate one's very pores. It was home for Federico, Eva, Rafa, Doña Maria and thousands of others.

Federico had been an active youth. He played basketball and was the star of his high school team. To his mother's dread and dismay, Federico loved the streets. She would hide his shoes in desperate attempts to keep him from being out in the streets all day and night, but he'd just borrow some shoes from a friend or hang out in his bare feet. What he enjoyed the best were the street rallies and demonstrations organized by the independence movement. There was something about these proud men and women with their Puerto Rican flags and defiant attitudes which made Federico want to be one of them. Though never really able to clearly state why, he always considered himself an *independentista*.

Upon graduation from high school, he received an athletic scholarship and was accepted at a prestigious east coast university. The atmosphere at the university was completely different from anything Federico had ever experienced. Competition replaced camaraderie, everyone was into making the grade, and in order to survive he became totally submerged in his studies and in basketball. He grew increasingly alienated from his old community, his friends, and even his mother. He entered medical school and throughout the years his visits to the old neighborhood became less frequent.

After finishing medical school, he was offered a residency in a large hospital coincidentally located near his old community. He became totally submerged in his career and the relatively comfortable life it provided him, enjoying the privileges of being a young professional. Though he was regularly confronted with institutional and individual racism, he had become like many Latino professionals— submissive, apologetic and (when the stress of living this contradiction began to wear on them) cynical.

All this changed for Federico with an unforeseen experience which impelled him to reflect upon and re-evaluate his life's direction and purpose. One evening, upon leaving the hospital, he heard on his car radio that due to a fire his usual route home was closed. He decided to take an alternative which would take him right through the heart of his old community.

As he stopped at a red light, a white van came swerving through the intersection at high speed. The driver of the van lost control and plowed into a parked car. The driver tried to back up but his engine died; within seconds several police cars came screeching to a stop just yards from the stalled van. A squad of "anti-terrorist" gunmen came pouring out of the cars with riot helmets, bulletproof vests and automatic weapons. Without hesitation or warning they fired a fusillade into the van, bursting its glass and piercing its metal sides. After what seemed to Federico an unnecessarily long time, the police stopped firing and cautiously approached the van. While covered, one of them carefully opened the door and stepped in. He came out with a man's body totally drenched in blood. He pulled him by the hair and threw him on the ground. The others began to pummel the wounded man with their boots and rifle butts. Federico could see from his car that the man was weakly attempting to ward off the blows with his arms. Outraged and shocked at what he saw, Federico grabbed his medical bag, jumped out of his car and ran to where the beating was taking place. The police slowed their beating somewhat, startled by this new arrival. One of the cops grabbed Federico by the collar and yelled into his face: "Get out of here you shitface spic before we kick your ass too!" Federico, caught unprepared for such violent and racist hatred, didn't know what to do. Then an fbi agent appeared. Realizing that the beating of a doctor—which was obvious from the medical bag—even a Puerto Rican one, was not good public relations, and noticing that an angry crowd was forming, the fbi agent ordered the policeman to let him go. Federico rushed to where the wounded man was lying and was horrified at what he saw. The wounded man was Puerto Rican, about 18 years old, with a boyish face. He was completely drenched with blood and seemed to have several bullet holes in him. Federico knew that if he didn't have him on an operating table soon he'd be dead.

Federico stood up as tall as he could and looked straight into the fbi agent's eyes and demanded, "I want you to get an ambulance here immediately and have this man transported to St. Mary's Hospital. NOW!"

The agent answered angrily, "I already have a patrol wagon on the way, Doc. We have procedures that we follow in cases like this."

"I don't care about your procedures. This man is going to die if he is not in a hospital in a few minutes. St. Mary's is just a few blocks away."

"Listen, this is a national security question! I advise you to mind your own business and stay out of this if you know what's . . ."

"Don't threaten me!" Federico said. "Don't give me that security bullshit. I want that man"—pointing to the ground—"in my hospital. I will take full responsibility and if you don't move him there I'll make as much stink about this as I can."

The fbi agent turned red with hatred and wrath; but seeing that Federico was not about to back down, and noticing the growing crowd which had begun to shout approval for Federico's demands, he grudgingly gave in.

At the emergency room of the hospital, Federico began to cut off his patient's bloody shirt, when the young man opened his eyes and tried to say something. Suddenly the fbi agent jumped between them. "Don't listen to him, Doc, he's nothing but a fucking terrorist!"

The wounded man, raising his head the best he could and using what strength he had left, feebly said, "You're the terrorist! I'm a soldier for the FRENTE and demand to be treated as a prisoner of war, and . . . and . . . ." He struggled to continue but lost consciousness.

Federico was taken by surprise. He couldn't believe that this young man who seemed just a boy was a member of the FRENTE which the government had virtually outlawed as a terrorist organization.

After surgery the wounded man was placed in a heavily guarded room. The hospital immediately filled with police, fbi and the media. Several agents attempted to speak to the wounded man but backed off when confronted by the intransigency of Federico, who was now feeling like he was on home turf. He was soon to realize how fragile that security really was. Several lawyers who came to the hospital were threatened with arrest and left to try and get a court order so they could see the prisoner. A picket was hastily organized by FRENTE supporters outside the hospital, driving the Anti-Terrorist Task Force into hysteria. That evening Federico met with the parents of his patient who had rushed to the hospital when they'd heard the news. It was through this that the fbi was able to identify their prisoner as Julio Alcedo.

Early the next morning, while Federico, who had been up all night, took a much-needed nap, the fbi seized Julio and transferred him to a federal prison. Federico was furious when he found out and filed a formal complaint when he realized that the hospital administration had given their approval. This was the beginning of his difficulties with the administration, which informed him it was hospital policy not to treat terrorists and advised him, for the sake of his career, to let the whole incident go.

But Federico couldn't "just let things go," and he began to work with Julio's parents and supporters. Julio took the position of prisoner of war, refusing to recognize United States jurisdiction over Puerto Rico or over combatants captured in the struggle to free the homeland. Federico was outraged to find that in cases involving "terrorists" normal judicial proceedings were *de facto* suspended. Julio was convicted and sentenced to life imprisonment for seditious conspiracy and other charges. This was Federico's first real experience with the state's legal machinery. The experience convinced him that there was nothing fair or just about the U.S. legal system; that it was in fact an administrative arm of the state's repressive apparatus which had a special and particular mandate: to jail political opposition and those for which the political-economic system no longer had any use.

It was after Julio's imprisonment that Federico began to develop relationships with Julio, his comrades, his parents and their supporters and became a target of the Anti-Terrorist Task Force. Federico was able to visit Julio and other jailed FRENTE members and through their discussions he gradually became radicalized. He became conscious of the irreconcilable contradictions in his working for a hospital that would not provide services to his own people— the same people who through their individual and collective sweat, toil, blood and sacrifice had made it possible for him to have the opportunity to acquire his medical skills! Discussing this preoccupation with Julio and others, the idea of a people's clinic in the community began to blossom.

As Federico lay back on the bench thinking about the hardships of the past year, he also thought it had been the most exhilarating year of his life. He felt, finally, that his medical skills were being used where they were most needed. Then his reverie ended and he heard that familiar voice once again:

"Hello folks, wonderful night, ah?"

It was Eva, who startled Doña Maria and made her respond excitedly: "Negra! What you doing walking around by yourself? You forget about the police. Come down here right now."

Eva walked down the small rickety stairs that led into the courtyard and sat next to Federico on the bench. To him, she

172

looked different. He couldn't remember if he had ever seen her more beautiful— her face without make up, her hair hanging loose, and wearing a simple sleeveless dress. That sensation he felt whenever he was around Eva swept over him, so that all he could do was just sit motionless. Eva noticed how he was looking at her and gave him an approving smile.

Then, just as she was turning to speak to Doña Maria and Rafa, a boy came running up to the railing which divided the sidewalk from the courtyard, and whispered while trying to catch his breath: "I'm looking for the doctor!"

"I'm the doctor," Federico said as he stood up. "What seems to be the problem?"

"A comrade just got shot by the police and needs you real bad!"

Though he had been working with the movement for over a year, Federico had never been asked to do anything illegal. Caught by surprise, he asked, "Why doesn't he go to the hospital?"— then wished he could somehow recall such a stupid utterance.

The boy exaggeratedly rolled his eyes upward and looked at Eva, then just as quickly looked away. For a second he hesitated, but finally responded: "He was shot by the police and if he goes to the hospital he'll be arrested. We can't take the chance, and . . . ."

Federico didn't let him finish. "I'll go, just let me go by the clinic" (*Through the back door,* he thought) "and get a few things. I'll meet you here in about five minutes."

As he began to walk away, Eva touched his arm, whispering, "I'll go with you."

"Thanks, *Compañera,* I could sure use the company." Federico thought right there and then that he shouldn't be bringing her into something "illegal," but his need to be with her on this night was stronger.

Three

The boy knew the neighborhood well and took an indirect route cutting through alleys and gangways in order to avoid the police. The boy was about ten years old, but tall for his age and well built, and there was something about him that bothered Federico. But he finally decided it was the boy's expressive eyes and mischievous smile that made him appear suspicious. Except for an occasional small group of young people or a couple seeking a moment of solitude, the streets were oddly empty of people or activity. Even the police seemed to have taken a break.

Federico and Eva hadn't said a word to each other since leaving the clinic. Federico finally decided to break the silence by going directly to what was troubling him.

"You know, this morning when we were talking I wasn't trying to run your life," he said. Eva slowed down, creating a little distance between them and the boy as Federico continued speaking. "It's just that not too long ago I thought of myself the same way you do. I lived like an ostrich with my head in the sand, only thinking about my career— today it seems funny saying this— having a good time, parties, vacations and whatever else I felt like doing and my money allowed me to do."

"I know you weren't trying to run my life," replied Eva. "I'm usually not that sensitive, but this morning I had a lot on my mind."

"Well, I'm sorry if I said anything to upset you. I— "

"No! No!" she interrupted. "In a way, what you said was exactly what I needed to hear this morning."

Federico, not fully understanding her, continued: "What is happening in Puerto Rico and here in our community can no longer be ignored. It's not just interesting conversation but a very real thing, a life and death struggle."

Eva was about to say something, but Federico continued speaking.

"For me, I needed to be shocked into reality. When I saw the injustice against Julio, I just couldn't continue to live as if these things don't matter to me. You know Julio, Julio Alcedo, Doña Maria and Rafa's son."

"I know him well. We were close years back."

"Oh, I didn't know that. I mentioned you to him several times" (*Man, why did I have to say that!* he thought) "and he never said he knew you."

Eva shrugged with a girlish smile on her face. "He has his reasons and I have mine."

"Anyway," Federico went on, "at first I resented how some of the people who work in the clinic seemed to be always getting on my case."

"I know the feeling," responded Eva.

"But with time, I began to realize that it wasn't that they were trying to run my life, but that if we don't develop a practice of bringing to light each other's shortcomings and errors, then we will not grow and overcome those errors."

"I agree with you, I really do. It's just that at times I feel like I'm no longer in control of my life. Other people are telling me what to do and what not to do."

"I feel like that sometimes myself," Federico said.

"I don't doubt it, but I think because you're a man and a doctor with a lot of responsibility and respect, it's not as hard on you as it is on me. Folks see me and automatically think I'm a dope. They don't even talk to me or try to know me, but because of how I dress, talk and carry myself I'm considered not worth the struggle."

Federico was beginning to realize that Eva was not what everyone, himself included, had supposed—but was in fact a sensitive woman who thought about herself and the world around her. He said, "I agree that people do jump to conclusions and don't take the time to talk and understand. But I think that part of the responsibility is on you, also."

"What do you mean?"

"Well, you should also take into consideration how your behavior draws people to conclusions, and . . . ."

Eva interrupted, irritated. "What do you mean by 'my behavior'? Because I don't fit into some neat little mold, everyone can't deal with me? Well, I think it's *their* problem and not mine. Why is it that I have to change? Why is it that the *woman* is always the one that has to change. Why don't you all change and accept me for what I am?"

"I think it has to be 50-50. Each side has to give and take a bit."

"Yeah, well, it seems to me that I always end up giving and getting nothing in return."

175

"Folks see what you do, say, and how you act, and come to certain conclusions."

"But what the hell do people know about what I do. Do you know what I do? I doubt it, you only know what you *think* is right—not what *is* right."

"What kind of bullshit is that?" Federico responded with a smile.

"It ain't no bullshit, brother! You've come to certain conclusions about me based on what you think you know about me. But when have you taken the time or trouble to ask me a simple question? Whenever we do talk, it's some small talk about nothing that matters. You've decided that I don't have any ideas or thoughts worth knowing about. I'm just something nice to look at, but that's it."

Federico felt embarrassed by her statement, feeling the sting of its truth. "If that's how you feel," he said, "I'm sorry."

"No, Bro! It ain't about being sorry, it's about what is real and what is not. You nor Doña Maria nor Rafa know a thing about me. You all just jumped to an idea about me and you can't let it go." She looked around as if unsure of her next words, and then continued. "Anyway, I wanted you to know these things tonight because I've learned from experience that sometimes we keep things inside and never say them to people we care about. Then before we know it, it's too late."

Federico felt a little tightening in his stomach when Eva said 'care about.' She continued: "Lots of things are happening in my life and I think the same will be true for you. I just want you to know that I *do* believe in the struggle, but the way I express my support is up to me, and you'll just have to trust me on that one."

Federico was about to respond when the boy who was leading them stopped in front of a large apartment building and let out a loud whistle. Suddenly a young woman stepped out of a darkened passageway. She looked as if she could have been the boy's sister except that while the boy was light-skinned with brown hair, she was dark with jet black hair. Federico thought of his own daughter upon seeing the young woman and wondered how long it had been since he had done that. She whispered something into the boy's ear, and giving Eva a smile that showed her white teeth, disappeared once again into the dark passageway with the boy following. Federico hesitated for a second. "Come on, Doc . . . don't be afraid," the boy said. Federico felt both embarrassment and irritation at the boy's comment and plunged after him. As soon as he stepped into the darkness he felt powerful hands grab his arms and others place a sack over his head. He tried to break free but his arms were pinned. He heard a voice whisper into his ear: "Take it easy, don't fight, we just want to talk to you." For a second he was confused— the voice sounded like Eva's—but how could that be? Then he thought maybe it was the young woman's voice.

Federico's hands were tied behind his back, tightly but not hurting him. He was spun in a circle, causing him to stumble, and when they stopped turning him he wasn't sure in what direction he was headed. He finally heard a door close behind him and he was led to a chair. The room felt cold and damp, which he couldn't understand since the days had been so unbearably hot. After only a few minutes (which seemed like an hour) his hands were untied and his mask removed. He rubbed his eyes; the light was dim but seemed bright after the mask. He was sitting in what looked like a basement across a table from three people.

Federico continued to rub his eyes. What little light there was in the room was positioned so that it projected only silhouettes. Nevertheless, he could make out three people all wearing scarves across their faces, and hats. Utilizing his years of studying anatomy, he guessed them to be two women and a man. The figure on the far left finally spoke, and it was indeed a woman.

"Please forgive us for the deception, Doctor, but we had to take precautions not just for our security, but for yours also. Do you know who we are?"

"Yes," he answered.

"Good, good. Well, let me first tell you that we have been watching you for some time now."

"I kind of figured that since we started getting those secret supplies at the clinic. Doña Maria and Rafa, those are the two community people who work in the clinic with me—Do you know them?" Not getting an answer and realizing he wasn't going to, he continued: "Anyway, they said that it had to have come from you."

177

"We would have liked to have been able to give you more, but we couldn't. We recognize the good work being carried out at the clinic."

"Thank you very much," said Federico, trying to disguise his nervousness. "But I'm sure you didn't go to all this trouble just to compliment us."

"Yes, you're right. And we appreciate your desire to get right to the point."

After a moment of silence, the center figure began to speak; also a woman. "Doctor, we have just two requests to make of you. If you agree to the first, than an agreement will be automatically taken for the second one." She continued in a slow, deliberate manner: "We are a clandestine politico-military organization creating the necessary foundations to wage armed struggle here in the United States, which will complement and support the struggle in the homeland. We see independence and socialism for our nation and the building of an anti-imperialist movement here in the metropolis as the only way the lives of our people will be fundamentally changed. While we have made great advances in the past few years, we still have a lot to do and many more sacrifices to endure."

The speaker hesitated momentarily, acknowledging Federico's nod of approval. "We have heard many good things about you. Not just your work in the clinic, but also your work with our imprisoned comrades. We also are aware of your personal sacrifice with regard to our comrade Julio Alcedo. Because of these things and the fact that we have a pressing need for a person of your skills, we want you to make a commitment to this work."

After a few minutes of contemplation, Federico responded: "Many times throughout the past year, I have thought about this very same question. I wondered if asked if I would say yes, and if I did what eloquent speech I would make. But now that it has happened the only thing I can say is—I would be honored to be part of the FRENTE." Even though he could not see their faces, Federico could sense they were all pleased with his response.

The first woman who had spoken, elation clear in her voice, said, "Welcome to the Army," reaching a gloved hand across the table. Federico took her hand and felt its strength. She continued, "Now comes our second request. We need you to leave on an important trip right away."

"You mean tonight?" Federico responded with surprise at the immediacy of his commitment.

"Yes, we can't take the chance of you being arrested here. We feel that the task force has just about had enough of the clinic and will do something to destroy it, and we don't want you around when that happens."

"How about Doña Maria and Rafa? What should I tell them."

"You don't tell them nothing. We want you to go back to your place, get whatever you need to travel light, and get out. We'll take care of things from there."

The man, who had not said a thing throughout the discussion, got up and came around the table. He began to brief Federico while the women spoke among themselves. Federico was told about organizational security, individual code of conduct, what he was expected to do if captured, and the plans for him to travel to different sites in the U.S. and in Puerto Rico to train comrades in first aid and basic treatment of wounds, and to explore the possibility of establishing a clandestine field hospital for the organization. Federico was overwhelmed with so much information and struggled to absorb it all. He was impressed by the FRENTE's foresight and planning.

When Federico could think of nothing further to ask, the comrade who had first spoken reached out and gave him a strong handshake, saying, "*Salud y Pa'lante, Compañero Combatiente.* The sister who brought you here will give you all the information about your departure tonight and where you'll be going."

"Eva!" cried Federico in shock.

"We don't use names, my brother. Please don't forget. Trust her, she is one of our best *Compañera Combatientes.*"

Once again a sack was placed over Federico's head, but this time his hands were not tied.

As he was being led away, Federico felt proud to be called a "*Compañero Combatiente.*" During his prison visits to Julio, he had been impressed with how the prisoners of war used the term among themselves as an expression of respect and solidarity. Now he had earned the privilege to use it and be addressed by it! He also felt great confusion over Eva. His feelings about her had always been mixed up, and now, with this new factor, he did not know what to say or do.

When the black sack was removed from his head, he saw Eva waiting for him. One of the comrades who had escorted him nodded affirmatively, bringing a broad smile to Eva's face.

Four

Eva and Federico walked back to the clinic slowly with the same boy leading the way. The route back was different than the one that had brought them there. Eva began to speak, but this time her voice was much more determined and businesslike. She began to explain the plan for him to leave town tonight, and where he would be going. He listened attentively, knowing that his life depended on doing the right thing. As they got close to the block where the clinic and Federico's house were, the boy slipped away unnoticed. Eva had stopped speaking before they had reached the block, and both had become submerged in their individual thoughts. When they reached the house, Federico looked at her—but she immediately turned away and started walking. He wanted to go after her and tell her what was in his feelings, but he just couldn't find a way.

He walked quietly into the house, hoping no one had noticed him. The comrades had given him two hours to get his things together and meet them on the other side of the community. *There're so many things that need to be done and so little time*, thought Federico. Accepting the fact that it would be impossible to do everything necessary, he resigned himself to do what was most important. He thought of sneaking into the clinic and leaving notes in his patients' files so that his successor would have a better grasp of their particular problems. But he just as quickly realized that he couldn't do that. He only hoped his people would understand the situation and know he would never abandon them.

He moved around his room quietly, not wanting to wake the Alcedos. He decided to carry only one bag so that one hand could be free at all times. He had never realized how many things he had accumulated in his little room. He laughed to himself, thinking that his first decision as a FRENTE member was to decide what to take with him. He realized that all who struggle must leave behind something that is a part of their past, in order to begin the future.

After showering, shaving and getting dressed he realized that he would just make it on time. He grabbed his bag and slipped out the back door, feeling sorrow at leaving the Alcedos without saying goodbye. They had become his parents, his friends and his co-workers. It was their support that had helped him survive that first year after he left the hospital, and worse, his divorce. But he knew that there was nothing he could do but look forward to the day they could be reunited in a free Puerto Rico.

He walked several blocks down an alley as the comrades had instructed. Reaching the front of a building through an empty lot, he noticed a car exactly where he was told it would be. Getting in the car, he began to search for the key under the seat, feeling a second of panic when he couldn't find it. Reaching under the passenger side, he found the key along with a small revolver. He breathed a sigh of relief when the key fit the ignition perfectly. He felt uneasy as he tucked the weapon into his pants. He had never felt comfortable around weapons— they seemed a contradiction to his profession. But now he would have to live the contradiction of being a healer and at the same time one willing and able to use violence. The demands of the struggle required it to be this way. Just as a revolution is itself a struggle between the larger interest of the nation and the daily necessities of its people, he would have to weigh the contending interests of being a doctor and a revolutionary.

About a block from where he sat in the car, he could see the police barricade. For over a year now, the police had been setting up barricades and road blocks to seal off the community at night. A few minutes later, he could see shadows moving in front of him, positioning themselves behind trees, parked cars and abandoned buildings. One shadow moved from behind a tree and into a passageway with a walk that caught his attention. "This time I won't hesitate," he thought, and he got out of the car quickly and followed. Walking into the passageway, he found himself staring down the barrel of a rifle.

"Hold it! Hold it! It's me, Federico," he whispered. The rifle was lowered and its owner stepped out of the darkness. Even though a scarf covered half the face, Federico recognized those angry eyes.

"You broke discipline, *Compañero*," said the masked one. Hearing the voice Federico knew he had made no mistake—well, at least no mistake in identity.

"I know," said Federico, embarrassed by his indiscretion. "I just couldn't leave without letting you know that I care a lot about you and think of you in a special way."

"I wanted to say the same to you, *Compañero*, but I couldn't. You are going to have to learn that in struggle discipline is always first. Not that we do not feel emotions . . . love . . . but if we are to survive and be victorious, we must make discipline the most important aspect of our lives."

Federico was unable to respond nor did he want to. He had never seen this part of Eva and felt even closer to her. When finally he began to speak, his confusion and his emotions were clear in his voice:

"I'm sorry—here I go again saying I'm sorry, that makes it twice in once day. I guess I'm new at this and still have a lot to learn." He paused, then asked, "Will we see each other again?"

"Oh yes, I'm pretty sure we will. I know I want to."

"I also want to."

"Then we will."

Federico stepped up to her, gently moving the rifle's barrel aside and pulling down Eva's scarf. He held her tightly and kissed her softly. It was for only a second, but for each it seemed an eternity. They held each other, unable to speak; there really wasn't anything to be said. At that moment, footsteps could be heard entering the passageway from its opposite end. Eva quickly stepped away from Federico, turning and pointing her weapon in the direction of the footsteps. Federico pulled his revolver from his waist, hoping he wouldn't have to use it, not just yet.

The footsteps belonged to a comrade with his face also covered, carrying a small automatic rifle. The comrade began to speak in an excited voice. "It's me, *Compañera*. Our intelligence service is back," he said with a faint chuckle. Behind him was the boy who

182

had escorted Federico and Eva earlier, and the young woman who met them at the passageway. They both looked at Federico as if wondering why his face was not covered.

The boy began to talk:

"It's just like it's been the last few nights. They're pretty relaxed and they don't have the street completely blocked. They're a real lazy bunch and they got tired of moving the barricade every time some cop wants to get through."

The young woman cut in: "It's the same bunch that are always harassing the children— real pigs! One of them searched my brother real rough and then tried to touch me." Eva reached over and placed her arms around the woman as she spoke. "I'm okay. I told him that if he touched me I'd get the comrades after him and then he'd really be in trouble. He chickened out."

The boy continued in his calm voice. "Each one has a rifle besides his side arm. I don't think they have anything bigger, but I can't say for sure." As he spoke he kept staring at Federico as if wondering why no one seemed to care that his face wasn't covered.

Eva gave each one an embrace and told them they had done well. As they walked away Federico was impressed and proud of his two little comrades, and he felt confident of his work, knowing that the struggle could engage all its people in the liberating process. The armed comrade motioned to Federico that it was time to move out. He reached into his back pocket and handed Federico a scarf, joking that the next time he caught him without a scarf, he'd personally shoot him. There was something a little too serious in his voice for Federico to take it completely as a joke. He quickly, but clumsily, put the scarf on.

Federico wanted to say something to Eva but she had moved away, busying herself with her rifle. He understood that it was time to go to work. He returned to the car, struggling with his nervousness, his new-found emotions for Eva, and his doubts about his ability to carry out this first task.

He could see Eva and the other comrade come out of the passageway and position themselves— he behind a parked car and she behind a large tree. Suddenly a combatant across the street began to fire, laying a steady barrage upon the police position,

183

which was followed by the throwing of a molotov cocktail that exploded into flames as it hit the police car.

Federico turned the key and felt the car's powerful engine roar into life. On his left he could see Eva behind the tree, laying down a steady fire from her rifle. The police, caught totally by surprise, were trying to return the fire and splinters were flying off the tree that Eva hid behind. Federico wanted to jump out of the car and be with her, but just as quickly he remembered her words about discipline. The police fire began to wither as they retreated, leaving behind their burning car. Eva began to wave her arms wildly that it was time for Federico to make his move. He floored the gas pedal and the car sprang forward, spitting back rocks and leaves from its tires. As he drove by, he could see Eva and several other comrades waving to him. His eyes switched frantically from the windshield to the rear-view mirror, savoring this last sight of his new comrades as they grew smaller in the mirror—and his new-found pride grew larger in his heart.

THE BEGINNING

184

Paul Magno

Advent for Prisoners

Narrow gate, jail gate,
Birth canal to authentic life.
Gate of Calvary, show us in,
Gate of Hananiah, Azariah, Mishael, receive us

Not unto the barren womb
    of Holy Mother State— all steel and concrete,
To be born again, Americans into America,
Bearing her stigmata:
Torture and murder for hands,
For feet, pillage and pride
And for death's certificate, most mortally,
Hate ensconced where hearts should be,

But into the life chamber
    of a true church,
Cultivating innocence until it comes to term,
Bearing us forth— viable at last,
Sisters and Brothers to others' lives,
No less
No more.

On the anniversary of Dorothy Day's
death, 1984. Modified, 1989.

Paul Magno

A Touch of Hunger

What I most miss
Was the chance to share an honest kiss
One over which we might have lingered
Would have left me sated to this day
and thru to kingdom come.

In weighing virtues, contentment against
a touch of hunger,
This missing kiss
Is sign to me.
(Theology, to term an event)
We desire tangible signs of God's presence,
Miracles we can latch onto and be placated.
So sated, we'd seek our own ends

Instead, Wisdom imparts to us
A touch of hunger for Her love.

Paul Magno

ACTS 19: A Contemporary Account

At this time there was serious trouble in Orlando because of the Way of the Lord. A certain aerosmith named Martin Marietta manufactured weapons in the likeness of the great god Pershing II, and the business provided generous salaries for the workers. So Martin exhorted them, together with likeminded people, saying,

> You know our livelihoods come from such work. Now you can see and hear for yourselves what this Pershing Plowshares community is doing. They say the Bomb is no god at all and have succeeded in persuading many people here in Orlando and throughout the country. There is danger, then, that this business of ours (bombmaking) will get a bad name. Not only that, but there is danger that the great god Pershing II will come to mean nothing and its greatness will be destroyed—the god worshipped by the whole country and all the world as well.

As the crowd heard these words, it became furious and began chanting, "Great is Pershing II of Orlando." The uproar spread through the whole city.

Paul Magno

May Day Observations from Jail

1

Martyrs— the biblical word means
   Suffering witnesses to truth
That is to say God
   To say Jesus
To say that a martyr points to justice
From persecution, from prison, from torture
   or from the grave
And demands it
   Even of the Most High

2

We bear witness to truth here
   And are tromped on for our troubles
By the state prosecutors, by the jailkeepers
   By the federal "authorities."

3

Is our faith of any use here
Or should we look elsewhere?

188

4

By fits and starts people are moving
    And being moved on our account.
Some prisoners say, "Damn the Bomb."
Some guards are not at peace with themselves
    Because they enforce political regulation against us.
A jail minister, after a week of us, re-examines presump-
        tions
    About the jailers, the jailed and justice.
Lawyers who shunned us on week one
    Flock to us publicly on week two
A priest proclaims our witness from the pulpit
    Taking flack from his priest-brothers
A Gainesville journalist counts our act
    In line with Jesus' conduct.
Statewide Pax Christi and the Freeze Campaign
Stand by us and work enthusiastically for us.

5

Human faces break out
    Tombstones roll back
Chains fall away
    And prison doors pop open.

6

Easter continues . . . .

Chapter Four

TEACH THE CHILDREN

*That no degree of pressure ever
will cause us to repudiate our
principles, does not in any way
lessen the heartbreak we suffer.*

— ETHEL ROSENBERG

David Gilbert

The Vortex

During the long intervals between visits, the only way to be in touch with my son is the phone. But like many kids his age, he isn't into talking on the phone. I would ask him what he did at school that day, what games he was playing, etc., but he wouldn't have much to say. I guess for him it was boring to report on something that had already happened when he'd rather be doing something with me. So we created epic stories together that we could develop in episodes over successive phone calls. Phone access has varied over the years, but typically I could call him once a week, with a 20-minute prison time limit on the call. We would get a good start on a story during a visit, and then keep it going with 20-minute episodes each week. I would try to end each week on a suspenseful point. One of our epics went on for 18 months. These stories are very much joint creations. Often my son will set the terms for what he wants included; at key crisis points I stop and ask him what the main character (which is he) does or says.

Here's a condensed version of several episodes from an epic we developed when he was eight.

INTRO: "Sean" (my son), "Kwame" (his best friend), "Katie" (Kathy Boudin, my wife) and "Roland" (yours truly) were on a cross-country surveying trip to find ways to replace the missing ozone in the atmosphere. We got caught in a tornado in the Minnesota mountains and, after a harrowing escape, helped evacuate local people into a remote valley forest. The local people had always been terrified of this forest and never entered it. We soon found out why—in the center of the valley a giant vortex was sucking everything within range into it, like a mini-Black Hole on Earth.

Sean himself was almost sucked in, and was only saved by clinging to a tree until we could get a rope around him. Then we noticed that our instruments were going wild—showing a severe ozone depletion in the area. Was that also a result of the strange vortex? We realized that the mystery of the vortex had to be explored. But only the government had the resources to do so, and they were strangely reluctant to look into it, ignoring all our reports. We had to mobilize widespread concern—through teach-ins, TV interviews, and demonstrations—to force the government to do something. The following episodes open with the resultant meeting with the government representative, Stevens.

Stevens said, "Yes, yes, we quite agree that the vortex must be investigated. But we have a little problem: all our trained explorers are tied up in a secret space project—so secret that you didn't even hear me mention it. We just can't spare anyone. We can provide the equipment but not the explorer. The only way the vortex can be examined is if Sean, the only person ever to be at its mouth and survive, volunteers to go down into the Black Hole."

Sean was about to shout back, "Are you crazy?! For an untrained person to go down there would be certain suicide!" But Roland gave him a kick under the table indicating that he should accept this government offer. Sean even made a macho little speech about how he loved adventure and was honored to take this risk for his country. That statement pleased Stevens, who said, "This is an outstanding example of our policy of accomplishing great things through government support for private initiative."

When the day for the exploration arrived, many people come to view it from the safe distance of a mile away. Katie was with Sean as the government outfitted him in a special explorer suit of high-tensile fabric that could withstand enormous pressure and heat. His face was protected by a thick plastic mask. Dressed in this high-tech outfit, Sean would be lowered into the vortex with super-strength titanium cables—and later (hopefully) pulled back out.

Once Sean was dressed, Katie said to the government man, "Please give me just ten minutes alone with my son before he leaves on such a dangerous mission." Stevens could hardly refuse. As soon as he was out of the room, Katie and Sean had to move fast—they quickly got Sean out of the suit and replaced him with a dummy. Sean scrambled out of the room through a trap door. The dummy had a tape recorder in it, so when Stevens returned he heard Sean's voice from within the suit proclaim: "Let's get it on!"

Thousands watched with baited breath as the figure of Sean was lowered into the vortex. Just as "Sean" descended, a colossal explosion rocked the mouth of the vortex and the whole valley. The figure was blown to smithereens; all that could be retrieved was the broken end of the titanium cable.

Stevens went on national TV to proclaim his shock and heartbreak at the loss of such a heroic young explorer. The government declared a national day of mourning for Sean, but even that wasn't enough. Stevens said that the vortex had proven too dangerous for anyone to approach it ever again. It and the surrounding area were to be sealed off forever, guarded by troops, and renamed "The Sean Roberts Memorial Protected Area."

So, as it had planned, the government used the incident to both get rid of Sean and to close off the vortex. But we had an advantage on our side: they thought that Sean was dead and that the three of us who remained were paralyzed with grief. As long as Sean stayed out of sight, we were now free to investigate. But how could four untrained people ever get to the secret of the vortex?

To be continued next phone call—

When the figure of Sean was lowered into the vortex, Kwame was sitting in the audience observing everything intently. He saw that it wasn't really an explosion but rather an *implosion*, with everything collapsing very rapidly inward. For all those hot gases to rush inward, there had to be an exhaust outlet somewhere farther down the line. Kwame estimated the volume, the direction, and speed of the gases and calculated that there had to be an exhaust vent exactly 5.3 miles SSE of the vortex.

Dressed in black and carrying picks and shovels, we snuck into the area at nightfall. At first we found nothing. But as Sean stepped over what looked like a rock, he was blown high in the air by a rush of gas and landed unhurt. We had found the camouflaged exhaust outlet. There was no possibility of climbing down the exhaust against the outflow, so we dug alongside it and broke through the ceiling of a giant underground room. Katie secured a rope and leapt down, then helped the others. We were in the center of a mammoth underground laboratory, with a huge computer and a complex control panel.

But our moment of discovery wasn't such a delight— for in the same instant we felt round nozzles sticking into our backs. We turned to see the barrels of giant laser guns trained on us. These were no little hand-held "Star Trek" guns but killer machines that could easily cut a person in half.

To be continued next phone call—

A strange, rumpled man emerged from behind the lasers asking "how dare we" intrude into his laboratory! We realized that our only chance for survival was to convince him we had no idea of what was going on. "You mean this isn't the engine room of the Grand Coulee Dam?" exclaimed Sean. "That tour guide really messed us up!" complained Katie.

The man, obviously relieved, introduced himself as Dr. Linnoleus and offered us a guest room for the night. To our (apparently) naive questions, he passed his project off as a computerized study of nocturnal flight patterns of bats, to which we responded with very bored yawns. He showed us to a guest room with cots.

Once inside the room, we saw that we were locked in; we also discovered that the room was bugged. Continuing to talk verbally as naive tourists, we used sign language to discuss our real plan of action. There had to be a way to explore the area! We spotted a grating covering an air vent in the ceiling. But the crawl space was very small; only Sean and Kwame could possibly fit through it. They would have to go alone.

The vent system was complex, almost like a maze. Kwame and Sean tied a string to the grating and unrolled it as they went so that they could find their way back. After a long crawl through the dust

196

and darkness, the main vent took them to a view of an incredible sight: a long, metallic tunnel passing through a lake of molten, bubbling metal. This was all surrounded by a strong magnetic field (they could tell by the effect on their watches), and there was a giant funnel for sucking in ozone.

Kwame and Sean crawled carefully back to our room, rolling up the ball of string as they returned. In the morning, Dr. Linnoleus let us out of the room and offered us breakfast. We asked a few polite questions about his bat study and he bid us farewell.

As soon as we left the area, we checked to make sure we weren't being followed, then made a beeline for the University of Minnesota. We couldn't wait to describe our discovery to two renowned scientists active in the ecology movement— Drs. Richard Greenberg and Elena Gonzalez.

"Amazing," said Dr. Gonzalez. "It has to be a giant particle accelerator fed through a lake of ionized metal, all magnetized and then boosted to a higher energy level by an ozone-fed explosion."

"We knew it was theoretically possible," exclaimed Dr. Greenberg, "but we never thought anyone would ever be mad enough to try it!"

"What do you mean? Try what?" asked Kwame.

"They're trying to create anti-matter. It must be a secret project to develop an anti-matter bomb!"

"What's anti-matter?" asked Sean.

Dr. Gonzalez explained: "At the birth of the universe, for every type of matter that was formed, its exact opposite was also formed— with the same structure but the opposite electrical charge and direction of spin. They're so perfectly opposite that if matter and anti-matter ever meet, they completely cancel each other out— boom, instant annihilation! Fortunately, matter gravitated to one universe and anti-matter to another, otherwise we wouldn't have a universe at all."

"It's the ultimate Doomsday Machine," said Dr. Greenberg. "If they can create anti-matter, they can build a bomb that will make nuclear weapons look like firecrackers. Once they start an anti-matter reaction no one knows for sure where it will stop!"

"These madmen in pursuit of their super-weapons threaten the very survival of the world," Katie cried out. "We have to find a way to expose this project and stop it!"

197

"Let's go tell the newspapers and TV," suggested Sean.

"No one would believe such a fantastic story— and all based on the observations of two kids!" said Dr. Greenberg.

"And once we showed our hand, the government would get us out of the way one way or the other," I added. "No, we have to stay under cover until we can come up with definite proof to show the public."

At the very same time this discussion was going on, Dr. Linnoleus was boasting to his head of security, Ed Williams, in the underground complex.

"I sure fooled those dumb tourists," chuckled Linnoleus.

"Fooled them, my ass!" retorted Williams. "I suppose that's why my people spotted a string trail in the vent system— a trail that was there in the middle of the night but gone in the morning. Those 'dumb tourists' of yours have been casing the whole complex."

"Well, why-why didn't you stop them?!" sputtered Linnoleus.

"Because I have a better plan," answered Williams. "Right now I'm having them tailed by a surveillance team. *They're* going to have to come snooping back here to get more evidence; *we're* going to need some cover for when we do our first anti-matter test. We're going to time it so that it goes off when they're here— that way we'll kill three birds with one bang: first, we'll get rid of the four of them forever; second, we'll cover our test by saying the explosion was caused by their meddling; and third, we'll discredit the ecology movement for all time!"

To be continued next phone call—

(Summary of Several Episodes: Drs. Gonzalez and Greenberg agreed to do more research on anti-matter while we would sneak back to the site for more evidence. But before we had even gotten off the campus, Sean realized that he had left his gloves at the Drs' office. Grumbling, we all went traipsing back— only to find the office empty and the window wide open. Drs. Gonzalez and Greenberg had mysteriously disappeared! A student saw us and shouted: "Those are the four suspicious characters who were here before.

198

Quick, call the cops." We high-tailed it out of there. We became the objects of the most intense man-woman-and-children-hunt in history. We felt like an antelope that had stumbled into a lions' den. The police were after us for the kidnapping of the two scientists, while it soon became clear that the surveillance team from the anti-matter project was also on our trail. There were all-points bulletins out, and descriptions of us on radio and TV. The only people who could clear our names were the two scientists, who were nowhere to be found. Over several episodes of the story we have a number of harrowing escapes. But, as the following episode opens, it has become clear that we cannot continue to elude them.)

Katie said, "It's time to turn the tables, from being the hunted to becoming the hunters."

"But how," queried Roland, "with just the four of us alone against the most powerful government on earth?"

"We have something going for us," offered Sean. "Remember, everyone in the world believes I was killed in the explosion at the mouth of the vortex."

We sat down and formulated our plan. When it was done, Kwame said, "So the government wants to find us, eh?— well, we'll come to them, and right at the vortex."

We then proceeded to make phone calls— done quickly and from different phone booths— to TV stations and newspapers throughout the state. It was Sean, unmistakably his voice, saying: "This is Sean Roberts and I am very much alive. If you want to know how that could be, I will appear at the gate to the Sean Roberts Protected Area next Saturday at noon."

Soon the excitement about "the miracle of the vortex" spread throughout the country. Thousands of people started to make their way to the back country of Minnesota by bus, by bike, by foot, and even by hang glider. Of course, the government security forces were questioning everyone coming into the area. They claimed that there was a bomb threat, but their real purpose was to intercept Sean and spirit him away. What they didn't know was that Sean was already at the gate— in a hidden underground compartment that we had dug out three days before. Just at noon, when everyone had gathered, Sean popped out of his hiding place and shouted: "You want to see the miracle of the vortex? Just follow me!"

The 4,000 government troops, who had looked so imposing just a day before, were easily pushed aside by the 100,000 people. The government man, Stevens, was aghast and ordered the troops to open fire. But the soldiers, whose families and friends were in the crowd, refused to shoot, and the crowd surged forward.

We knew that once the people actually saw the anti-matter complex they would believe us and that such exposure would end this dangerous project. But Dr. Linnoleus met the crowd at the entrance. "Be reasonable," he said. "Would I lie to you? This is just a peaceful industrial project, but if you enter you could all be harmed by the radiation." The crowd wavered and the moment of decision was about to be lost.

Just then a voice came on the intercom shouting, "Yes, he *would* lie to you." It was Dr. Elena Gonzalez, imploring, "People, people, please come in; it's important; you have to see what's happening here." Everyone rushed in and saw that she, along with Dr. Greenberg, had been tied up but had managed to get loose and get to the intercom system. Government agents had kidnapped them to try to force them to work on the anti-matter project, but they had steadfastly refused. The scientists led the people to the edge of the sinister complex, explaining to all exactly what it was and how it worked.

Sean felt a tremendous sense of relief after these frantic weeks of being hunted and knowing a terrible secret. Now that this dangerous and frightening project had been exposed it would definitely be stopped.

At that very instant, they felt a deep and powerful rumbling well up from the ground below them.

"Oh, my God, I don't believe it," shouted Dr. Greenberg. "The government scientists have set off the anti-matter reaction!!!!"

To be continued next phone call—

(P.S.: Needless to say, we figured a way out of this one too . . .)

Laura Whitehorn
Scene from the Intifada, 1989
marking pen on paper, 6″ x 9″

Elizam Escobar
La Tortura del Sueño, 1988
acrylic on canvas, 70" x 48"

Elizam Escobar
El Heresiarca,
acrylic on canvas, 72″ x 48″

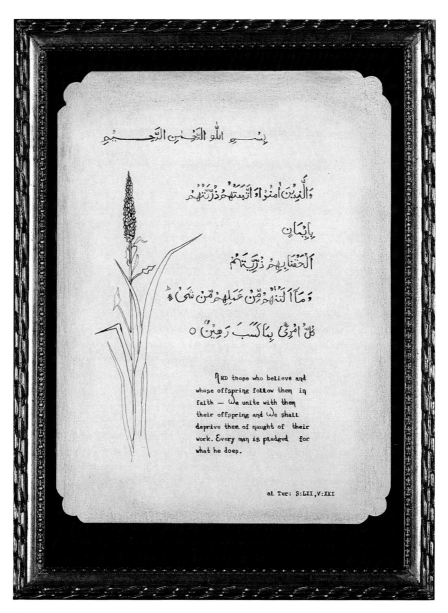

Dhoruba Bin Wahad *(formerly Richard Moore)*
Untitled, 1985
ink on paper, gilded frame, 11 ″ x 15 ″

Laura Whitehorn
Untitled, 1988
acrylic on paper, 16" x 14"

Sundiata Acoli
Milk Goddess Talking to Earth, 1988
acrylic on canvasboard, 20" x 16"

Sundiata Acoli
Royalty, 1984
pastel on paper, 7½″ x 9½″

Leonard Peltier
Big Mountain Lady, 1988
oil on canvas, 18″ x 24″

Leonard Peltier
Grandma Jumping Bull, 1989
oil on canvas, 24″ x 30″

Tom Manning
Georgia O'Keefe, 1988
ink on paper, 9″ x 12″

Tim Blunk
Mary Ann as a Little Girl, 1988
watercolor on paper, 6″ x 10½″

Elizam Escobar
Pez # 3 (Imagen Pasional), 1984
acrylic on masonite, 48″ x 32″

Tim Blunk
Se Desaparecen, 1987
ink, acrylic & pencil on paper, 5″ x 6½″

Susan Rosenberg
Victory to the FMLN! Stop the Death Squads! 1988
ceramic, 12″ diameter

Tom Manning
U.S. Policy in San Salvador, 1989
watercolor & ink on paper, 10" x 8"

Tim Blunk
Sandinista, 1986
acrylic on canvasboard, 16″ x 20″

Wadiyah Jamal

A Living Nightmare

"He couldn't hold me for his hands were hand cuffed to his sides, despite the fact that he had not long come from surgery. He couldn't kiss me for his face was a maze of dried blood, lumps, swellings and bandages. For several days we would speak only through knowing nods, silent eyes, that communicated a strong, stiff will to survive."

The night began like most others. It offered no hint of the disasters the day ahead would bring. Mumia went to work driving a cab to make ends meet. I hated passionately the idea of him driving a cab, as I had been told and had read about the horrors of cab drivers being injured or killed.

Little did I know he had nothing to fear from a robber, for this town's so-called peace officers had other, more grim plans for him. It became clear what those plans were in the wee hours of Wednesday, December 9, 1981.

I waited for Mumia's call— as he called me often from wherever he was. (If he was near, he'd stop home to make sure we were all right.) But the calls I got, definitely not Mumia, shattered my world. The first one was strange, the voice of a white man saying, "Uh-huh! We got you now!" What could he have meant? Was it the wrong number, I wondered. I worried.

A woman then called and asked, *Is Mumia there? No he isn't. Do you know when he'll be in? Yes, I do.* Little did I know. Her voice was thick with emotion, *Is this his wife? Yes it is.* She left her name and number and asked that Mumia return her call. She then hung up, but not completely. For some reason I hung on, only to hear her talking to another woman. The other voice asked, *Are you sure it was Mumia? Yes, it's him, I'm sure.* Then my phone disconnected from theirs.

I was frantic. What were they talking about? I called the number she left and asked her what was going on. She told me Mumia, according to her source, had been shot on 13th & Locust. She gave me little to go on; either she didn't know much or was afraid to say.

Was this a nightmare? Was I in the midst of some maddening dream? Or was I the victim of someone's cruel joke. I truly would have preferred either of the above to the reality.

Shortly after, a reporter who had worked with Mumia called to verify that Mumia had been shot in his chest and was in Jefferson Hospital. No *How.* No *Why.* No *What.* I could believe only that my fears of him being hurt, robbed or killed while driving a cab had come true. I was sick to the bone with pain and fear, too afraid to even turn on the TV or the radio. What should I do?

I called my sister Jeanette Africa, who got me a ride to Jefferson. It wasn't until on the way to the hospital that I learned, from the car radio, that Mumia had been accused of shooting and killing a cop.

How unreal. How dare they lie on him, accuse him of taking a life, when he taught me and our children to love and respect life, and that life loves and respects us. I was in shock, but my concern was with Mumia. Was he dead or alive? Just how fatal was the bullet that burst its way through Mumia's body?

At Jefferson I waded through a sea of reporters and policemen. They informed me Mumia was being prepared for surgery. I demanded that they let me see him. NOW. After about a half hour of delays I was escorted by two policemen to where he was. The walk down that hallway was the longest walk I ever made. Was he still alive? Was it too late? Finally, we reached the end of the hall, only to be greeted by a so-called "colleague" of Mumia's and more cops— both uniformed and plain-clothed—who informed me that Mumia was behind the double doors that stood before me and that, again, I couldn't see him because he was being prepared for surgery.

I waited impatiently, paced, prayed. A man stepped up to me identifying himself as Mumia's doctor and told me what he planned to do to Mumia. Why is he telling me these things? Why can't I just see Mumia? Why wasn't he with Mumia? I was in total confusion.

The double doors blasted open. Mumia laid flat on his back, each hand stiffly strapped to the bars alongside them. His face was swollen twice its normal size, with a gash in his forehead the size of my index finger. I could nearly see his skull. I was paralyzed from head to toe. He was lying there looking like a strange being from another world; tubes were leading from his chest, his nose, his mouth and arms. Tubes were everywhere.

I stared in disbelief. His eyes were puffed and closed, and hiss of oxygen filled the large hallways of Jefferson. Was this Mumia? Was this really happening to us? I called to him—*I love you.* His voice faint, he responded: *I love you.* Then, away they took him down the hallway, police all around him. I walked with him until we reached the elevator door. *I love you,* I cried to him. He made no response. No movement.

As the door closed in my face, I was faint. One of Mumia's so-called colleagues caught me and helped me back to the waiting room. He told me he was going to city hall to get a lawyer friend of his—who turned out to be a shyster.

I used to wonder how a person could hurt so bad, they'd want to take their own life. I bear witness to that hurt, because I just wanted to lay down and die. I have long since then wished I could tear my heart from my chest, put it in the chest of those without understanding, and those who opposed us, and say: *Here, feel what I can feel!*

Calls came from everywhere. Oh, yeah! People came out of the woodwork, blurting out their love and devotion just to promise lies and more lies. Talk and more talk. I didn't want to hear that crap, though some of it was very convincing.

I found myself waiting hours and hours (for what seemed like years and years), sticking like glue to the phone, not really wanting to answer it for fear of the fatal information the caller on the other end of the line could bring. Finally the verdict of whether Mumia would survive surgery had come. He was recovering! I couldn't get to him fast enough, only to be detained and told I couldn't see him.

Why in hell did these people hate us so? Why can't I see Mumia? Was he dead? Haven't we suffered enough already?

I was told that I could possibly see him the next day. The night was endless. When would the time come for me to see Mumia? The separation was, and is now, painful. I wondered, would he be alive? I couldn't get a grip. Why had life turned so swiftly against us? I waited up all night. When the so-called officials gave me clearance to see Mumia, I went to him immediately.

I must have cried an ocean of tears. Finally, I could see him, not impressed in the least with the stitchings. By that I mean the patchwork done on his head, his chest being held together by staples, tubes and more tubes. Nevertheless, I was grateful to have him anyway I could, for he was alive!

He couldn't hold me for his hands were handcuffed to his sides, despite the fact that he had not long come from surgery. He couldn't kiss me for his face was a maze of dried blood, lumps, swellings and bandages. But I could, and would, kiss him. I was ordered by police not to touch him. What could they have been thinking? I dared to and I did kiss him with all the love I could muster.

I was seeing my life fading before me. Mumia's voice was silent, for a clear, plastic tube blowing a phlegmatic mix of blood and fluid blocked his way. I was truly shattered by what I saw, not to mention cops trying to hide rifles and machine guns behind and between their legs.

The walk down Jefferson's hallways got seemingly longer each time I walked it. For several days we would speak only through knowing nods, silent eyes that communicated a strong, stiff will to survive. And survive we must. Nothing we had ever endured prepared me for this living nightmare.

Miraculously, even to the doctor's surprise (and to my pleasure), Mumia healed and regained his strength quickly. His irrepressible grin glowed again, almost as if he wasn't the victim of a police bullet that took him nearly to death's door. For weeks, I ignored newspapers, TV and radio. All I knew was that my man nearly died and that now that he was well again. I honestly expected him to return home and we would be happy again. Only a person in pure shock would be so naive as to believe that. But other shocks were in store for me . . . .

It was unbelievable that my husband would be in prison, for he was beaten repeatedly, shot, and police tried to kill *him* in his hospital bed in the first few days of his hospitalization. His battered and bruised face bore solid testament to the beatings he received. His chest was a brown lump of mangled flesh. It wasn't until he was transferred to Guiffre Detention Unit, however, that he could even write again!

I went into action with the help of my loving Brothers and Sisters of the Family Africa— MOVE— speaking to whomever would listen about what happened to Mumia on December 9, 1981, and to ask support. Many people had been harassed during this time, and that instilled fear in all too many of them in one way or another.

I arranged a press conference. Reporters were there from all the local TV, radio and newspapers. I was misled to believe that they would be fair and impartial and investigative when— no wonder I was nervous (as they so graciously printed)— they came at me like blood-sucking leeches. Except for the committed revolutionaries of MOVE, the Family Africa, I found little support. The press, the many who were taught and led by my husband until recently, were interested only in the system's version, the police reports of what had happened that night. What happened to Mumia was of no import, it seemed. As I was unaccustomed to speaking publicly, my nerves were like electricity, but somehow I got my point across, probably because my rage was far greater than my nervousness.

On the basis of police stories, which changed constantly and therefore changed the press reports, Mumia was already convicted long before the trial. What I found remarkable about that nightmarish period of pain and threatening death was the absolute war of words that raged in the pages of the city's press. The now-defunct *Bulletin* and the not-to-be-missed *Journal* were two of the most misinformed, racist scandal sheets in memory. Their coverage followed form, not to be outdone by the *Daily News*, which, in a moment of "civil consciousness," called for my husband's execution. In an editorial long before the trial, anyone daring to speak in support of Mumia Abu-Jamal was branded Black Racist. This was definitely any tabloid's new low in "fair, objective, impartial journalism."

Throughout it all Mumia remained, and yes remains, an inspirational example of the True Fighting Spirit. However, his colleagues, interested more in serving their white media masters than the truth, played ostrich, and dug their craven faces in the sand.

Mumia's court-appointed attorney, a little dwarf of a man with a deceitful, crooked halfgrin, was from the start someone I couldn't trust. He was a fancy dressin', gold chain wearin' house nigger, it seemed to me. And I disliked his style immediately. From the start his vibes were negative ones to me. I saw through the smooth, too smooth, talk and busted him in quite a few lies. As Mumia and I first met him together—"I love you Mumia"—yes, he too swore his love and devotion to Mumia. But the feeling I got was as far from love as one could get. I warned Mumia of my feelings.

Mumia would later fight a vain attempt to rid himself of this fool. But the judges defended the lawyer's failing and weak efforts. Mumia was placed in the unenviable position of having to defend himself from a lawyer he didn't trust. The lawyer told us: *I can promise certainly that you'll get bail so you can continue to heal at home. You don't have to worry, you've got a good reputation in the community.* Bail would be no sweat. Oh, it sounded so good to me, and I'm sure to Mumia as well. But it was one of many lies. A lie known even as it passed from the lawyer's deceiving heart into the air. The farce of a trial resulted in another call for Mumia's execution.

My husband could have no faith and trust in this system's law. That's why he chose to put his trust and faith in MOVE's law. Mumia could not rely on the strategy of a sell-out shyster, and chose the only strategy that was reliable, the strategy of John Africa.

Mumia is and will continue to stay strong, as so very many have weakened. As a man of principle, he has worked continuously to oppose this system and stand firm in his positon as a seeker, teller of truth. He is without doubt known for his force of truth and honesty, his compassion for people, and his sensitivity for the

206

oppressed, as he is one of us. Mumia gives voice to the voiceless, and as a people we must be heard. Mumia will tell our truth.

I've searched endlessly for an ending to this saga. But there is none. As my memories of this hell linger on, I shall forever live them. Victory is certain!

from DREAD TIMES,
Front Line News Service

Sarah Berkman-Zeller

The Visit

The glass, a barrier
  keeping me from touching you.
The glass, a shield
  prohibiting me from hugging, kissing
  feeling in a physical way, but
  never mentally.
The glass, a wall that can and will be
  broken.
We will touch, we will hug and we
  will hold each other.
But just remember until then,
The glass can keep us from touching
  but never, never from loving.

written at age 11

Carmen Levasseur

Poem for Mom

Oh, how many flowers.
Don't worry she would say
the true beauty is in your heart.
I wish it would all stay the same.
The gentle breeze touches my cheek,
the cool grass under my toes.

A hawk circles above,
she is going home to her children.
They are hungry, she provides.

I love my mama,
we are a pair.
We run through the flowers
barefoot,
as if nothing matters— does it?
When I am with Mama, nothing does,
nothing in the world.
I am hungry,
She provides.

age 12

Dylcia Pagan

The Littlest Warrior

Many moments of my days are spent contemplating your face.
i remember your beaming eyes and precious nose.
Your strong little body, which at an early age had the semblance of
    strength.
You had a gaiety in your soul,
that led me to believe that warrior genes are happy ones.
i remember your first step,
your first smile,
your first words of defiance:
"No Mama" you proclaimed.

Early on you had a softness about you that i shared when you
    caressed me,
seeking comfort in my arms and at times just comforting me.

Yes, you have comforted me although i never asked because we
    have been intertwined with each
other since the first moment of your existence.

And now you have reached the age of reason,
but i know not what you look like or where you are.

210

Dylcia Pagan
The Littlest Warrior, 1989
pencil on paper, 6″ x 7½″

211

i envision you with curled locks of dark mahogany— with a halo of
    red sparks!
Hands strong! capable of holding a gun,
Limber! ready to move.
Joyful! because you possess a spirit of triumph and victory.
(It is difficult to write of you because when I begin to express that
    which i hold inside,
emotionally i am overwhelmed.)

i wonder if you know our names,
that of your true parents
You have come from an Act of Love— totally conscious of your birth.
You were chosen to be born— contrary to all the obstacles in the
    way.
You arrived "triumphantly."
You were embraced by our comrades,
our friends.
You are our Little Warrior!

Before you is a challenge, my Son,
a responsibility to yourself and our people.
Right now this may not be clear to you,
in due time as you continue to grow,
you too will see the necessity for change.

Even though i have not glanced in your eyes
 or held you in my arms
or cared for you in times of fear or hurt,
i have done so in my mind
because i feel your spirit in me.

You are a fortunate child,
because many love you.
Some have crossed your path,
others extend their love for you
by their commitment to struggle.
Oh Littlest Warrior of My Heart!

212

i embrace you from a distance,
hold you in my heart,
awaiting the time when we will meet again,
eye to eye, spirit to spirit.

i will know you at first glance,
at any given moment;
because i have seen you
in the children of the world of struggle.

Happy birthday, dear son
Feliz Cumpleaños, Hijo Querido
February 28, 1986

Kathy Boudin

The Amazing Story of the Bog Man

One day, about 4 years ago, a man named Andy Mould was working at his job. He was digging peat in a bog near Manchester, England.

Before this story goes on any longer, you have to learn what "peat" is and what a "bog" is . . .

What is peat? Peat is a thick moss. When it dries it is very good for heating a house. You can burn it like wood or coal. In some countries people use peat to heat their houses. Peat also helps vegetables grow; it is a fertilizer. Some people, like Andy Mould, make their living by cutting peat and selling it. Just like some people earn a living by cutting down trees or digging for coal.

What is a bog? A bog is like a swamp or marsh. It is land that has lots of water in it so it is very soft. Peat grows in a bog.

Now, back to the story:

Andy Mould made a living by cutting the peat and selling it so that people could heat their houses or make their vegetables grow bigger.

On that day, Andy was about to throw a load of peat into a cutting machine when some of the crumbling moss fell away, and Andy saw . . . a human foot.

Andy was very surprised. He stopped what he was doing and called for other people to come and look. Soon some scientists came and as they looked more carefully, they found the whole body of a person: the body, head, arms, legs.

And the most amazing thing was that the body was two thousand and two hundred years old!

214

And the other amazing thing was that the skin was almost perfectly kept, after two thousand and two hundred years.

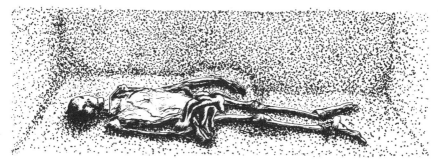

The skin was a little brown and kind of leathery. The face was changed a bit because it had been in water for two thousand and two hundred years. But you could tell pretty much what he looked like from his face, his skin texture, his body. You could even tell what the food was in his stomach.

This is a drawing of how scientists imagine that the Bog Man looked.

Scientists named the man "Lindow Man" because the name of the bog where they found him was Lindow Bog. People also called him the "Bog Man."

Scientists had a lot of questions about the Bog Man:

1. What kind of life did he lead?
2. What was his work?
3. Was he rich or was he poor?
4. How did he die?
5. Why did he die?

A lot of different kinds of scientists worked together to try and answer these questions. Being a scientist means looking for clues and then figuring out what the clues can tell you. Different scientists are interested in different kinds of clues. So it helped to have different scientists working on these questions. Trying to answer these questions is probably like setting out on an exciting adventure.

Here are the names of some kinds of scientists and what they look for:

1. archaeologist: they study things like tools, pottery, buildings, jewelry, and other things that come from a long time ago. They use these clues to try and understand how people used to live.

2. anthropologist: they study how people used to live: how they acted, what they ate, what were their religions, what did they look like; languages spoken.

3. pathologist: they study what happens to the body when someone is sick or hurt.

4. historian: they study the past—what happened in different countries, and they try to understand what happened and why events happened.

5. chemist: they study what something is made of, especially the things you can't see without a microscope or other ways of seeing things that are so small that we can't see it just with our eyes.

All these scientists and more helped to answer the questions.

First the scientists looked at the Bog Man's body. His body was healthy and strong. That clue gave them the idea that he had been able to afford good food.

He had no calluses or blisters on his hands. That clue gave them the idea that he had not been a common worker who worked with his hands.

No other wounds or cuts or scars were found on his body, except the injuries that caused his death. That clue gave them the idea that he was not a soldier.

All these clues together made the scientists think that he was probably a rich man, a member of the group of people who ruled his country.

What do you think from these clues?

But the scientists wanted to know more. Two scientists became interested in the Bog Man's last meal. They found a partly digested piece of cake in his stomach. And, one part of the cake was badly burned.

Some of the scientists knew a lot about how people had lived when the Bog Man lived. The Bog Man was part of a people called the Celts. Just like there are Americans, French people, Chinese people, there were Celts.

And it turned out the piece of burned cake in the Bog Man's stomach gave them a very important clue.

The Celts had a religious group called the Druids. The Druid priests had a tradition: they had a cake called bannock. It was thin and flat.

They cooked the cake and allowed one part of it to burn. Then the Druid priests would break the finished cake into pieces.

They put all the pieces into a leather bag and passed the bag around. Each priest would take out a piece without looking. The priest who drew the burned piece would then be put to death as a sacrifice to their gods.

Then some scientists did some experiments and found that it had taken only 8 minutes to cook the bannock cake. This was about the time needed to prepare the burned bannock in the traditional way.

They also found that the Bog Man had eaten the cake about 30 minutes before his death. And that is about how the tradition was supposed to work.

217

From all of these clues they decided that the Bog Man had been a Druid priest and that he had died because he picked the burned piece of bannock cake and he was then sacrificed to the gods.

What do you think about this conclusion from the clues?

How did the Bog Man die?

It turned out, when scientists studied his body, that he had died in three ways: they cut his throat; they crushed his neck; they drowned him.

What did they learn from these clues?

Their religion said that it was good to please the gods. They believed that if you killed someone in a ceremony as a sacrifice to the gods, that was a way to show respect for a god.

The Druids believed in several gods. The God Tarainis was usually honored by hitting someone hard.

The God Teutates was honored by drowning someone.

These clues made the scientists think that the Bog Man must have been considered so valuable that he was offered in sacrifice to three Gods, so he was killed in three different ways.

You may be wondering how can a human body stay preserved for thousands of years in a peat bog?

The answer is that peat has certain chemicals in it—iron and sulfur—and it can preserve the skin and a lot of the body.

Some questions are still not answered: The Bog Man had an armband made of fox fur.

One scientist thinks he can figure out the real name of the Bog Man from this clue of the fox fur. But he hasn't figured it out for sure yet.

What do you think? Will we ever know the Bog Man's real name?

Would you like to be a scientist and study clues?

What would you like to learn about?

Atiba Shanna

From One Generation to the Next

Ours is a struggle with continuity, unbroken except occasionally in our own minds. We have, and must continue, to struggle from one generation to the next; evolving in time and space, a people in motion, regaining independence and making history.

Ours is a mass struggle, a people's struggle, a struggle involving the participation of the young and the old, the female and the male. Ours is the struggle of an entire people, a whole nation oppressed and moving toward a new way of life on a planet made mad by greed and fear.

Our struggle involves our elders, the refugees who were forced to abandon the National Territory, head north and northwest, during the "migrations."

They were REFUGEES, those who "migrated" from the National Territory during the WWI and WWII years. Our elders were REFUGEES during the years of the "Black Codes" when they fled the National Territory.

The cities of amerikkka are full of New Afrikan refugees who entered them during the '30s and the '40s, escaping the klan and the southern prison. One step ahead of the hounds, a few minutes ahead of the lynch mob, is how many New Afrikans came north. Refugees, from the National Territory.

New Afrikans now living in Peoria, Brooklyn, Oakland and Des Moines were born in Clarksdale, Mississippi, and Greensboro, North Carolina. Twelve-year-old bloods boarded trains in New Orleans, Mobile and Atlanta, loaded with stained brown paper bags of cold chicken, cardboard suitcases, and dreams of big cities where work was available and where white folks weren't so mean.

219

New Afrikan women who cooked in big pots for white folks in Charleston, came to New York and Chicago, only to cook in "greasy spoons" or in the quiet kitchens of more white folks, for the same few dollars a week and all the left-overs they could carry.

What of our Past? What of our History? What of our Future?

i can imagine the pain and the strength of my great great grandmothers who were slaves and my great great grandmothers who were Cherokee Indians trapped on reservations. i remember my great grandmother who walked everywhere rather than sit in the back of the bus. i think about North Carolina and my home town and i remember the women of my grandmother's generation: strong, fierce women who could stop you with a look out the corners of their eyes. Women who walked with a majesty; who could wring a chicken's neck and scale a fish. Who could pick cotton, plant a garden and sew without a pattern. Women who boiled clothes white in big black cauldrons and who hummed work songs and lullabys. Women who visited the elderly, made soup for the sick and shortnin' bread for the babies.

Women who delivered babies, searched for healing roots and brewed medicines. Women who darned socks and chopped wood and laid bricks. Women who could swim rivers and shoot the head off a snake. Women who took passionate responsibility for their children and for their neighbor's children too.

The women in my grandmother's generation made giving an art form. 'Here, gal, take this pot of collards to Sister Sur'; 'Take this bag of pecans to school for the teacher'; 'Stay here while i go tend Mister Johnson's leg.' Every child in the neighborhood ate in their kitchens. They called each other 'Sister' because of feeling rather than as the result of a movement. They supported each other through the lean times, sharing the little they had.

The women of my grandmother's generation in my home town trained their daughters for womanhood. They taught them to give respect and to demand respect. They taught their daughters how to churn butter; how to use elbow grease. They taught their daughters to respect the strength of their bodies, to lift boulders and how to kill a hog; what to do for colic, how to break a fever and how to make a poultice, patchwork quilts, plait hair and how to hum and sing. They taught their daughters to take care, to take charge, and to take responsibility. They would not tolerate

220

a 'lazy heifer' or 'a gal with her head in the clouds.' Their daughters had to learn how to get their lessons, how to survive, how to be strong.

The women of my grandmother's generation were the glue that held the family and the community together. They were the backbone of the church. And of the school. They regarded outside institutions with dislike and distrust. They were determined that their children should survive and they were committed to a better future. (From "Women In Prison: How We Are" by Comrade-Sister Assata Shakur, printed in *The Black Scholar*, April 1978)

We became refugees from the National Territory; We came with dreams and We wanted "to forget the past," to forget the oppression and terror, to forget the snarls of red necks and the strangefuit of poplar trees. Far too many of us forgot that the stuggle goes on, from one generation to the next. We forgot that We were simply refugees, and not yet free.

The '40s, '50s and even early '60s were years that saw New Afrikan faces rubbed with Royal Crown so they wouldn't be "ashy"; saw our heads plastered with Murry's, saw noses and lips as repulsive objects in the thin-shaped beauty standards of amerikka.

These same years saw us move gradually farther from our first stops upon leaving the trains and buses; they saw the families that came north move farther "out south" and into dwellings just abandoned by whites; they saw us move further from each other and the strength which allowed us to survive and maintain the consciousness of ourselves as one people, struggling from one generation to the next, until We are free.

Being colonial subjects situated so near the seat of empire has blurred our vision. Slaves in "the richest country in the world"— while still slaves— are "better off" than slaves elsewhere. Amerikkka is the "big house" of the plantation it has made of a good part of the world. It is more difficult now than in the past for us to feel acutely the chains that bind us— enough so that We begin again to pass on the history, to begin again to socialize the children and hand down the awareness that comes with being taught the survival/resistance techniques needed to overcome the obstacles to our independence presented by the settlers who rule.

From one generation to the next is how We must move, until the nation is sovereign.

Build To Win!
Free The Land!
Atiba Shanna
February 14 ADM

Ethel Rosenberg

If We Die

You shall know, my sons, shall know
why we leave the song unsung,
the book unread, the work undone
to rest beneath the sod.

Mourn no more, my sons, no more
why the lies and smears were framed,
the tears we shed, the hurt we bore
to all shall be proclaimed.

Earth shall smile, my sons, shall smile
and green above our resting place,
the killing end, the world rejoice
in brotherhood and peace.

Work and build, my sons, and build
a monument to love and joy,
to human worth, to faith we kept
for you, my sons, for you.*

Ossining, NY, January 24, 1953

*later changed to "for our sons and yours."

Alan Berkman

Teach the Children

Memory is a source of both joy and pain in prison. Perhaps even of wisdom.

I remember 1971 as a year when the seasons were wrong. The fall started in August when the dying began.

It started on August 21st when George Jackson died. It swept from west to east, rather than north to south.

In D Yard in Attica, spring came on September 9th. There was a blossoming of hope and human regeneration. But September 13th was cold and wet and dark grey. The clouds of tear gas and rifle smoke were whipped about in the wash of the attacking helicopters, and killed off the fragile life. On September 13th, the leaves turned blood red in upstate New York.

The next time I saw anything like it was on May 13th, 1985, here in Philadelphia.

The official lying began immediately: "The guards had had their throats cut." Rockefeller conferred with Nixon and now the true sewage and sickness of ruling-class America spilled out. The official spokesman announced that the prisoners (mostly Black) had castrated the guards (all white). Not only were the 43 deaths now justified, but there was absolution of the historical wrongs committed by white men against Black men.

It was 48 hours before an honest pathologist told the truth: everyone, guards included, had been killed by the troopers. No one was castrated.

I raise this to point out that "they" lie. "They" are a wide variety of government officials. The press invariably prints what "they" say as the truth.

I'm in prison with Wilfredo Santiago and some of the male MOVE members. According to offical reports, I'm a fanatic left-wing terrorist. MOVE is an urban terrorist cult, and Wilfredo is a cold-blooded killer.

It's not true, and it's important to realize it's not true. "They" dehumanize us as a way to distort what we stand for, and to justify their own actions. It may be easier to recognize a propaganda war when nonexistent MIGs are created in Nicaragua and a military airfield in Grenada. But, it's just as important to know it happens here.

Please—think long and hard before believing the characterizations of anyone who becomes the target of government attack.

There was violence at Attica. The state's violence was massive, random and designed to terrorize.

The prisoners used violence—or the threat of it—to seize the prison, but the only guard who died during the rebellion fell from a catwalk trying to escape. Life was respected, even as the official slaughter proceeded. Perhaps only the oppressed who must struggle to live, can truly value life.

This system will impose on us—and on the rest of humanity—as much injustice as we allow it to. Frederick Douglass pointed that out long ago. I believe we need to resist. Sometimes our resistance will be moral, sometimes physical, and increasingly both. I think we can see in Attica that the violence of the oppressor and of the oppressed are not the same.

The US government is attempting to make the proud concept of "revolutionary" synonymous with the "terrorist." And "terrorism" of course is only used to refer to the violence of the oppressed.

Che Guevara said that revolutionaries are motivated by feelings of great love. In my experience with revolutionaries from Asia, Africa, Latin America and the US, this has always been true.

Revolutionaries do not believe that the ends justify the means; we believe that the ends shape and determine the means.

There is much room for discussion among us about both strategy and tactics, but I don't believe the government's campaign against "terrorism" can be any part of it. The government wants to fragment us, weaken us, limit us to the protests permitted by the FBI guidelines. We are all surveilled, but those who breach those guidelines are actively repressed. The Sanctuary movement, the Plowshares activists, and revolutionary underground groups and their supporters, have been each targeted. There is not necessarily unity on either strategy or tactics among us, yet, I believe we share a commitment to social justice, and a willingness to confront the government. The government is not neutral—it is the opposition, and it uses the legal system and the FBI as instruments of control. We should not ignore legal means, but we also have to learn to create our own areas of confrontation.

In the people's history, Attica will be viewed more as a slave rebellion, than a prison rebellion. It was Watts, or Newark or Detroit, inside the walls. It had all the power and righteousness of the yet-to-be-completed struggle of Black people in this country for human rights and self-determination. But perhaps more clearly than ever before, along with the Black prisoners were Puerto Ricans, Native Americans, Mexicans, and whites. A front of the oppressed was forged in the midst of an institution where segregation was still officially sanctioned. That is the nightmare of ruling class America, and the dream of the rest of us.

We need to claim our history.

The oppressed national groups in this country have been fighting for years to dig out the true history of resistance from under the layers of official distortion and neglect. Progressive whites need to do the same.

If we let it be buried, Attica—and all the struggles from the period of 1955 to 1975—will become just superficial phenomena in mainstream history. The true contradictions of this system were exposed then, and we can't let them be mystified again.

226

If we allow that, we will be a people outside of history. To make history requires both a past and a future. The dominant forces in this society have no future to promise and can only evoke a false and idealized version of the past.

The future lies with the oppressed; the lessons of the past can point the way.

We owe it to our children. Teach the children.

From a statement in court, 9/13/86

Chapter Five

IDEAS ARE WEAPONS

I could not live in Amerika
without attacking it.

— SAM MELVILLE

Hakim Al-Jamil

who killed mcduffie
(a definitive question)

his brain was bashed
cranium crashed
skull fractured/broken
all the way around
but they said those who beat him
didnt kill him
so who killed mcduffie?
maybe it was the same ones
who didnt kill
clifford glover/randy heath/jay parker
claude reese/randy evans/luis baez
arturo reyes/bonita carter/eula love
elizabeth magnum/arthur miller &
countless others
when they musta tripped or
their fingers slipped
maybe it was the same ones
who didnt kill
jose torres/zayd shakur/fred & carl
hampton/jonathan & george/joe dell
twyman myers/spurgeon winters &
a few thousand others
perhaps it was those who didnt kill
lumumba/che/amilcar/biko/fanon

231

mondlane/marighella/cordero &
quite a few thousand more
do you suppose it may have been those
who didnt kill
the indians & mexicans
who didnt
steal the land &
claim that they discovered it
who didnt steal afrikan peoples
halfway across the planet
who didnt loot our customs/cultures/
religions/languages/labor/& land
who didnt bomb the japanese/
vietnamese/& boriqua too
do you think it might have been those
who didnt kill at attica/watts/dc/
detroit/newark/el barrios
at jackson state, at southern u
at the algiers motel
who didnt shoot mark essex for
16 hours after he was dead
ask them & they'll tell you
what they didnt do
but they cant tell you
who killed mcduffie
maybe it was one of those
seizures unexplainable where he
beat himself to death
it wouldnt be unusual
our history is full of cases where we
attack nightsticks & flashlights with our heads
choke billyclubs with our throats till we die
jump in front of bullets with our backs
throw ourselves into rivers with
our hands and feet bound
and hang ourselves on trees/in prison cells
by magic

so it shouldnt be a mystery that
nobody killed mcduffie
he just died the way so many of us do
of a disease nobody makes a claim to
the police say they didnt do it
the mayor says he didnt do it
the judges say they didnt do it
the gov't says it didnt do it
nixon says he didnt do it
the fbi/cia/military establishment
says they didnt do it
xerox/exxon/itt say they didnt do it
the klan & nazis say they didnt do it
(say they were busy in greensboro & wrightsville)
i know i didnt do it
that dont leave nobody but you
& if you say you didnt do it
we're back to where we started
looking for nobody
who killed mcduffie
you remember nobody dont you
like with de facto segregation
where they said the schools were segregated
but nobody did it on purpose
like when they said there's been
job discrimination for years
but nobody did it intentionally
but nobody we're looking for

the one with the motive to kill mcduffie
& you see, we must find this nobody
who slew mcduffie
because the next person nobody will beat,
stomp, hang or shoot to death
wont be mcduffie
it'll be you or someone close to you

so for your own safety,
you should know the pedigree of
who killed mcduffie
you should know the reason of
who killed mcduffie
you should remember all those forgotten
who died of the disease nobody makes a claim to
so we wont be here asking
who killed you.

(Reprinted with permission of New Afrikan
Prisoners Organization)

John Africa

On the Move

THE MOVE ORGANIZATION IS A POWERFUL FAMILY OF REVOLU-
TIONARIES, FIXED IN PRINCIPLE, STRONG IN COHESION,
STEADY AS THE FOUNDATION OF A MASSIVE TREE. A PEOPLE
TOTALLY EQUIPPED WITH THE PROFOUND UNDERSTANDING OF
SIMPLE ASSERTION, COLLECTIVE COMMITMENT, UNBENDING
DIRECTION.
OUR WAY IS TRUE, DIRECTION SAFE, OUR POWER OF PURPOSE
COMPLETELY FIXATED, AS WE ARE THE MOST ORGANIZED
BODY TO EVER WEAR THE TITLE OF HUMAN WITH TOTAL
COMPREHENSION.
WHILE THE SO-CALLED EDUCATORS TALK OF LOVE, MOUTH
THE NECESSITY FOR PEACE, WE LIVE PEACE, ASSERT THE
POWER OF LOVE, COMPREHEND THE URGENCY OF FREEDOM.
THE REFORMED WORLD SYSTEM CANNOT TEACH LOVE WHILE
MAKING ALLOWANCES FOR HATE, PEACE WHILE MAKING
ALLOWANCES FOR WAR, FREEDOM WHILE MAKING ALLOW-
ANCES FOR THE INCONSISTENT SCHACKLES OF ENSLAVEMENT.
FOR TO MAKE ALLOWANCES FOR SICKNESS IS TO BE UN-
HEALTHY, TO MAKE CONCESSIONS WITH SLAVERY IS TO BE
ENSLAVED, TO COMPROMISE WITH THE PERSON OF COMPRO-
MISE IS TO BE AS THE PERSON YOU ARE COMPROMISING WITH.
SICKNESS IS NOT TO BE ALLOWED, IT IS TO BE ELIMINATED,
HATRED IS NOT TO BE CONSIDERED, IT IS TO BE ABOLISHED,
THE ENSLAVING PERSON OF WAR IS NOT TO BE CONCEDED,
ACCEPTED, TEMPORARILY OBSCURED BY THE ILLUSION OF
PEACE, IT MUST BE COMPLETELY CUT DOWN, DIRECTLY DONE
AWAY WITH, TOTALLY DESTROYED THROUGH THE REALITY OF

PEACE. TO ATTEMPT TO PROMISE THE TRANQUILITY OF PEACE IN A LIFESTYLE THAT FROWNS ON THE MEANING OF ABSOLUTE, SCOFFS AT THE MENTION OF PERFECTION, GETS UPTIGHT AT THE MERE SUGGESTION OF ONE DIRECTION, IS TO ADMIT TO DECEPTION, NULLIFYING YOUR HONESTY. ANY GOVERNMENT, COMMUNIST, CAPITALIST, SOCIALIST, IMPERIALIST SO-CALLED NEUTRALIST, THAT PROMISES PEOPLE PEACE WHILE TEACHING THE PEOPLE THERE'S NO SUCH THING AS PERFECTION, PEACE, AINT PROMISING YOU PEACE, THEY ARE ASSIGNING YOU TO THE DECEPTIVE FALLACY OF POLITICAL CONFLICT, POLICY OF WAR, SANCTIONED SLAVERY. FALLACIES THAT ARE CONSTANT-LY BACKING UP ON THEM AND WHEN CAUGHT IN THESE LIES YOU ARE ASKED TO MAKE ALLOWANCES, CONSIDERATIONS, TOLD THAT NOBODY'S PERFECT, PEACEFUL, EVERYBODY MAKES MISTAKES.

HOW CAN YOU EXPECT PEACE FROM A WORLD SYSTEM THAT ASKS YOU, DECEIVES YOU, HARASSES YOU INTO INVESTING YOUR LIFE IN A MISTAKE, A FALLACY, IMPERFECTION, A LIE? WHAT KIND OF INCENTIVE CAN YOU MAINTAIN IN SUCH CONFLICTING CONFUSION, HOW IS IT POSSIBLE TO HAVE HOPE IN A SYSTEM THAT IS CONFLICTINGLY HOPELESS, HOW CAN YOU HAVE FAITH IN A SO-CALLED ESTABLISHMENT THAT IS DISASTROUSLY UNFAITHFUL, INCONSISTENT, COMPLETELY UNESTABLISHED?

WHY MUST YOU ATTEMPT TO BELIEVE IN A GOVERNMENT, A MONARCH, A RULER THAT IS TOTALLY UNBELIEVABLE, UNGOV-ERNABLE, UNRULEY? IT IS FOOLISH TO THINK YOU CAN TRUST A GOVERNMENT THAT HAS CONSTANTLY PROVEN TO BE UNTRUSTWORTHY. SO LONG AS YOU ATTEMPT TO INVEST YOUR LIFE IN THE FAILING DECEPTION OF EXTERNAL GOVERN-MENT YOU CAN EXPECT FAILURE, AINT NOTHIN' SAFE, THE WHOLE THING IS DISASTROUS, FOR THERE IS ONLY ONE GOV-ERNMENT, ONE SYSTEM, ONE ESTABLISHMENT, THE GOVERN-MENT OF SELF, SYSTEM OF COMMITMENT, ESTABLISHED DIRECTION OF COMMON CONSISTENCY.

THE AFRICANS INVESTED THEIR LIVES IN GOVERNMENT AND THE RELICS AND RUINS OF THAT CIVILIZATION STILL REMAINS, THE CHINESE INVESTED THEIR LIVES IN EXTERNAL GOVERN-

MENT AND THE ONLY THING THEY GOT TO SHOW IS STARVA-
TION, OVER-POPULATION AND COMMUNISM; THE ROMANS
INVESTED THEIR LIVES IN EXTERNAL GOVERNMENT AND 2,000
YEARS OF BLOODY TRAGEDY LATER CAME UP WITH AN EVEN
GREATER TRAGEDY IN THE PERSON OF MUSSOLINI, NAZISM,
AND MORE MINORITY SLAUGHTER; GREAT BRITAIN WAS THE
SO-CALLED WORLD POWER AT ONE TIME, YEARS LATER
THERE'S STILL BRITISH BUT THEY AINT SO GREAT.   NOW
THERE'S AMERICA, HUSTLING THEIR BRAND OF EXTERNAL
GOVERNMENT AND ALREADY THEY'VE HAD FOUR PRESIDENTS
ASSASSINATED, ONE ATTEMPTED ASSASSINATION, TWO
ATTEMPTED IMPEACHMENTS OF PRESIDENTS, ONE OF THEM
CAUGHT IN A PACK OF LIES, DISGRACED, AND FORCED TO
RESIGN ALONG WITH THE SCANDALOUS DISGRACE OF HIS VICE
PRESIDENT AND 27 OTHER STAFF MEMBERS WHO ARE EITHER
DOING TIME IN JAIL, ABOUT TO GO TO JAIL, OR ABOUT TO
COME OUT OF JAIL.
POLITICIANS WHO DRAW UP LAWS AND ATTEMPT TO MAKE
CONCESSIONS WHEN THOSE LAWS ARE USED ON THEM, FOR
GRAFT, EXTORTION, CONFLICT OF INTEREST, SLUSH FUNDING,
FILLING THE BALLOT BOXES WITH DEAD PEOPLES VOTES, WILL
ADVOCATE THE IMPORTANCE OF A LIE DETECTOR TEST, FAIL
IT, AND ASK YOU TO MAKE ALLOWANCES FOR HIS FAILURES.
SO LONG AS THE PEOPLE ALLOW POLITICIANS TO MAKE
MISTAKES, YOU CAN EXPECT MORE LIES, CORRUPTION, BALLOT
STUFFING, LIES ABOUT CAMPAIGN FUNDS, MONEY DERIVED
FROM BENEFITS, STOLEN PERSONAL ASSETS AND THE COST OF
THEIR NEW HOMES.
POLITICIANS WHO BUILD ARMIES TO SO-CALLED POLICE ONE
COUNTRY FROM THE INVASION OF ANOTHER, IGNORE THE
CRIES OF POLICE BRUTALITY COMING FROM THE CITIZENS IN
THE COUNTRY THEY ARE SUPPOSED TO BE PROTECTING FROM
THE INVASION OF POLICE BRUTALITY, THE IMPOSING ARMY.
WATCH THESE GANG LEADERS IN THE WHITE HOUSE COMMIT
CRIME, PUT THEM ON PENSIONS AND PUT STREET GANGS IN
JAIL, ALLOCATE MONEY TO BUILD MISSILES FOR THE SO-
CALLED PROTECTION OF THIS COUNTRY AGAINST INVASION,
AND IGNORE THE INVASION OF SLUMS, BOASTING ABOUT HOW

MANY ATOMIC SUBMARINES YOU'VE GOT TO PROTECT AGAINST THE INVASION OF AN ENEMY AND BEING INVADED WITH THE ENEMY OF UNEMPLOYMENT.

BUILDING WAR SHIPS TO PROTECT AGAINST THE DANGER OF INVASION, AND BEING INVADED WITH VD, FBI, TB, CIA, TNT, CD, DDT, DRUG ADDICTS, ALCOHOLICS, RACISM, SEXISM, DECEPTIONISM, CON MEN, CROOKED GOVERNMENT, QUESTIONABLE POLICE ADMINISTRATORS, GRAFT, CORRUPTION, EXTORTION, MURDER, RAPE, PROSTITUTION. BEING INVADED WITH EVERY CRIME EXISTING, KILLING, MAIMING, LOOTING, TEARING DOWN, BURNING OUT, EXPERIENCING AN INVASION OF THE WORSE KIND WITHIN THE COUNTRY, AND DUPING THE PEOPLE INTO THINKING INVASION ONLY COMES FROM WITHOUT.

FIGHTING TO PROTECT YOURSELF FROM AN INVASION OF THE COUNTRY THAT YOU INVADED, OVERTHREW, STOLE FROM THE INDIANS.

SINCE THESE POLITICIANS DON'T SEE NOTHING WRONG WITH COMPROMISE LET 'EM COMPROMISE 20 OF THAT 40 POUNDS OF STEAK THEY GOT STORED AWAY IN THEIR DEEP FREEZE TO A FEW OF THE POOR, HUNGRY SUPPORTERS. SINCE THEY DON'T SEE NOTHING WRONG WITH CONCESSION LET 'EM CONCEED SOME OF THAT MONEY THEY GOT STORED AWAY IN THEIR BANK TO A FEW OF THEIR POOR, LOYAL, HUNGRY SUPPORTERS; LET 'EM COMPROMISE ONE OF THOSE CARS TO THOSE CRIPPLED, LEGLESS VETERANS OF WAR THESE POLITICIANS ARE TO BLAME FOR, GIVE HALF OF THEIR PAYCHECKS TO SOME OF THEIR HUNGRY, LOYAL SUPPORTERS THAT ARE OUT OF WORK.

SINCE THEY LIKE MAKING CONCESSIONS LET 'EM TAKE ALL THAT MONEY THEY SPEND ON THOSE UNEARNED VACATIONS AND BUY SOME OF THEIR SUPPORTERS A HOUSE, THEIR CHILDREN WINTER COATS, GRANDCHILDREN A SAFE PLACE TO PLAY; LET 'EM INVITE THEIR SUPPORTERS FAMILIES TO THEIR HOUSE FOR A MONTH TO SEE HOW THEY LIVE, SEND KIDS TO THE COUNTRY; LET 'EM SPEND A COUPLE OF MONTHS IN THAT SUMMER COTTAGE YOU POLITICIANS AIN'T USING WHILE YOU ARE VACATIONING IN ENGLAND, FRANCE, GERMANY, THE VIRGIN ISLANDS. SINCE THESE POLITICIANS DON'T MIND

MAKIN' DEALS, MAKE ONE, NOW YOU'VE VOTED FOR THEM. TELL 'EM YOU LOST YOUR JOB, TELL 'EM TO PAY YOUR RENT FOR THE NEXT SIX MONTHS, YOUR PHONE BILL FOR THE NEXT SEVEN MONTHS, YOUR OIL, GAS, ELECTRIC BILLS FOR THE NEXT YEAR.
THE NEXT TIME THE PAYMENT ON YOUR CAR IS DUE SEND IT TO THEM. THEY ARE YOUR REPRESENTATIVES, LET 'EM REPRESENT YOU. WHEN YOUR MORTGAGE IS DUE SEND IT TO THEM.
SINCE THEY DONT SEE NOTHIN WRONG WITH MAKING ALLOW-ANCES LET EM MAKE AN ALLOWANCE FOR THE RAPIST WHEN THEIR DAUGHTER IS RAPED, CONVINCE THEIR WIVES THAT EVERYBODY IS ENTITLED TO A MISTAKE WHEN THAT MUGGER SNATCHES HER POCKETBOOK WITH HER VACATION MONEY IN IT. LET 'EM MAKE ALLOWANCES FOR THOSE DRUG ADDICTS THAT BURGLARIZED THEIR HOUSES, THEIR CARS, THE IMPOS-ING PARTY THAT BREAKS INTO THEIR OFFICE, FINDS SOME SCANDELOUS DOCUMENTS AND EXPOSES THEIR DEAL MAKIN CAR CASS.
WHEN THEIR MOTHERS ARE HIT BY CARS, FATHERS KNOCKED IN THE HEAD, SONS BEATEN UP BY GANGS AND WANNA PROSECUTE, TRY CONVINCING THEM NOT TO, WITH THAT NOBODY'S PERFECT ARGUMENT, CONVINCE THEIR UNCLES TO COMPROMISE WITH DOCTORS THAT ARE SUPPOSED TO BE TREATIN THEM FOR A PAIN IN THE BACK AND CUTS OFF THEIR HAND. TELL THEIR AUNTS TO MAKE CONCESSIONS WITH THOSE BEAUTICIANS THAT MADE THEIR HAIR FALL OUT. SINCE YOU POLITICIANS DONT SEE NOTHING WRONG WITH MAKING ALLOWANCES MAKE ALLOWANCES FOR YOUR WIFE WHEN SHE PUTS YOU IN COURT, A LIEN ON YOUR PAYCHECK, AND SUES YOU FOR EVERYTHING YOU GOT. YOU PEOPLE OUGHT TO MAKE THESE CAPITALISTS STOP LYING ABOUT THIS FALLACY OF EQUAL OPPORTUNITY WHILE COMPROMISING YOUR EQUALITY IN SOME POLITICAL INVESTMENT.
SINCE THE COMMUNISTS DONT SEE NOTHING WRONG WITH COMPROMISE, MAKE 'EM COMPROMISE SOME OF THE WEALTH OF LEADERS, THAT, ACCORDING TO THE COMMUNIST DOC-TRINE, WAS SUPPOSED TO BE EQUALLY DISTRIBUTED TO

239

BEGIN WITH. SINCE THEY WANNA TALK 'BOUT THE POLICIES OF COMMUNISM, LET EM STOP TALKING BOUT SHARING IN THE LAND, EQUAL DISTRIBUTION, MEANS OF PRODUCTION AND START PRODUCING, SHARING, DISTRIBUTING EQUALLY. TELL THE IMPERIALIST TO TAKE THAT IMPERIALISM, THAT FOOLS THESE UNRULY MANIACS INTO THINKING THEY CAN RULE OTHERS, SERVE OTHERS, WHEN THEY AINT SECURE THEM-SELVES AND LEAVE PEOPLE ALONE.

SINCE THE SOCIALISTS BELIEVE IN MAKING CONCESSIONS, ENDORSE THE FALLACY OF ALLOWANCE, DIG COMPROMISING, LET 'EM COMPROMISE SOME OF THAT MONEY THEY GOT IN THE BANK, MAKE ALLOWANCES WHEN THE HAVES ARE MUGGED BY THE HAVE NOTS, CONCEDE ALL THOSE UNNECESSARY MATERI-AL POSSESSIONS THEY'VE WRAPPED THEIR LIVES UP IN.

IF THEY REALLY WANT THAT EQUAL DISTRIBUTION THEY TALK SO MUCH ABOUT, WHY ARE THEY PUSHIN' THIS EDUCATIONAL SYSTEM THAT TEACHES GRADE, RANK, STATUS, POSITION? IF THESE GOVERNMENTAL IMPERSONATORS, MORALISTIC FRAUDS, PHILOSOPHICAL COUNTERFEITS WANT TO CONTINUE TO BOMBARD THE PEOPLE WITH ALL OF THEIR THEORIES MAKE 'EM PRODUCE, HOLD 'EM TO THEIR PROMISES, MAKE 'EM SHOW YOU THAT THEIR THEORIES WORK OR GET AWAY FROM YOU. SINCE THE COMMUNISTS CLAIM THEY DON'T LIKE CAPITALISM, LET 'EM STOP TEACHING ABOUT CAPITALISM; SINCE THE IMPERIALISTS CLAIM THEY DON'T LIKE SOCIALISM, LET 'EM STOP TEACHING ABOUT SOCIALISM. IF THIS REFORM WORLD SYSTEM REALLY WANTS TO GET RID OF RACISM, LET 'EM STOP TALKING RACE, IF EVERYBODY WANTS THE POWER OF LOVE SO BAD, LET 'EM STRIKE THE FALLACY OF HATE OUT OF THEIR VOCABULARY.

Editor's Note: As requested by members of MOVE, this manuscript is printed exactly as written.

Terry Bisson

RSVP to the FBI

On being subpoenaed to give information to a Federal Grand Jury investigating revolutionary movements inside the USA

Thank you for handing me this invitation
to talk to you

But I am otherwise engaged.

Thank you for offering me this opportunity
to have a heart to heart
with the murderers of Martin Luther King
and Fred Hampton,
not to mention Crazy Horse
Michael Stewart and Eleanor Bumpurs
and nameless millions
who do have and will have names

But I am otherwise engaged.

Thank you for inviting me
to sit down with the brothers
of the somocistas
(as you describe yourselves)
their long knives eager
for the blood of teachers

the blood of nuns
the blood of Sandino
which is right now running
bright like a river in the veins of young
Nicaragua

But I am otherwise engaged.

Thank you for giving me this opportunity
to spit on the graves of Sacco and Vanzetti
to dishonor the memory of the Rosenbergs
or of my ex father in law
who spent 10 years not being an actor
rather than 10 minutes being a collaborator

But I am otherwise engaged.

Thank you for inviting me to run with the hounds
howling through the ruined cities
trying to hunt down the
FALN, the BLA
the ten or the hundred most wanted
most ready and willing and able
to resist with arms
and heart and ideology
your world
wide crimes

But I am otherwise engaged.

And seriously, thanks
for giving me this chance
to stand fast with the Puerto Ricans
who have gone to jail silent since 1936
rather than drink from your bootprints
To stand fast with the New Afrikans
who like Nat Turner "never said a mumbling word"
To stand fast with the Palestinians

242

steadfast in Israeli prisons
the Irish deep and defiant in Long Kesh,
the Africans on Robben Island
scorning your offers with songs
To stand fast with the children of Lumumba
and Che and Malcolm X
not to mention my own children and your own as well

Thank you for this chance to stand
not with the defeated but the defiant
who pick up the gun
who pick up the pen
who pick up the baby and the struggle
Thank you for this chance
to stand with humanity against you

Don't mind if I do.

Herman Ferguson

Excerpts from a letter

During my 19 years in exile in Guyana, I had many positive experiences which broadened my political perceptions and sharpened my nation building skills. I found Guyana in 1970 to be a progressive Third World nation with a socialist orientation and a firm commitment to the non-aligned movement. Because of Guyana's membership in the non-aligned movement, and as a result of the level at which I functioned in the government, I was privileged to meet many of the Third World heads of government. Notable among them were Fidel Castro, Nyerere of Tanzania, Mugabe of Zimbabwe, the president of Zambia and many others too numerous to list.

Most importantly, I met and spent a good deal of time with brothers and sisters who were experienced freedom fighters in their own countries. They had come to Guyana seeking political asylum from such diverse places as South Africa, Namibia, Angola, Mozambique, Southern Rhodesia (before it became Zimbabwe), Ethiopia, Eritrea, Somalia and Sri Lanka, just to name a few.

While I found this exposure rewarding and educational, I could not help but feel saddened by the fact that almost none of these courageous fighters were aware of the Black struggle in the USA against racism and imperialism with our goal of self-determination, self-defense and land on which to build our nation.

Their limited knowledge of any agitation among Blacks in the USA was about Martin Luther King, Jr., and his efforts to integrate into the system. It was frustrating to realize that in their opinion Blacks in the USA are a part of the system that is raping the rest of the world. The American communications media has done its job well.

Tears would fill my eyes when I would think about our unsung and literally unknown freedom fighters: brothers and sisters like Assata Shakur, Mtayari Sundiata, Sekou Odinga, Abdul Majid (Nicky LaBorde), Bashir Hameed (James York), Zayd Shakur, Dhoruba Moore, Geronimo Pratt, Sundiata Acoli, the New York 3, the RNA 11, other members of the Black Liberation Army and the many, many other young people who knew they had to move the struggle a step farther than we had done in the '60s.

I knew then that I had to come back, to return and say to those young people by my physical presence, although I knew I would be thrown into prison immediately. I wanted them to know that I understood and supported their activities totally and to let them know they were correct in whatever action they took against this evil racist system. I am proud of them. I salute them and I hope to live long enough to see them on the outside resuming their revolutionary work which has been interrupted by this temporary period of imprisonment. I also include all of the Latinos (especially Puerto Rican Independentistas), Native Americans and white political prisoners behind the walls because they fought for freedom against imperialism and injustices.

In the meantime, I have kept active while in this prisoner-of-war camp. I exercise daily and I read everything in an effort to catch up on the America of the 1980s, which I know so little about. I am not dismayed or disillusioned by what appears to be a stagnation or even a recession in our struggle. Batista, Duvalier, the Shah of Iran, Somoza, and so many other despots were toppled when it appeared their regime was in its ascendency. America today is in deep trouble and the stepped up genocidal war against us through the introduction of crack, high powered automatic weapons and AIDS into our communities is ample proof that America is trying to conceal her decline as a world power by focusing attention on us as the threat to America's "good life," just as Hitler used the Jews to justify his spread of Nazism.

I am also giving much thought to the need to inform the public about America's hidden political prisoners who are lumped together in her prisons and categorized as common criminals. Once we are able to make the clear distinction between a common criminal who commits crimes against the person or property for personal gain, and the political prisoner as one who, by any means necessary, attempts to change or destroy an unjust system to liberate his people, then we can reach out for understanding and support from the international community of nations. The challenge to America's claim that she has no political prisoners would expose that position for the lie that it is.

Already I have written Congressman Ron Dellums calling his attention to this matter and asking him to raise the whole question of political prisoners at the congressional level so that the arrests, convictions, sentences and conditions of imprisonment of those persons we deem to be political prisoners can be investigated for the purpose of introducing legislation to change our status and recognize us for what we truly are, that is, persons who by words and/or action have taken a position against this racist government.

I intend also to write the National Council of Churches asking them to address this issue through the many churches it represents. This could be their way of involving themselves in the wave of liberation theology which is sweeping throughout Latin America today.

Give my strong regards to all political prisoners and activists out there. Tell them to be strong and firm in their political beliefs. I am with them all the way.

Russ Ford

Declaration of a Draft Registration Resister*

I, Russell F. Ford, state as follows:

1.   I am now facing a possible maximum five years in prison for refusing to fill out and sign a 5-by-8-inch piece of cardboard (see attachment #1, Selective Service form I).

2.   I was born July 4, 1963.

3.   I celebrated the American Revolution and my own eighteenth birthday on July 4, 1981. At that time I was aware of the personal implications of the Military Selective Service Act and knew that the prevailing view of the United States courts upheld the constitutionality of draft registration.

4.   In refusing to register for the draft with Selective Service, I understood that this could be considered a crime under United States law.

5.   In refusing to register, I was trying to prevent crimes that are actually at issue— the waging of interventionary wars and the use of nuclear weapons by the United States. I believe that my resistance to military preparations by the U.S. government is in accordance with the Fifth Commandment ("You Shall Not Kill"); the First Amendment (free exercise of religion, speech, and conscience or belief); and the Nuremberg Charter (the moral necessity not to

---

*Made by Russell Ford in US District Court, Hartford, CT, April 7, 1983, before the Honorable M. Joseph Blumenfeld.

participate in crimes against peace or humanity planned or perpetrated by one's own country). The defendant is not versed in legal matters and is uncertain how the Fifth Commandment, Bill of Rights, and Nuremberg Charter relate to U.S. law.

6.   I believe that war resisters are acting in the spirit of our history as Americans. If Harriet Tubman, a black abolitionist, could risk death guiding fellow humans through the Underground Railroad to freedom in the North and Canada, violating as she did the Fugitive Slaves Act, then certainly I can risk a few years imprisonment for violating another federal law. If enough of us act today, then perhaps our children will no longer see their children conscripted for war, as today we no longer sell children into slavery.

Samuel Adams, Harriet Tubman, Susan B. Anthony, and Rosa Parks did not think of themselves as saints or heroines. They were ordinary people who knew wrong and struggled against it. Yesterday they were criminals and traitors. Today we honor them and the hundreds who were with them. Yet today we jail disarmament activists for painting "U.S.S. Auschwitz: An Oven Without Walls" on a Trident missile submarine. We prosecute people for nonviolently sitting-in at the U.S. Capitol Rotunda demanding that government and municipal buildings be used at night as emergency shelters for people with no homes.

7.   For draft-age men to conform to Selective Service draft registration would be to demonstrate that we have not learned from the history of U.S. military involvement in Vietnam and the genocide carried out by this country against the people of Vietnam, Cambodia, and Laos. The draft is not practical without young men willing to submit to it. Conscription is necessary for the state to force men into the military for a war they would not choose to fight, as was the case in Vietnam. Opposition to the draft system is as important today in preventing a new war as it was to ending the war in Vietnam.

Registration is a step towards the draft—a testing of the political situation to gauge who is ready, who will object, how many will resist. According to the government's own figures, more than five hundred thousand men have not signed up though required to. Perhaps one million more did not give their social security numbers.

248

Several million more have moved without telling Selective Service their new addresses.

As the government has been unable to convince the people that the law is in their best interest or in the interest of the country, the government has had to begin an enforcement program of doubtful legality (the defendant refers to decisions in the cases of David Wayte and Rusty Martin, putting in question the prosecution of selected vocal nonregistrants; and the recent injunction in Minneapolis federal court against enforcement of the "Solomon Amendment," a bill denying federal student aid to any person who does not prove compliance with the Selective Service).

8.   An inspiration to my resistance has been my friendship with John Bach, housepainter, of Hartford. John was a student at Wesleyan University, as I have been, and in 1969 was convicted of refusing to cooperate with the Selective Service draft system. He was sentenced by the Honorable M. Joseph Blumenfeld, as result of which he was in prison for thirty-five months. Although that experience has certainly had a lasting influence on his life, it did not reform him, and neither has it deterred me from similar action.

9.   I submit that to convict and jail me would be to repeat a mistake made fourteen years ago. Our consciences do not allow us to live our lives in any other way. We do not seek jail, but we cannot avoid it. It is your choice. We have not lied, we have not hidden our actions, we have not caused threat or harm to any living being. If it is illegal to refuse to fill out this Selective Service form, if it is illegal to make as clear as I know how that I will not kill, then it is the law that must change.

10.   I submit that I have better ways to occupy the next thirty-five months of my life than continuing my witness in jail. The money spent to convict me and keep me in jail could be better spent for food, shelter, and education. I think that all of us—judge, jury, prosecutor, defendant, clerks, secretaries, guards, witnesses—would do better to involve ourselves working against real injustice, especially to search for ways to resolve conflicts without threat or violence. I ask you, a person of the law: how has history (and the law) judged the men who jailed Rosa Parks for sitting in the front of a Montgomery, Alabama, bus? What purpose did you fulfill by

keeping John Bach in jail for his refusal to participate in the Vietnam War?

11.   I request that you dismiss charges, and join John Bach and me for lunch and conversation at a convenient time.

Respectfully submitted,
RUSSELL F. FORD, pro se

"In the name of Allah the beneficient, the merciful."

Bashir Hameed

The Struggle is Jihaad, and Jihaad Starts Within Ourselves!!!

> *"And why should ye not fight in
> the cause of Allah and of those
> who, being weak are ill treated
> and oppressed. Men, women and
> children, whose cry is: Oh Lord!
> Rescue us from this town, whose
> people are oppressors; and raise
> from thee one who will help."*
>
> — HOLY QURAN, IV: 75

The fundamental principles of Islam are revolutionary. This fact is never presented by the mainstream media, and is seldom or rarely presented in most of the literature seen by people in Amerika. Islam is invariably portrayed as being the basis of "terrorist thought," the oppression of women, and a fourteen-hundred-year-old religion out of touch with reality.

Today, throughout the world, Muslims are struggling against oppression. Be it the Zionist occupation of Palestine or the Soviet occupation of Afghanistan, neocolonialist Saudi Arabia or secular Egypt, Islam is on the offensive. Those governments which exploit their own people, e.g., Morocco, Tunisia, Egypt, or the reactionary Brahmins of Saudi Arabia, are all governed by stooges and quislings of the industrialized West.

251

In the recent uprising in Algeria it was Muslims who were calling for fundamental changes in the governmental structure in order to bring about a better quality of life. In Afghanistan it is the Muja-hideen who have put the invading Soviet Army to flight; and we witness the Soviet puppet government in Kabul shaking in its boots. It was the motivating force of Al-Islam which sent the Shah of Iran into exile and disgrace. Today, throughout the Middle East, Islamic Fundamentalism is the guiding light and force at the core of the people's struggle to throw off the yoke of their reactionary/secular governments. Why is Islam the guiding light? Because people want more than can be provided by secular oppressors who offer nothing more than spiritual and social decay.

The struggle or method used by Muslims to bring about this revolution is called Jihaad! This Jihaad or struggle must first of all begin in one's own heart and mind. This revolutionary concept governs how man is to deal with man, his wife, his family, and extends to his relationship to society. The reformation of ourselves must be our first and foremost Jihaad.

> *"Because Allah will never change the grace/ condition which He Hath bestowed on a people until they change what is in their (own) souls. And verily Allah is he who heareth and knoweth all things."*

HOLY QURAN, VIII: 53

Islam does not confine its struggle to a single race, nation or geographical area. Its revolutionary concept of the oneness of man-kind was sent to and meant for the whole of mankind, regardless of class or race. It is a way of life that governs man's social, economic and political affairs. Muslim society is governed by a set of principles and guidelines decreed by Allah. Pragmatism, political expediency or narrow nationalism has no place in Al-Islam. There is no such thing as a separation of Church and State. There is a synthesis of all facets of social life. The whole of Islamic society is governed by the exact same set of rules, rules decreed by Allah. Theft is theft for the whole society, whether it be carpenter, mason or those who lead the community.

252

"Mankind was one single nation and Allah sent messengers with glad tidings and warnings; and with them He sent the Book in truth to judge between people in matters wherein they differed."

HOLY QURAN, II: 213

Islam is the religion of peace and harmony among mankind. Islam *commands* Muslims to strive against those who are unjust, those who oppress, and those who assume authority and rule without the consent of the people.

Here in Amerika the u.s. government has declared war on people in general and on the poor and people of color in particular. Daily, we watch and see vice and an onslaught of crimes against the sanctity of humanity. We witness the steady deterioration and pollution of the environment; the Earth itself is dying. This state of affairs could not be under Islam.

We witness Amerika's collusion with the exploitation and oppression of people both here and around the world. In Chile, Palestine, Azania (South Africa), El Salvador and Guatemala to name a few places, people are struggling, desperately, to find that synthesis. . . .

Muslims are commanded by Allah to wage Jihaad in order to bring about Allah's decree.

"Go ye forth (whether equipped), lightly or heavily, and strive and struggle, with your goods and your person, in the cause of Allah. That is best for you, if ye (but) know."

HOLY QURAN, IX: 41

Muslims cannot *peacefully coexist* in an oppressive society. There is a sinister, criminal and genocidal war prevailing today and especially against the minority community by this government and reactionary elements of society. It is the Muslims' decreed duty to wage Jihaad against these forces.

Our beloved martyr Sayyid Qutb of Egypt, who was hung by that country's secular government in 1966, stated: "(M)any Muslim

253

apologists and defeatists . . . want to confine Jihaad to what today is called 'defensive war.'" He further states: "Islam is not merely a belief, so that it is enough merely to preach it. Islam, which is a way of life, takes practical steps to organize a movement for freeing man." The reason for Jihaad exists in the nature of its message and in the actual conditions it finds in human society, and not merely in the necessity for defense.

> "O ye who believe! What is the matter with you,
> that, when ye are asked to go forth in the cause
> of Allah, ye cling heavily to the Earth? Do ye
> prefer the life of this world to the hereafter? But
> little is the comfort of this life, as compared with
> the hereafter."

HOLY QURAN, IX: 38

Alicia Rodriguez

Patriarchy

You have molded and dominated
much of recorded history
with its attitudes, beliefs, and
institutional practices
gripped tightly within your
control.

Your ideology—based on male
superiority and female inferiority
— is one that
serves to socialize men and women
into conformity and acceptance of
certain patterns of behavior.

Etched in recorded history
is your litany of negativism
directed against women!

From Abraham onward,
your claims of "natural"
physiological and genetic
superiority are reflected in the
dehumanizing and alienating
practice of woman's subordination
and inequality.

Sequentially, you exploited
the historical moment when
communal economics was eclipsed by
private property.
As a consequence,
women were reduced to mere
private property— a commodity.

Hidden behind an ecumenical cloak,
you impregnated within
major religions the belief
that woman is to blame for
the fall of man,
for the existence of sin,
for the birth of evil,
and for the origins of punishment.

Your legacy,
still bears the universal
fruit of passivity, dependence,
subservience and inequality,
exacerbating divisions inside
ourselves and against one another.

In opposition to you,
revolutionary women are
breaking out of the symptoms
of deep-rooted
inertia and paralysis.
They are constantly evolving,
understanding that
meaningful changes cannot
be forthcoming through
reforms.
We have only to look
at the past for proof!

2/89 Dwight Correctional Center

256

Alicia Rodriguez

Continuum

The past
is inseparably
locked into the present.
The future?
The mere fruit
of the past.
Ignored, it is
lifeless.
Internalized, it offers
revolutionaries a tangible
measuring tool and a window of
experiences to discard
or build on.
Behind prison bars
it becomes amplified; generating
a kind of high voltage
with the capacity
to resuscitate
and invigorate,
especially after a spell
of physical or mental torture,
tension of yearning human contact,
frustration of
receiving news
of a comrade's pain or suffering,
the report of another imperialist

attack against the
oppressed class.
The inseparable nature
of time is also somewhat
intimidating; it does not really
offer a place to hide or ignore
our contradictions.
It serves as a model of importance
in developing and maintaining an
attitude of self-discipline and
self-criticism.
The inseparable nature of
time is synonymous
with the solidarity prerequisite
to a people's struggle for national
liberation.

2/89 Dwight Correctional Center

Alicia Rodriguez

Paloma Borincana

Se acerca otro año más sin tí,
pero jamás podremos olvidarte.
Nos parece insoportable e injusto
tu auséncia y aunque manos malvadas
todavía nos siguen colonizando nos
hemos sostenido con tu recuerdo.

Ayer to vimos cruzando por el horizonte
luciendo un semblante blanco y puro.
Dentro de tu pacho vimos que guardadas
celosamente las nuevas armas para tu
pueblo en lucha.

Se acerca otro año más Palomo Borincaña,
jamás podremos olvidarte. Ya el año se
está poniendo viejo y queremos brindar
revolucionariamente la entrada de una
nueva esperanza.

12/88 Dwight Correctional Center

259

Kuwasi Balagoon

Your Honor

your honor
since i've been convicted of murder
and have taken the time to digest
just what that means
after noting what it means to my family
and how it affects people who read the newspapers
and all
i see now, that i've made an awful mistake!
and didn't approach this matter of a trial
in a respectful, deliberate or thoughtful manner
didn't take advantage of the best legal advice
and based my actions on irrelevant matters
which i can see now in a much more sober mind
had nothing to do with this case
i must have been legally insane thinking about:
the twenty five murders of children in Atlanta since Wayne Williams
    capture
the recent murder of a man in Boston by police
the two recent murders in Chicago by police
the shooting of the five-year-old little boy in suburban Calif
the lynchings in Alabama
the mob murder of a transit worker in Brooklyn
the murders of fourteen women in Boston
feeling that this is evidence of something
and that there must be a lesson in all this— i thought murder was
    legal.

260

Kuwasi Balagoon

---

with no questions

the leaves are changing
to sheaves of fire
rust 'n indigo
in waves
And all at once
And one by one
different in their deaths
like all times
and loved ones
and memories of places
faded from lack of presence
and fallen from the attention of today
to lie like a quilt on the earth
and winter
and change to the rich pungent ground
that feeds realities to come
with no questions.

11/82

Chapter Six

DREAMS ARE STRUGGLE TOO

Hurl me into the next existence. The descent into hell won't turn me. They won't defeat my revenge, never, never. I'm part of a righteous people who anger slowly, but rage undamned. We'll gather at his door in such a number that the rumbling of our feet will make the earth tremble.

— GEORGE JACKSON

Laura Whitehorn

Claustrophobia

Do   not   think   of   air—
 air clean of smoke, and dirt, and
   years of sour meals lingering,
   of too many people in pain
   and in frenzy.
And don't think of sunshine in fresh air,
 because as soon as you do,
 your body stiffens,
 stretches,
 yearns to become
   the explosion you are accused of,
 yearning to explode
   so much inhumanity, the walls and bars,
   leaving ruins
   which would really be
    tender shoots of growth,
    people freed from these structures
    of chains,
 people smiling with life
   and without irony.

D.C. Jail, 6/23/88

Laura Whitehorn

The Enemy

An army spokesman, meanwhile, said soldiers
acted improperly when they tied a 50-year-old
Palestinian demonstrator to the front of a jeep
in Jericho, in the West Bank, before driving off
last week. But he said no disciplinary action
would be taken.

—The Washington Post, 9/5/88

Can someone explain to me
what the inside of an "Israeli's" heart
   looks like?
Is there any light left in it
   at all,
or is it so dark that human feeling itself
   is obscured—
      along with the history and the lessons
      I thought millions of people had died
      so that we could learn?

Can someone explain to me
what the inside of an "Israeli's" mind
   looks like?

THE ENEMY

Has it forgotten, in less than half a life-time,
   the cattle-cars, camps, and ovens,
   the deportations,
   "collective responsibility and punishment,"
   brutality so rancid
      the human mind can't bear
      to comprehend it?
Or has the mind, remembering, decided
   (cold as marble mausoleum walls)
   to win by domination,
   to vanquish,
   using those self-same cruelties,
   stripping life
      of all its essence, hope, and meaning,
   leaving only greed,
      an army of occupation,
      and hollow, colonial supremacy?

Having grown up
   in white Amerikkka,
I'm afraid I know
   the answer.

Laura Whitehorn

Sisterhood Is Powerful

Brenda has one cigarette, and shares it
   with a woman she's never seen before,
   who sits on her bedroll,
   abscesses freshly bandaged,
   thin
   and shaken.
Sisterhood is powerful.

Lurinda brags she's hard, won't give
   away a thing without a trade. But she's
   the first to slide
   into the cell next door
   to see that the new arrival, withdrawing,
   has what she needs
   to get her through the sickness.
Sisterhood is powerful.

And I, the communist, have learned
   to give not just the easy things
   but the hard,
   to give what I didn't think
     I had enough of,
   to give of myself,
     the only commodity left to me.
You'd have to see it to believe
   how sisterhood is powerful.

7/6/88

Laura Whitehorn

Baltimore City Jail
August, 1985

A breeze sneaks in my prison window,
    carrying a late-Summer aroma
        of green things basking and baking in hot sun,
        of wildflowers, long since become
           familiar everyday sights,
        of asphalt radiating heat
           that will be remembered fondly
                in colder weeks to come.

But the longings stirred in me
    by the breeze with its gift of odors
reach far beyond the freedom I can see
    outside my window, in the weeds and grass.

They reach to feet marching
        stamping
        running
           through hot dust
      to masses arming, fighting
        in Azania
        to revolution
        in Azania.

They reach to El Salvador
    to celebrate successful actions
      carried out by the guerilla forces
        of the people of El Salvador
          against marines,
            advisors
              imperialists drunk with power
                in El Salvador.

They reach to the streets of Harlem
          and Detroit
    to chanting
      clapping
      celebrating
        New Afrikan Freedom Fighters' Day
    to growing revolution
      in Harlem
      and Detroit.

These longings are not for freedom
      from the walls and bars alone,
    but for the freedom
      that comes from fighting
        for real freedom.

Hanif Shabazz Bey

The Throwing of Stones

During the Muslim pilgrimage to Mecca there is a ceremonial rite performed called "the throwing of stones," in which the Muslim pilgrim is to gather forty-nine small stones and throw them, in a very meticulous ceremonial method, at three pillars set up at intervals along a distance of three hundred yards through the town of Mina, in Saudi Arabia.

There is an atmosphere of indescribable excitement attached to this rite. For although theologians refrain from calling the ritual anything other than "the throwing of stones," in the vernacular of all Muslim countries, including the Hizaz region itself, it is referred to as "the stoning of Satan." The stone pillars themselves are known in some countries and provinces as Satan. Popular legends describing the rite invite the faithful to stone Satan.

During the throwing of stones the expressions on faces range from strain to torture, as the Pilgrims believe that they should manifest their antagonism toward the source of their past errors and faults. In their own way, they are demonstrating how they intend from now on to make a complete break with the forces of evil.

The courageous young freedom fighters inside occupied Palestine, known as "Shebabs," have added a revolutionary touch to the old tradition of throwing stones. Just when the Zionist settlers were under the impression that they had totally crushed the liberation movement inside occupied Palestine, these adamant young fighters with mere stones as weapons have challenged the Zionist oppression of their homeland.

271

The Zionist soldiers who the "Shebabs" hurl their stones at are seen as the same forces of evil that the Muslim Pilgrims seek to redeem themselves from. Although the throwing of stones against the formidable Zionist war machine may seem like a futile effort, the Zionist settlers understand the symbolic significance in the throwing of stones. This is why Yitzhak Shamir, the Zionist Prime Minister, has said that this latest rebellion by the Palestinian masses is not a mere form of civil disobedience, but an act of war. Mr. Shamir and his other Zionist kindred realize that these stones represent the seeds of resistance, just as the ones David hurled at mighty Goliath.

The Palestinian people display selflessness and sacrifice, demonstrating to the oppressed people of the world that once the conscious level of the people has been raised, no war machine or threat of death can extinguish the flame that burns for freedom.

Marion

Tim Blunk

for comrades who ask, "what is to be done?" during this particular historical conjuncture, a (partial) list of practical things to do

throw a stone
throw another
fire a poem
slash a tire
raise a fist
raise your voice
raise a child
wear a mask
paint a slogan
paint a dream
honor the martyrs
build a barricade
build a network
claim your history
claim the streets
sing a message
shoot a bullet
sow a seed
set a fire
break a window
break a sweat
rent a safehouse

print a leaflet
forge a document
shelter a fugitive
bind a wound
love a friend
hold a lantern
hold your ground
clean your weapon
practice your aim
strike a chord
strike a blow
tell the truth
trick the man
hold a meeting
take a beating
hold your tongue
watch your back
watch the sky
cut a trail
leave no traces
pick a target
launch a rocket

learn from workers
teach a comrade
mark the time
free a p.o.w.
steal the files
steel your heart
hound a landlord
feed the homeless
squat a building
join a cell
learn a kata
memorize the code
cut the bars
vault the fence
clear the perimeter
swim the river
disarm a cop
disable a missile
create a diversion
tell a joke
secure a march
walk the picket
pick a lock
bait a trap
spring an ambush
blow a horn
make a plan
plan a back-up
wreck the tracks
lose a tail
find your hope
raise the stakes
change your name
wipe for prints
test a theory
challenge a dogma
cut the wires

slip the noose
slip the checkpoint
use your fear
tighten the drum
plant a thought
tend the orchard
cherish a tear
commit it to memory
check your ego
study the map
deal with the traitors
silence the snitch
start from scratch
carry your weight
take on some more
fight to love
say it again
cross the line
take us with you
don't look back

6/87 U.S. P. Marion

Tim Blunk

liberated territory

Chalatenango, Jabaliyah
Hafenstrasse, Loisaida

liberated territory

more than the absence of fear
the love between us
more than the space around us
the place that is ours
this camp, our street
nuestras hamacas, our house
our lives, this cell
a terrain of relations
where the conspiracy begins and returns
we carry it with us
to another squat
on *las guindas*
to the refugee camps
to the prisons

more than the space between us
not a vacuum at all
the place where our eyes met
one river, *ein Traum*
i walk with you there
along the Elbe
in Chalatenango, Jabaliyah
beyond the searchlights
in this prison yard
under four stars and a quarter moon
where we go to do
what must be done
where we solve the philosophical problem
of the other
in the soup kitchen, the safehouse
the polyclinic, the women's shelter
the guerrilla

liberated territory

the place where our eyes will meet
a relation of justice
a promise born of integrity
a house made of stone
a defensible position
more than the power within us

9 november 1989

Tim Blunk

---

untitled

1

As a child
I threw stones into the air
trying to influence the flight of birds
and bats

2

My friend and I launched our arrows
into the sky straight up!
disappearing from sight for endless moments
pulling the arrows from the ground
buried to the fletching
we savored the danger.

3

As a young man
I fired my rifle into the heart of despair
we defended the rarest forms of light
we searched for the lost ones
we gave up nothing.

4

Now without a sling
a bow, a rifle
I cast my longing to the sky.
Would they serve me better
than poetry to reach
the threads of blue,
of moonlight and crystalline ice
that connect us?

5

These are the risks worth taking:
to exult in the being of others
to give freely
to hope with abandon
to love with audacity.

5/25/89
Washington, D.C.

Kojo Bomani Sababu

New Afrika

A small nation in the minds of 30 million people. Somewhere in the bottom of North America. Formerly called the Black Belt where Afrikans dispersed through diaspora were forced to settle and used as slaves to fill the coffers of European colonial-settlers. While the settlers acquired their wealth through primitive accumulation, enriching themselves in finance, technology, societal organization, their slaves weren't permitted to read, write or articulate culture.

New Afrikans— a people dispossessed of the higher authority of life, disenfranchised, dislocated from family, distorted from reality. Apprehending only that no dreams corresponded to a future, due to their harsh conditions and the torturous lives they had to lead.

There were examples of Maroons, who extricated themselves from foreign domination. The rebellions of Denmark Vesey, Nat Turner, John Brown commenced a liberation statement— pursued by many New Afrikans to reclaim land, assert independence, profess self-determination. Malcolm X taught us the significance and value of nationhood, what national sovereignty implies, bequeaths upon a people.

True to this call, our national independence movement has grown geometrically from its union with geopolitical affairs. The freedom fighters for New Afrika are making sacrifices to make sure no abortion occurs this time. The Republic of New Afrika will emerge as a viable entity in the house of nations and not be a stillborn dream. LAND, INDEPENDENCE, SELF-DETERMINATION, NATION-HOOD IS OUR CRY UNTIL WE FREE THE LAND!

This prose is dedicated to all who have struggled to see oppressed people free. In addition, to those who've sacrificed their lives in the contribution of building an Afrikan nation in North America!

Linda Evans
Vigilancia para el Pueblo, 1989
pencil on paper, 12″ x 9″

Susan Rosenberg

Puerto Rico, A Fantasy Dream

Flowers bloom for us
The times we are human joy
The resistance grows from us . . .

— NAVAJO POEM FROM BIG
MOUNTAIN

. . .Oh flower of Santiago
As the petals fall,
Grow your thistles with the bloodsap
You have given to the violated earth.

— EDGAR MARAVAN, CHILEAN POET
AND POLITICAL PRISONER

Torture and repression come in all forms. From the physical to the psychological to sexual. Repression also comes in all forms, and is inherent in the very system we live under. Its degree may vary, but its purpose is to control and dominate whole oppressed nations, whole peoples, and classes and sectors. Torture is for the purpose of destroying the revolutionary oppositon and terrorizing the people. Revolutionaries resist torture, the people's movements fight repression, and when the people resist both we can defeat the imperialist enemy. Women (and men) are resisting torture and fighting repression all over the world. In Azania, in Chile, in El Salvador, in Palestine. Women resist torture to protect those we love, to defend our lives, our organizations, and the lives of our

282

people, for our objectives, goals, and commitments. When we endure today, we grow tomorrow—because what is left after the degradation, after the vilification, after the pain and the loneliness is their fear, and our anger and strength. Because they see the inevitability of our rise and their fall. Revolutionary character arises from revolutionary struggle. Creating the collective capacity to transform ourselves and our organizations will only come about when we recognize that we have more to lose by maintaining the staus quo then by fighting it, and when we sink the roots of practice that is committed to fighting at all levels against injustices of colonialism, white supremacy, and imperialist war.

We were standing in El Yunque. A forest, a rain forest—El Caribe, Isla Grande, Puerto Rico. The beauty was sublime. Hot and cool, lush and damp. Dark and filled with mystery. How many thousands of people had stood in the same spot, looking at this beautiful waterfall. My friend was talking, he was giving a history lesson. It was about the Indians, their fierce independence, their resistance to the Spanish colonization, their life and their customs. Los Tainos de Boricua. How well I could understand the rich historical and current resistance to the rape and genocide of U.S. imperialist domination. Of how the Puerto Rican people living in a nation militarily intervened by the largest and most powerful country in the world would have to fight and give everything to win independence. Why clandestine forms of struggle were critical and why the rearguard was necessary. Puerto Rico is a small island.

And then I was dreaming. I was sitting on a rock looking at a cool clear blue pool of water in a rain forest. Maybe I looked up too quickly, maybe the dream made me dizzy, or the heat. Nothing moved: not a leaf, not a cloud; it was still. The air had caved in. In that stillness I sat up and looked around. Around the pool, ringing the whole rim, were roses. Red roses. They were hanging over the pool. Some were so heavy that the tips of their petals grazed the water. In the serenity and quiet, liquid started dripping from the flowers. Red liquid flowed from each petal into the blue water until the water was purple, magenta, red—and the roses were colorless.

283

The quiet evaporated as vapors started to rise from the pool and it began to spin and churn; little whirlpools started first in one spot and then another, as though fish from under the surface were snapping for air. In one great movement from a deep rumbling underneath, the pool transformed itself into a river—a rapid, fastmoving narrow river. A red river. It snaked and twisted into the waterfall in El Yunque. And in watching this violent action of nature I looked closer and saw that inside the water as it crashed downward, thousands of roses were falling into the water. These roses were yellow, white, red, pink. Inside each flower was a face. Each face part of the crying times we live in. Each face with its own story. Distraught, disappeared, dispossessed. And in my dreams I thought of Doña Consuelo's poem "For Every Tear a Bullet," and I couldn't listen to their cries. I began to cry, feeling helpless and powerless, and alone, watching all this beauty—drowning, drowning in a waterfall of blood. Of the avariciousness, greed, oppression and the exploitation of a system convulsing in on itself.

And then I looked up. At the apex where the forest and water merged. Standing with rifle in hand was a woman, her face masked, her long black hair wrapped tightly around her head. With one flowing movement her arm made an arc and several men and women appeared. Together they stood on the edge and unrolled a huge net. The net was made of thick twine knotted in a hundred places. Together they pulled on each knot to be sure all were secure. The woman began to sing and as she sang the others threw the net over the waterfall and caught the flowers as they merged with the flowing currents. Then they hauled and pulled and strained to raise the net through the downward crashing water. It seemed that the flowers were heavier and the job much harder than it appeared.

I was back at the pool. The water was blue. Instead of the roses there were many lilies of the valley and they spread out away from the water. In the field of lilies the woman of the waterfall was sitting. When I woke up I thought, Puerto Rico will be free—for the clandestine fighters today, tears, flowers, bullets, all. For the people tomorrow.

Venceremos.

Spring, 1986

284

Susan Rosenberg

April/Spring/Hungerstrike

There are nights when freedom
is close as a lover's breath
When desire and imagination
merge
and the prisoner rides a tempest,
a tidal wave of
memories.
A spirit in the dark
A conspiracy of spirit.
Sleep is happily elusive

But it is cold, and the cold
intrudes, invades
and brings with it the present

Two marvelous friends
that have never met
will soon
die.
They will die from hungerstrike
and no spirit conspiracy
will save them

But in the cold
all those that conspire
in the dark secretive regions of cells
in and out
will continue.
How it is
will not be in vain.
No.

1989

Susan Rosenberg

Sparks Fly

A calm shuddering deep within
a chill that rises in the midst of dryness
an inner core anger, slowly turning into a fury.

There is no peace without justice
there is no justice without freedom
there is no freedom without dignity and liberation
there is no victory for those who never attempt

When they took us we weren't ready
But—we were more ready than others
We didn't go quietly, but no one stopped them
Some said "they brought it on themselves."
Others "better them than us."
And still others felt the sparks fly
and said we are not lost in the stars.

1987

Susan Rosenberg

Of Poems

Poems are a gift for me in the late time.
My time for myself. I think of night
and how it draws its knees up near me,
and settles, in, singing its light and its mysteries.
I think of the countless numbers
of us who put down the pen to pick up
other tools, and how of necessity we are
returned to the pen.
I think of the poet who said
"I curse the poetry of those who do not take sides."
I think the torture, the degradation, and the
humiliation that the enemy inflicts on us all
is to teach us, to force us to lose the memory of ourselves.
So, in that poetry becomes a weapon that guides
us to the future.
Opening the heart to love, to justice, to dignity,
and to a freedom the enemy knows nothing of.
To be willing to give everything to achieve
that allows poetry to course through all
of us like a revolutionary elixir.

Albert Nuh Washington

Smile

i am locked in a cage
Where even the sun can't penetrate
And no music to brighten my mood
Yet i smile.

i am free in my soul
remembering songs of revolution,
comrades who died, lived, loved,
sacrificed, cared and even smiled:
The thought of them makes me smile.

3/22/88, MCC

Albert Nuh Washington

Faith

How cold and bleak seem the days
Winter is gone yet a greyness hangs
like a coat of sadness upon us
We have suffered another seeming defeat
But take heart, sunny days are ahead
Soon flowers will bloom, trees will bud
And the coat of sadness will fall
like a ripe fruit in which
we'll experience the sweet taste of victory.

4/20/88, MCC

Albert Nuh Washington

Listen

Boy, take that wax out of your ears
Can't you hear the pain and suffering down through the years?
You hustle nickels and dimes to get you a sip
Steal your momma's rent money for some drug trip.
You don't remember Malcolm, hardly know King
And the murder of black men, women and children
     to you, don't mean a thing.
Won't raise a hand against the brutalizer
But will cut my throat (if i bump into you) for being an apologizer.
The truth of the matter is, you don't want to hear
Beat your woman and child to mask your fear.
Keep shucking and jiving pretending you got it made
While working blackmen are sent to an early grave.
I could go on and on and tell you it all
But i realize it's like talking to a wall.
You don't want to hear you don't want to listen
Don't want to be bothered in your self-made prison.
So if as a people we want dignity and pride
Our first order of business is sweeping you aside.

5/8/87 Auburn State Prison, NY

Albert Nuh Washington

BLA

Black
    is a political condition,
    a state of oppression and consciousness
    a nation seeking to become,
                A people who hope.

Liberation
    is freedom from oppression
    freedom to define, to determine one's destiny
    free from despair
                A slave to hope.

Army
    is a politically armed unit
    to defend and preserve
    after it achieves
                Liberation for those who hope.

3/14/86

Albert Nuh Washington

By Way of Introduction

Who are you, I am asked
If I give a name
It only tells what I am called
Having had many names
It still does not say
Who nor what I am

To the oppressed I am the angel of deliverance
To the oppressor I am the angel of destruction
So who I am
      depends on who you are . . .

8/22/75, Folsom Prison;
from THE SOUL OF THE BLACK LIBERATION ARMY

Albert Nuh Washington

That Which Is Shared

In one's memory are many things
of joy and pain but most of all
That which is shared.
It doesn't matter what the occasions were
For the act of sharing is significant unto itself
To share; love as between man and woman,
bread in times of hunger, a sword in the midst
of war, the dream of freedom when slavery rules
the land, the idea of victory when overwhelmed by
great forces— strengthens one's faith.

That which is shared
Is only but a moment
In the span of a lifetime
Yet remains throughout.

5/19/76

Albert Nuh Washington

Nelson 'n' Winnie

He said "if not for you
(meaning her)
I could not have made it"
(All those years in prison)
And she travelling twice a year
to see him and enduring her own pain.
He for so long kept in isolation
She banned (in her own country)
Giving to each other love
That cannot touch with hands
Yet can penetrate the soul.
He unable to see his daughters grow
She, fearful for their safety.
But not afraid to stand for what's right.
When apartheid crumbles it will be
Nelson 'n' Winnie's love
for their people, their land and each other
That will have proved to be stronger
Than the racist clique and its Washington allies.

4/8/86

Albert Nuh Washington

Spiderman

I have never been bitten by a radioactive spider
So i cannot climb walls
Or defeat a bunch of bad guys at once
But like Spiderman i have a sense of humor
Yet i'd give up some of this humor
To be able just for a few hours
To climb walls and bend bars
So as to leave this place without humor
And laugh at their wonder of
                how did he do that?

3/18/86

296

Albert Nuh Washington

If I Could

I would if i could
Walk from the mountain to the sea
Just to see the high tide
And return to sit on a plateau
To watch the grass dance across the plains
Build me a shelter in the forest
Clear some land to grow food
Take me a mate whose laughter comes naturally
And can sing from her soul.

And if i really could,
I'd dismantle your political systems
Turn off your electricity
Steal your batteries and all your conveniences
And leave you with a few books of wisdom
So that we may leave each other in peace.

4/7/86

Liz Davidson

Prison Visit

I've always admired those
who persevere out of a severe hope
In the world remade.
It spins in their dark and secret heart: intimately textured,
    sturdy as bread to the teeth,
While with shrewd eyes and scraped knuckles they build it up day
by day.

That long view isn't my gift. Instead,
I am sustained by the delights of our present life.
Fierce love and friendship, sudden sweep of action, freedom
savoured
    under the tongue—
And by that passion of belief, my anarchist ancestors.
My talent is to help summon for a moment the demon of the
    absolute:
Heat and light together, something bright
That hangs in the air.

Still there was an hour
When it came towards me all at once.
A river of swift green water—
Sun leaping at my eyes—
Hope so sudden it left me gaping.

That morning I was visiting a friend in jail.
A bright morning, a long bumpy bus ride, and hours still to wait.
The prison roosted sadly in a vast complex of misery
And I wandered away to explore the grounds.
Strangely, nobody stopped me.

I discovered a bit that had fallen into ruin.
A hidden courtyard, empty windows with the bars rusted out.
In the center wild green grasses
Flowers raw and bright
And over all the sweet randy heat of a northern spring.

A maple stands here, leaves just unfurled,
Small as a mouse's ears
And a green to make your heart ache.
I leaned against it almost asleep,
Sun scalding above, beneath me the cold earth sluggishly waking.
Right in the middle of the courtyard the cracked concrete
Had been pushed jaggedly up— somebody's burrow.
I watched, and a woodchuck came out,
stretched in the sun and observed me,
Her fur tipped with gold.

Drifting towards sleep, I daydreamed an idle myth
Of after the Revolution.
People would live here; it could be a good place—
A garden with tomatoes and blackberries
And washing hanging bright from the windows.
In that arched doorway a woman leans, hand on hip,
And watches a black cat rolling in the fresh-turned earth.
He is disturbing the pumpkin seeds, but she smiles and lets him
    stay.
I even picked out a sunny corner room for myself,
Filled the windows with geraniums and rosemary,
And laid a braided rug on the floor.

But first, I thought, we will pull down the walls of the prison.
Block by block, down to the earth.

The sun was lower, soon
I'd make my way back to my friend.
Right now it's count, I thought: stand by your bed
Eyes carefully blank for the guard.
I checked that I had the two picture IDs required,
Brushed the grass out of my hair, composed my face to escape
    notice.
Stood up stiff and chill, knowing

I would never be among those to surge up the prison steps
And break open every door.
In our lifetime the wall will always be there
Cutting off half the sky.

But standing in the silence of afternoon
I thought suddenly: perhaps, perhaps,
It will happen. Not in my life, but perhaps—

I thought of them returning to the campfires from a long day's work
    on the wall
Walking slow and easy and tired.
"Two meters today, a good day," one calls out.
For a moment the distance between us seems insignificant
As though the woman leaning in the doorway has looked
Straight up into my eyes.

She walks over and takes my wrist gently
And turns my cold hand palm up.
Her fingers are warm and earth-stained at the nails; she touches
    them to mine.
My dear, she says,
Don't you know
Our work is the same?

3/88

Liz Davidson

Deeper Waters

When one of us first went to jail
It seemed that he had gone to another country
Or as though the slave ships from Arcturus had swept down
And beamed him off to the sixth dimension.

A number of things happened in the ten days he was there
The ordinary bad things that happen to people in jail
He was put in the hole for being uncooperative
They took his clothes away and he was cold
And none of us were allowed to see him.
Those of us left outside were furious with activity.
We threw ourselves at the bureaucracy and became entangled.
We scrabbled for lawyers and bail; we hadn't learned to wait.

Our class backgrounds were showing.
No one we knew had ever been to prison.

Later on it became a part of everyday life—
Thirty days, six months, two years.
Visiting hours were taped to the refrigerator,
Instructions on how to send commissary money,
And what kinds of books were allowed in.
We sang on the long car trips to distant prisons
And waited for hours in the visiting rooms
   Drinking coffee or talking
   Reading or trying to write letters.

We learned from those who waited with us
To wear masks of impassive patience for the eyes of the guards.
"We will wait forever, if necessary," our masks said,
"To see those we love, to hold them for the quick permitted
    embrace.
You will not outwait us, and we will show you nothing.
Not tears
Not anger
Only patience hard as rock."

This we learned from them, and also
Still to grin at the baby across the room
Who clutches her father's nose, whose cheeks are as soft as the
    darkest pansy.
Still to admire her father's yellow shirt
Crisp as toast, bright as the sun,
Which he put on this morning to delight his wife's eyes
To give her the subversive gift
Of color.

As we sit together, as we breathe slowly together the stale air
We realize that it is our lives that have been the anomaly.
For those who are not white, who do not have money
Prison has been there always.

We learned that it would be a given in our lives, that moment
When the cellblock door shuts between us.
But still, a part of us refused
To comprehend the endurance of more than a few years
Locked up.

Now
Friends of friends are doing forty years, or life
In places designed to twist their minds to ruin.
Women I almost know, one whose father
I have seen weep.
Women sho still continue to write witty letters
Discussing with precision and hope that latest protest

Remembering a desert walk in the spring
Or expressing a sudden yearning
For steamed clams.

At a certain moment we realize
That if we are serious and passionate in what we do
The state will try any means to destroy us.
What allows us to continue then
Is simply to know that our struggle
Is worth it.

3/88

Liz Davidson

Elephants

After the revolution elephants will live in the White House.
I do not mean that they will be kept there
I mean that they will take it over.
Soft and heavy they will walk up the stairs.
They will curl their trunks around the doors
And tread them down.
In the oval office
The great seal will lie shattered on the floor
And the desk will crack
Under a casual footstep.

All winter they will stay inside
As they breathe the air will turn moist
Moss will cover the peeling paint
Grass will push its way through the cracked floors
The stairs will run with water and ferns
Orchids will sprout from the mouldering heaps of papers
And
The young ones
with their delicate high-domed whiskery heads
will sedately blink their long-lashed eyes
as they meditatively munch up
the portraits of famous statesmen.

After the revolution
Elephants will live in the White House
And when Spring comes
They will walk out under the wet star-shivered sky
And scream their joy to the new moon.

West Townshend, VT

"In the name of Allah the beneficient, the merciful."

Sekou Odinga

Why Struggle?

*And why should you not fight for the cause of Allah and of
the feeble among men and of the women and the children
who are crying: Our Lord! Bring us forth from this town
(country) of which the people are oppressors. Oh, give us
from Thy presence some protecting friend. Oh, give us from
Thy presence some defender.*

—S. 4: 75

Maybe the question should be: Why not struggle? Struggle in the
political context that I use it in is the act of opposing oppression in
any form through some conscious activity geared to end or lessen
that oppression. It can be violent or nonviolent in form.

Obviously, just the act of struggling will not necessarily end
oppression. But, without struggling, we can be almost assured that
the oppression will at least continue.

To effectively struggle we must make a correct analysis of the true
nature of our oppression and come up with correct tactics to combat
this oppression.

It must also be known and remembered that oppression as well as
struggle moves in predictable patterns. That is, it moves from lower
to higher. This is to say that if allowed to continue, oppression will
get oppressively worse. To effectively struggle, we must start with
what we have and continue to build our opposition until we reach a
level that will crush the oppressive machinery. We must also be

building the positive progressive machinery to replace the oppressive one.

History teaches us that we usually need more than one form or level of struggle. The forms of struggle are dictated by the oppressive conditions and what we are replacing them with. For instance, if we want to end racism and replace it with integration, we need particular tactics. If we want to separate from racism and place ourselves in a non-racist nation of our own, this calls for other tactics.

So, the questions—What are we struggling against, and what are we struggling for?—become the first questions we must answer. Once we answer these questions, we can move on to the next, which are—How to end what we are against, and how to build what we are for?

Next, we should determine who are our enemies and who are our natural allies. Then, we must find ways to attack and defeat our enemies and to unify and cooperate with our allies.

Toward New Afrika

Some of us have as our goal the political separation of our people from the imperialist government known as the U.S. of A., and the establishment of our own nation—New Afrika. We struggle to have this nation on free, liberated territory (land). There are some prerequisites before this can happen. Number one is that the masses of our people accept this goal as their own and be brought into the work of establishing this goal. This calls for massive political education and organization. Our people must be educated to the need, benefits and possibilities of our own nation and the proper organizational structure must be put into place to lead the people to our final goal.

The building of the proper organizational machinery at this point, should be a priority. I do not believe that any particular groups exist today that have the necessary machinery in place to lead our people to nationhood.

I do believe that the religious community has the best existing machinery from which to build. I know that for many people, especially those on the left, religion has no place in the day-to-day

307

politics of our struggle. But, as a Muslim revolutionary, I believe that there is a clear cut need for *true* religion to play a much larger role (if not the major role) in our struggle.

For one thing, "the church" has an independent economic base. Churches have the heart, ears and respect of our people. They have physical organizational machinery— that is, land, office equipment, communications tools, etc. They also can help build the moral strength and integrity that has so often been missing in our struggling comrades. Just think of how many comrades have had problems because of drugs, alcohol, sex, stealing, lying, fighting each other, etc. The list could go on and on. My point is that when one accepts *true* religion as a guide in his day-to-day life, he will have little or none of the problems I have just mentioned.

I guess the next question is: What is *true religion*? To me, true religion is religion as taught and practiced by the prophets of old, from Adam, Abraham, Moses to Jesus, and Muhammad. (May Peace and Blessings be on them all.) When we check out the history of the Prophets, we find that most of them were revolutionaries. They stood for an end to oppression of the masses and the setting up of a righteous government or nation.

I do not know if there is any person or group willing or capable of taking on the role of trying to organize and lead the masses from the religious community, but I do believe that it is possible and that the greatest revolutionary potential lies in the religious community. It is up to the people to demand more from their Church, Mosque, Temple, etc.

Clearly, the three greatest movers of our people in modern history were religious leaders— Martin Luther King, Malcolm X, and Elijah Muhammad. We can learn much from these brothers. We should study their history and learn from their successes and mistakes. We should then take the best of their examples and build on them for the purpose of helping to survive and build.

> *Those who believe do battle for the cause of Allah: and those who disbelieve do battle for the cause of Satan. So fight the minions of the devil. Lo, the devil's strategy is ever weak.*
>
> —S. 4: 76

Elizam Escobar

---

from
The Other Dreamer

You go to bed with the deaf mute one
and wake up with a strange canvas
that you place in the mail
you think you have fulfilled your obligations
but no, there's nothing to fulfill
you know it well.

You have breakfast in a hurry
and by the hand
you take me to the elevator
which is not as good as mother's.

I see you opening the door, coming in
and not coming in
but today I think you are not coming in
because my mother is crying, in Greek
or in Jewish
and you are not coming in Puerto Rican
because no one knows in what direction
to the sea and the ocean
you have gone. (I look slowly at you,

in a hurry, sleepy, with rancor,
you see me leaving prison
you look at me, you kiss me, there is
something I still don't understand;
I am 5 years old.)

Elizam Escobar

---

de
el otro sueñista

Te acuestas con la sordo-muda
te levantas con un lienzo extraño
y lo depositas en el correo
crees que has cumplido tu deber
pero no, no hay deberes que cumplir
lo sabes bien.

Te desayunas aprisa
y me tomas de la mano
hacia el ascensor que no es tan bueno
como el de madre.

Te veo abrir la puerta, y entras
y no entras
creo que no entras hoy
porque mi madre llora, en griego
o en judío
y tú, no entras en puertorriqueño
porque nadie sabe hacia dónde
del mar y el océano
has salido. (Te miro lentamente,

con prisa, con sueño, con rencor,
me ves salir de las prisión
me miras, me besas, hay algo
que no entiendo todavía;
tengo 5 años.)

Elizam Escobar

from
Nietzschean Poems

the universal is the necessary chimera

the dove is universal
dreams
the eye, angst
the way of looking
the ego

however, I
a man
with various egos
and the brain divided in two
asks himself:

    tonight, of what good is the universe to me?
    why should I hold with my hands
    the earthquake of my passion?

the universal dove
is nervous in my country
dreams are nervous
the eye
angst
the way of looking
the collective ego is nervous.

Elizam Escobar

---

de

poemas nietzscheanos

lo universal es la quimera necesaria

la paloma es universal
el sueño
el ojo, la angustia
la forma de mirar
el ego

sin embargo, yo
un hombre
con varios egos
y el cerebro dividido en dos
se pregunta:

    de qué me sirve el universo esta noche?
    para qué aguantar con la manos
    el terremoto de mi pasión?

la paloma universal
está nerviosa en mi país
el sueño está nervioso
el ojo
la angustia
la forma de mirar
el ego colectivo está nervioso.

Elizam Escobar

Yo me muero a veces ...

Yo me muero a veces
cuando apago la luz
y dentro de mi volcán
las cenizas.

Me muero en las mañanas
cuando se monte la luna toda
en mi celda
redonda cuadrada
y apenas tengo espacio.

Me muero en las noches frías y cúbicas
e
m
u
e
r
o
e
n
l
a
s

n
o
c
h
e
s
f
r
í
a
s
y
c
ú
b
i
c
a
s

Cuando resucito
descubro como un oso
el rayito de luz
que me comienza.

1984

Elizam Escobar

Sometimes I die ...

Sometimes I die
when I turn off the light
and inside my volcano
the ashes.

I die in the mornings
when the moon comes in whole
into my cell
rounded squared
and I hardly have room

I die in the cubic and cold nights
d
i
e
i
n
t
h
e
c
u
b
i
c

a
n
d
c
o
l
d
n
i
g
h
t
s

When I resurrect
I discover like a bear
the little lightning ray
that starts me over.

1984

Obafemi Senghor

Apocalyptic Children

THEY sniff catastrophic refuge
into their brains
but the oppressions of
meaninglessness and improverishment
remain.
FUTURE flowers of humanity
are in pain
from trying to escape from the ghetto—
a brutal imprisonment chain.

NEON concrete walls
cry their powerless rage
at the history of a SYSTEM
writing another genocidal page
while the PRESIDENT sings
human rights and fundamental freedoms
on the world's political stage.

OH where is AQUARIUS with its
revolutionary years of rage
to demand that no more APOCALYPTIC
CHILDREN be made ?
AND when will the CHILDREN COMING
be saved ?
AND WHEN WILL PATRIOTISM TO THE AMERICAN
GOVERNMENT, STOP BEING A SLAVE ??

December, 1988

319

Chapter Seven

REMEMBER THE FIGHTERS

*Those who protest at injustice
are people of true merit. When
the prison doors are opened, the
real dragon will fly out.*

— HO CHI MINH, PRISON DIARY

Prince Cuba

Universal Struggle
edited with notes by Campos-Garcia

Faith, belief, sacrifice,
to the deity of Universal Struggle,
and the Apostle Martí,
the murdered saviors, Che and Sandino,
and the Church of Marxist-Leninismo,
and its Pope, Fidel;
Singing the praises of Patriarch Bolívar,
and the liturgy of "Fatherland or Death!"
are the fallen fighters,
Albizu, Villa, Sendic,
Marighela, Allende,
Tupac Amaru, and Moctezuma.

But "Manifest Destiny" be damned:
they came, they saw, they conquered,
and built an empire on the foundation
of divided peoples.
"They divided the lands among themselves by lots,"
and crucified the saviours of the people,
saying words like "peace" and "justice,"
"Bread and Liberty,"
while Pax Americana sacrificed the hearts of nuns
and priests, at the altar of the wailing Wall Street,
and the moneylenders of the Temple of the Almighty Dollar
drank the blood of the martyrs in Tiffany chalices.
Babylon has fallen.

323

Vandals sacked Rome,
and the Sun has set on the British Empire.
The threads of Fate shall be unrolled, unraveled,
and de-controlled,
until the Coliseum on 59th Street is also in ruins.

Babylon or Bust,
We've passed this way before;
deja vu, and god-knows-who,
we'll go there again.

Batista, and Taco
made their pact with the Devil,
and made life hell for the people.

Vampires, Ton Ton Macoutes, Death Squads;
Murderers of babes, rapers of nuns, poisoners of the Earth;
Satan unleashed, come to rule and oppress,
the righteous peoples of the planet Earth.

Those without sin, please cast the first stone,
and render unto Caesar what is his.
In the name of the God of Universal Struggle,
of the Apostle Martí,
of the saviours Che and Sandino,
of Fidel, and Bolívar,
and the prophets Albizu, Villa, and Sendic,
Marighela, and Allende, Tupac Amaru,
and Moctezuma,
to whom he appeared, saying:

"I am the God of Universal Struggle;
I help those who help themselves.
I live in the Spirits of those who struggle.
There is no progress without Sacrifice.
'La Patria es Sacrificio.'
Take this machine gun and bomb
and pray with them to the God of Universal Struggle,

and in the names of my Prophets,
and you shall soon be Master in the place
where once you were a slave to the Devil."

[Cuban revolutionary **José Martí** (1853-95) coined the term "in the belly of the beast" when he was in exile in New York; **Don Pedro Albizu Campos**, Puerto Rican Nationalist leader; **Pancho Villa**, Mexican revolutionary, murdered in 1923; **Raul Sendic**, Uruguayan Tupamaro; Brazilian revolutionary **Carlos Marighela**, author of the Urban Guerrilla Minimanual; **Salvador Allende Gossens**, progressive Chilean leader, murdered in 1973; **Tupac Amaru**, Indian leader in resistance against Spanish in South America; **Moctezuma** (misspelled "Montezuma"), last Aztec emperor of Mexico, murdered in 1520. **Manifest Destiny**, racist doctrine justifying expansion of U.S. The crucified Jesus's clothing was divided among the Romans by lots. **Pax Americana** parallels the "Pax Romana" of the Roman Empire.]

Mumia Abu-Jamal

Things Go Round

Juxtapositions.

Changes.

Life is a jumbled bunch of tickets in a dark derby, awarding to each player, that loved/feared winning ticket-change.

What change could be as total, as absolute, as the "clang!" of steel, shutting, barring, blockading life's central purpose— to be free?

Many of us, rebels, political prisoners, prisoners of conscience, anarchs, social prisoners politicized by their slip into the abyss, bear witness to the power of change.

Some of us stubbornly resist that which is irresistible.

Better to resist the beating of one's heart, or the blink of an eye.

Change, that force of nature, may be channeled— but not resisted. Change— to strengthen; to build; to become clearer in purpose; to grow more human.

Several years ago, I sat in a crowded basement of the American Friends Service Committee headquarters in Center City, Philly, in the midst of a press conference. I had come with other reporters to meet and interview several of the heroic Independentistas of the 1950s attack on the U.S. Congress, a demonstration of Puerto Rican will to be free of the clutches of U.S. Empire.

Oscar Collazo and Rafael Cancel Miranda spoke on their long incarceration, and on being the longest-imprisoned captives in U.S. pens. Collazo, his thick spectacles making his eyes appear

326

larger, and Miranda, with his almost white head of thick curls, had spent over a quarter century in fed joints, emerging still committed to independence. (Heroine Lolita Lebron was also freed, but did not attend the press conference, as she had commitments on the island.)

They, like Republic of New Afrika Chairman Imari Obadele, were among the many long-imprisoned political prisoners of which onetime U.N. Ambassador Andrew Young spoke when he noted that thousands of political prisoners were being held in U.S. gulags.

Juxtapose.

Miranda, Collazo and Obadele are free.

The writer writes not a script for a radio broadcast, but his own thoughts, from a gulag, behind the cage.

CHANGE.

Miranda, in a 1986 interview (not mine), offered valuable insights into how he coped while in Babylon's dungeons for over 25 years. I shamelessly borrow from my source, to share with you, from one who's been there:

> If you go there thinking you're tough, you're going to find someone tougher than you. King of the World. But if you go there thinking you're soft, you're in trouble too. The point is how not to be too tough, nor be too soft. The other prisoners learn to respect you when you treat them right. Once they know you're not afraid, that you treat them right because you want to treat them right, they dig you. They dig you immediately. When they know that you don't come there to shove them around, you don't think "I'm better than you because I'm here for a political reason." I'm saying how I act. They know they can have confidence in you, that you won't snitch. They respect that.
>
> . . . Don't start daydreaming . . . You're daydreaming, "Wow, how great it would be if I were out, if I were with my woman, how good it would be. . . ." Forget it!

You start daydreaming, wishful thinking, then you lose reality. But you better not lose reality, because that's the only way you can handle it. Not by escaping, escaping in your mind. Forget what could have been. You're here! Find ways to keep your mind busy. . . . Try to be free, but don't be too anxious to be free. Because then they've got you. Campaign to be free, but don't become too anxious and desperate . . . . Because if they see a weakness in you, they will go through that weakness.

I was afraid of one thing—I was afraid of losing my sensibility. More than anything else. Afraid that if I came out of prison, I'd come out without giving a damn about anything. Because you will have to go through certain things. You have to see so many nasty things— beatings, behavior modification, things like that. You're afraid that you'll become too hard.

Then when I got out and we went to Chicago— there was a blind Puerto Rican girl, who used to write me. Martita. She used to write to me when she was very young. And she used to call me Uncle Pito. My nieces and nephews used to call me Uncle Pito. And I got to love her, like a real niece. I heard she was blind but I had never seen her. And that was the very first day we came out of prison, we stopped in Chicago. The community and the school made a welcoming party and it was crowded with many people. And I still hadn't seen Martita, the little blind girl. I wasn't really thinking of her. And all of a sudden, here is the little blind girl, calling, "Uncle Pito! Uncle Pito!" I cried. I cried when I saw that little girl who couldn't see me, looking for me.

All of that time in prison, and I hadn't stopped being a
human being, a real human being.*

28 years in one of America's grimmest gulags—almost three
decades which transformed a young man, into an elder nearly 50
years old. Miranda changed—but his revolutionary spirit, the best
part of him, his humanity, survived.

A younger generation of political prisoners from different
struggles and campaigns now inhabit America's gulags.

Some are relegated to mind-numbing, soul-sapping joints like
Marion, where the infamous "Behavior Modification Units" are
used to "modify" the political ideology of anti-imperialists like the
Resistance Conspiracy Case defendants. They continue to resist.

The draconian Lexington Control Unit, which worked with near-
deadly efficiency on Silvia Baraldini, Susan Rosenberg, and
Alejandrina Torres, and left several of the radical women seriously
ailing and weakened, if not in spirit, certainly in flesh. They
remain committed to struggle.

Africans like former L.A. Panther Deputy Defense Minister,
Geronimo Pratt, ex-NY Panther Dhoruba Bin-Wahad, and BLA
soldier Sundiata Acoli remain caged in state gulags across
America, more than 20 years after trials orchestrated by the
infamous FBI Cointelpro program, which featured introduction of
tainted evidence provided by paid government informants. They
remain committed to Black Liberation.

In joints scattered across Pennsylvania, members of the rebel
Naturalist clan, the MOVE Organization, languish under 100-year
sentences, simply for being MOVE members. The sentencing judge
said as much when he told reporters after delivering 900 years to
9 male and female MOVE defendants in 1981: "They were tried as
a family, and I sentenced them as a family." (Perhaps it would be
more honest to say they were sentenced for *being* a family.) This

---

*From a talk with Rafael Cancel Miranda, San Francisco, 1986; reprinted
in *The Real Dragon New Year's Book*, 1989.

is especially significant as MOVE women never charged with weapons offenses, received sentences identical to the men, i.e., for weapons possessions.

They remain rebels, committed to *John Africa's* Way, Natural Law.

Without a doubt, after so many years, all have changed, even as they remain resolute in resistance to a corrupt, twisted system. They are inspirations to us all. Let our resistance enhance our humanity.

We learn.
We change.
We grow.
We persevere.
  We win.

Ona Move! Long Live John Africa's Revolution!

Mumia Abu-Jamal

Sister Mona Africa

Militant, fiery, foe of this system,
Advocate of resistance, dead set against them;
Sister Mona went to battle,
No slave, yet free
Never chattel!

Fighting for freedom,
Hers and others,
She sought freedom of MOVE
Sister/brothers;

For this they burned, framed,
Gave her time,

Proving that, in America, survival is
        a crime.

January 1988

Jonathan Blunk

A Letter to My Brother in Prison

Listen.
I don't pretend
my life is harder
than the unrelenting sameness of your days
but hear me out.

Between us
is what each of us has made
and left undone.

I, too, must
gauge the innocence
of thieves and grasp
at words to weigh
suffering and love.

You must also
master this living
each day, choosing the stones
that will still be left standing
at sunrise.

We each fear
for this world
and do the work we're here to do,
imagining the day will come
when we will stand together
by a river,
with no need
to speak.

Mtayari Shabaka Sundiata

By Choice You Are Assata

By choice you are a Black freedom fighter.
You choose to rebel against a
criminal system in the name of
freedom and dignity for self and kind.

By choice you are a Black woman,
fighting to raise other Ndugu na
Dada by revolutionary example to cast
off their garb of perversity
in their blind pursuit of the
amerikkan nightmare.

By choice you are the purifier of
our Afrikan humanity, your every
act my Sister was designed
to restore life to a nation killed
by wrong ideas.

By choice you are the matrix out of
which many Black warriors will
emerge, in their right hand they will
bear the seal of the New Nation.

By choice you are a doctor that is healing
thousands of sick minds
mutilated by the germ of
oppression.

By choice, Assata, you are the reality
that we must face if we are to survive
and ultimately, Assata, create a world where
freedom and dignity will reign supreme
for Afrikan people.

By choice, Assata, you refuse to listen
to the voices of the political
scavengers feeding on the debilitated
minds of those hopeless
souls raped in the arena of
democracy by the amerikkkan
nightmare.

By choice, you liberated Afrikan
warriors from the graves
of nigger minds
you shattered the bastile of ignorance
by injecting revolution into the minds,
souls, and bodies of an oppressed nation.

By choice, you are our symbol of truth,
your every body movement says to the
Black man blinded by the brutality of
the white whore that has kept him
prostrated before the vagina of a
dying society, raise your eyes from
the filth of the amerikkkan dream and
watch my body movement, watch me move
to the beat of a different drummer.

By choice, Assata, you turned us into a
brave and proud army.
Now we move with the same rhythm that
moves you against the amerikkkan dream.
We too are dedicated to the death of
the monster called oppression.

By choice, we now turn to face the
nation of our survival
and the synthetic melodies of the
amerikkkan dream fades in the back
ground as we move with the celestial
beat of sun-ra, to outer space, outer
their space of oppression into our
space of beingus,
Afrikan People.

Larry Giddings

Roque, Federico and Victor

Cousin,
      Federico
            A bullet
                  tests your love
                        of Gypsies

Your brother,
      Victor
            guitar song
                  hollow gourd flute
                  the drum
                  hands lying before you
                        on the ground
                              as you sing
                              to your severed
                              people

Laughter,
     Roque
          eyes of wonder
          invincible humor
               knew
               that the president
                    of the U.S.
                    was a little
                         bit more
                         the president
                              of El Salvador
                              than the president
                              of El Salvador

Roque,
     overflowing energy
          knew
          that when there was no more room
               for the dead
               the living
                    must
                    move over
Spain
     Chile
          El Salvador

Your voices
     echo
          in
               my nights

Ricardo Flores Magon

We listen
   to your presses
   rumbling
   in the night
Your Indio father
   in your thoughts
Your mother
   of the land

Tierra y Libertad!!

The sound rings
   in your blood
   until
   it rings
   in ours

Tierra y Libertad!!

Yaqui, Maya, Zapotec
   Zapata, Villa
   your friends
   your people

Tierra y Libertad!!

A chorus of people
   answer again
   and again
As your presses
   turn

Tierra y Libertad!!

You shout from
   the cell
   Porfirio Diaz
   assigns you
You shout from
   the cells
   the North Americans
   assign you
   in Arizona,
   California,
   Texas,
   and finally
   Kansas

Tierra y Libertad!!

Your shout is echoed
   in the drumming
   of the Kickapoo
   and the land
   productive
   and stolen
   like your life

Magon! Presente!

Tierra y Libertad!!
Tierra y Libertad!!
Tierra
   y
     Libertad!!

Larry Giddings

Rock

A picture of a Palestinian youth, confronting soldiers in Israeli uniforms, with his slingshot drawn, brings forth a jolt of recognition from within me. I see, clearly, all the frustration of my youth, gripped with white-knuckled fury in the hands of a Palestinian. He points at a target he cannot overcome; yet, he must let fly—the rock.

It is as if I have become the rock, first shot and then bounding off of a soldier's helmet into a street and forgotten. A rock, taken from quarries and gathered at random, placed stone upon stone to build the wall of a house. The house which Palestinians built and lived in was demolished by the soldiers. Now, the rubble provides the rocks being shot at Israeli soldiers.

This picture reminds me, there are more rocks; they are my brothers, they are my sisters, we are many and we may be used more than once.

Larry Giddings

No Borders

Language of life
   notes of recognition
I look in eyes
   Feel the earth
   shifting
Speaking the same tongue
   without wonder
   darkness flees

Muted tones of oceans
   Crete, Mauritius, Bali
The sky blinks
   while
   Gypsy guitar
   sheds our tears
   cries our laughter

Sisters in Palestine
   Brothers in Angola
   Friends in Japan
   Dreams in German
   Hopi Time

Heart beats singing
   People
   reach out
   No borders

David Gilbert

Born on Sunday*

Oh that Saturday, that Saturday—
why can't we make it go away?
Don't want to believe it— though
It's all too real.
Where did our warrior go?

Born on Sunday; died on Saturday;
struggle the whole week through.
Gave "24/7" and more.

As bad as Death is . . .
no way it could take Kuwasi head on.
No one took Kuwasi head on.
He'd dodged a couple of bullets,
caught a couple too,
always kept moving.
No, Death must have snuck up on him,
must have snuck him
to take our warrior away.

---

*Kuwasi means "Born on Sunday"; Balagoon means "Warlord." He died at
Auburn prison on Saturday, December 13, 1986.

Born on Sunday; died on Saturday;
struggled the whole time in between:
Struggled and loved, danced to the beat, laughed,
and then struggled even harder—
whole life through, struggled for his people
to be free.

Gentle warrior—
writing poems, cooking oxtail stew, tussling with
kids (when he could)—
gentle warrior, valor in action.
No,
he didn't like violence,
not even a little bit,
just hated oppression a whole lot more.
So he fought and fought and fought
and never looked back.

Born on Sunday; died on Saturday;
created the poetry of struggle all week long;
said New Afrika had to be free.

Our warrior, revolution personified,
and mainly, well mainly he just loved people.
Not only "the people" in the abstract,
but people,
his people,
common people,
and all kinds of individuals
with their faults and foibles, soul and creativity.

Said New Afrika would be free;
said all forms of oppression must be overturned;
said let the human spirit flourish!

Born on Sunday; died on Saturday—
how could we lose him so soon?
Death snuck up and snatched him.
Yet his life is much greater than death:
Can still hear Kuwasi's giant laugh,
ringing across from the other side.

Died on Saturday; born on Sunday,
wherever people struggle to be free.

12/31/86

Shaheem Malik Jabbar

Poem to Mtayari

My brother is gone

Let me close my eyes
Let me close my eyes
So I can see him
Remember him
Love him

Remember him as he was
The blackness of his face
The strength of a Blackman
A revolutionary a freedom fighter

Now I open my eyes
My brother is gone

Let me close my eyes
Once again
So I can remember the love
He had for his people
The commitment in his heart

My brother is gone

They killed him

I will always remember him.

Richard Williams

Mairead, St Patrick's Day, 1988

The SAS thought that by pumping
bullets into your prone body
they were also killing a cause.

How ignorant they are
You can't kill a revolution
by killing a revolutionary
Bob Sands' example must give them pause.

But no, those english shits
ran up and killed you and your comrades
on a foreign soil ignoring all laws.

Though we'll miss you, you didn't die in vain
your light and truth will never be suppressed
we'll keep fond your memory
as we continue the wars.

Richard Williams

The Sea—Again

I was brought up in New England
    by the shore
    And many nights I think
        of the fog and the mist
            of the smell of the sea
        of the sound of the waves
    And I need to be free.

I remember the feel of sun-drying
            salty-wet skin
    And the good ache of my back and hands
    While rowing a dory on the water
    of the cold spray upon me caused by
    wet oars being wind-whipped
    As they are drawn out for another stroke
And I know I must be free— again.

Mike McCoy

A Vision

One

After what felt like hours of tossing and turning, Sonovia Oden-Muhammad woke to curse the still darkness of the room which would not let her sleep, the darkness which would not quell the problems which cried incessantly for attention in her mind. With both hands she pushed herself up and leaned her head against the bedboard. She reached to the night table beside the bed and found the cigarettes she had left there earlier. With her bony, crab-like fingers, she grabbed the half-crumpled pack and shook one of the cigarettes loose to light up. The square felt soothing as she sucked in the smoke and expelled it through her nostrils and mouth into the pitch blackness of the night.

The recent nationally-televised broadcast by President Webster agreeing to concede Mississippi, Georgia, Alabama, South Carolina, and Louisiana to blacks in america had intensified antagonisms between the two largest national liberation groups jockeying for control of the five states called the Republic of New Africa (RNA). The Malcolm X Movement for Social Democracy (MMSD) was headed by liberals, cultural nationalists, entertainers and other petty bourgeois New Africans who were left destitute by the severe recession which had flattened the u.s. Their inability to satisfy their class aspirations and the need to counter the popular appeal of the New African Revolutionary Army (NARA) had forced this class to organize in support of national independence. Although the Marxist-Leninist stance of the NARA cost it the support of imperialism which the

349

MMSD enjoyed, this "weakness" was overshadowed by the support which the NARA held among the masses of New Africans.

Sonovia sat with both knees tucked under her chin; and as she lit another cigarette she decided to drown, to mercilessly strangle, her current problems with memories of the past. She thought of the eight years spent in prison for a "crime" she had not committed. The district attorney had argued that since the bank robbery and killing of the police were committed by her husband, and since the weapons and bank money had been found in their apartment, she could be charged as a co-conspirator. "An accessory after the fact," the district attorney called it. But that was a long time ago; and besides, the political consciousness Sonovia acquired while in prison provided a foundation which had sustained her for the last 15 years in the movement. Whenever Sonovia's mind wandered to prison, inevitably she thought of Tobiku, a New African who was among the most profound revolutionary theorists she had encountered both in prison and out. Tobiku had a command of political science, history, sociology, and economics equalled by few. It was Tobiku who pushed Sonovia to be consistent and thorough in her approach to study. And even though Tobiku had been dead now for 15 years, Sonovia could still hear her voice: "We can't organize in the traditional way brothers like Marcus Garvey and Malcolm X did. Perhaps their methods were appropriate for their time, but the colony is more complex today, and effective organizing demands that we have a firm grasp of social, political and economic problems."

The wisdom of those words had proved itself through the years as Sonovia and a small, dedicated group of New African communists had built the New African Revolutionary Organization (NARO) into a mass-based one by the creation of alternative institutions which addressed the social, political and economic problems of the community. NARO had correctly rejected as unrevolutionary the politics of despair which relied on fear to organize the masses; instead, they held high a view of the future which was radically different from life under colonialism— a future where social relations weren't based on racism, sexism, or exploitation. It was this projection, along with NARO's ability to create a strategy which moved the masses closer to liberation, that gradually won them the

350

hearts and minds of New African people. Some members of NARO had also realized early that their political, economic, and cultural institutions could not thrive without the support of a peoples' army. And so it was that the New African Revolutionary Army (NARA) was created; and though u.s. imperialism had murdered over two million New Africans trying to destroy the army, its ranks now swelled with tens of thousands of New African patriots dedicated, to the death, to an independent Republic of New Africa.

The night had finally passed and the sun was beginning to rise. Sonovia yawned and stretched both her arms above her head. She could hear from the slight movement in the next room that the two guerrillas assigned to guard her were preparing breakfast. Since the assassination a year ago of Jamal and Salam, the two most senior members of NARA, Sonovia had assumed command of the army. Her brilliance as a revolutionary theorist and tactician was respected by her comrades and enemies alike.

Sonovia sprung from the bed with the agility of a cat and for the next half hour she stretched and practiced her martial arts as she had done now for the last 15 years. Her regret was she had no dumbbells to work with since they helped build and maintain upper body strength. But since the assassination of her two comrades, she never slept in the same place twice and to lug dumbbells around would just add unnecessary weight to the automatic weapons she always carried.

With the last spin kick she lit another cigarette and went to prepare bath water.

After removing her underclothing she stepped back from the medicine cabinet to examine her light brown five-foot-two-inch frame in the mirror. Modern eating habits and regular exercises over the years had kept her body lean and firm. But war had taken its toll. Before Sonovia had gone underground, two white policemen had thrown acid in her face after sodomizing her and beating her unconscious, thinking she was another "nigger hooker" they had trapped in an alley. Cosmetic surgery had helped correct much of the damage, but some scar tissue still remained on the sides of her face. Bags had begun to develop under her eyes, and her breasts, of which she had always been so proud, no longer stood to attention when that tingling sensation spread throughout her body. Despite

351

this, she was considered an attractive woman who at forty could still turn heads and elicit unwanted catcalls.

She turned the bath water off and used both hands to ease herself into the tub. The hot water soothed and relaxed her. It had been two weeks since she had had a chance to bathe. At one time she would never have imagined going so long without bathing. But she, along with so many other comrades, had discovered that in war the will to survive and win becomes an obsession, until the most ordinary habits are disrupted and pushed aside.

Sonovia leaned back to rest her head on the edge of the tub, closed her eyes, and thought about the up-coming events of the day. Although President Webster had conceded independence to the RNA, a statement was expected by NARA on whether it would form a coalition government with the MMSD. Sonovia found the idea of sharing power with the MMSD disgusting, since its role in the war had been minimal, and on occasion it had collaborated with u.s. imperialism to assassinate members of NARA— most recently, Salam and Jamal. It was NARA, along with the national liberation struggles of Puerto Ricans, Native Americans, and Mexicans in the Southwest, and with the support of the North American left, that had brought u.s. imperialism to its knees.

Despite this, Sonovia knew that politics was largely the art of compromise. The MMSD would have to be reckoned with. Sonovia decided to meet clandestinely with a reporter this morning who had shown sympathy over the years to NARA. Sonovia knew no amount of publicity would influence imperialism to favor NARA over the MMSD. But it was necessary for NARA to take advantage of publicity to fight against the negative propaganda imperialism always hurled against it. She scrubbed her body and let the water out of the tub. After she looked herself over in the mirror, with a few adjustments to her dreadlocks, she felt satisfied with her appearance. There was knock on the door and she turned and said, "Come in."

"Commander, your breakfast is here."

"Thank you, Toedoe. Have you and Kiswana eaten yet?"

"No, we haven't."

"Then bring your breakfast here and eat with me." Sonovia knew they would like this. Despite the popularity she held among her comrades and New Africans in general, she had never developed an

352

exaggerated view of herself—largely because she never related power to herself. She always stressed to comrades that the masses were the real source of power; and that through the clarity, integrity, and commitment to struggle of cadres, they could be helped to assume their revolutionary role in history as the primary agents of change.

She thought for a moment over the circumstances in which Toedoe had been assigned to her. He was a young ex-professional football player who had joined NARO and, after demonstrating his commitment, was asked to join the army. This same dedication and enthusiasm for work allowed him to rise through the ranks of the army—until one day in a meeting someone mentioned that Toedoe was gay and had recently contracted AIDS. Looks of disgust and grunts of dismay reverberated throughout the small room, and someone yelled he should be kicked out. Sonovia rose to her feet and said, "That's ridiculous." She balled up her fists and placed them before her on the table and said: "Heterosexual relations aren't inherently better than homosexual relations. What determines the quality of any communion is whether it's based on honesty and mutual respect. If a comrade has a homosexual affair which isn't exploitative and represents no security threat—that's a right he or she has." Sonovia paused for a moment, then went on: "What concerns me is not his sexual preference, but that we have a comrade somewhere alone and vulnerable because we can't deal with his sexuality. And that to me is not revolutionary! Someone give me his address."

A street number was scribbled on a piece of paper and handed to her. By now the men and women in the room were either turned away from Sonovia in shame, or openly glared at her with hostility or approval. She took the address and left the meeting. Thirty minutes later, she stood knocking on an apartment door.

The door opened, and Toedoe was surprised to see his commander—and happy someone had stopped by. They embraced, and as they separated Sonovia smiled and watched him closely thorough her tinted prescription glasses. For a 270-pound football player, his embrace was weak and he appeared withdrawn. She correctly guessed that this was due to depression rather than to any advanced stage of the disease.

353

Toedoe spoke first. "Commander, I was just preparing something to eat. Would you please join me?"

"Just some coffee, comrade. I already ate."

She followed him into the kitchen and sat at the table while he placed a coffee pot along with a spoon and cup in front of her. She could see how difficult it was for him to mask his feelings as he sat across from her with his head bowed, twirling spaghetti around a fork. She knew that most her comrades had accepted the possibility of death when they joined the army: but she knew also that this death was abstract and did not have the same degree of certainty to it which death from AIDS had. She reached across the table with a fork and ate from his plate. He realized from this gesture that she knew, and the weight of loneliness and dejection which had been building found release. He dropped his massive head into the palms of his hands and the sobs which rocked his body threatened to collapse the tiny table. With her hand Sonovia lifted his head and said, "Comrade, the two things a revolutionary must never fear are death or prison. It's an eventuality we all face. Dry your eyes. I have an assignment for you."

Two

While they ate breakfast Sonovia thought over what the doctor had said of Toedoe's condition. "He can still function for several years as long as he eats properly and takes his medication regularly." The three of them finished breakfast and were ready to leave. They checked their weapons to ensure they were operative and each put on a bullet-proof vest. The apartment chosen for the night was located in a New African town in Texas near the Mexican border. For security reasons, Sonovia rarely left the national territory; but for the last week she had met with heads of progressive governments in Latin America to build support for the RNA. Kiswana and Toedoe stepped through the door first and Sonovia followed. The three walked briskly down the corridor and descended two flights of stairs to the front entrance of the apartment. They walked the thirty feet to the bullet-proof Mercedes, and Kiswana climbed into the driver's seat while Toedoe and Sonovia got into the back. Initially Sonovia had felt uncomfortable about the use of such an expensive car, but after it was explained that the car was chosen for its small size, durability, and quick acceleration, she had reluctantly conceded. The Mercedes moved slowly over the speed bumps NARA had placed in the parking lot to prevent would-be speeders from injuring children who played there. As the car slowed to exit the parking lot, Kiswana felt that familiar surge of pride she always did when in liberated zones. Just before the entrance to the projects stood a large sign which read:

> YOU ARE NOW ENTERING A LIBERATED ZONE UNDER THE PRO-
> TECTION OF THE N.A.R.A. WHILE HERE, THE FOLLOWING RULES
> WILL BE OBEYED—

The militarization of third world communities had at first been reluctantly accepted by New Africans who hoped that it would solve the drug problem. But as the National Guard and other u.s. security agencies began to attack progressive community activists and organizations, New Africans began to believe more of what NARA was saying: "The government's war on drugs is in fact a war against the community. It's not a war against poverty, racism, unemployment, and other horrendous conditions which push so many of our people into drugs."

The success of NARA in creating revolutionary programs to deal with the problems of drugs, housing, medical care, etc., had helped to establish its leadership credentials among the masses of people. The colonial administration of New African mayors and other elected officials had gradually collapsed faced with the success of hundreds of popular people's institutions. Crack and other drugs did not exist in the hundreds of liberated zones built inside the empire. And people of all ages who lived there felt safe. Money for rent no longer went to the housing authority; instead it went to NARA to maintain services ranging from people's clinics to what became the pride of all liberated zones— the people's store which never ran out of food. This was the reality which motivated New Africans like Kiswana, who was previously a crack addict, to change. When Kiswana was asked to become a member of the army she knew the RNA was a distant dream, but NARA made it concrete enough to believe in and fight for. It was a vision, in her mind, just within reach.

The Mercedes weaved smoothly through the Monday morning traffic to the destination where the reporter was to be brought for the interview. Despite the effects of more than 20 years of urban warfare and President Webster's position on the RNA, the streets were remarkably calm as the Mercedes moved through the business district of Fort Worth. Over the last year, tens of thousands of whites who sensed a NARA victory had been burning their property and migrating from the Southern states in angry protest—"I'd die before I live under a nigger communist regime," the white migrants would say. Two-thirds of NARA had been sent to the national territory to stem such acts of vandalism as well as check the violent reaction of the Klan to an independent RNA. Sonovia smiled when she thought of the KKK. They were tough until they met a people armed and prepared to fight back.

The apartment building where the interview was to be held could be seen ahead. Children played in the parking lot and mothers sat along the building talking with one another. Toedoe eased the car alongside an old beat-up Ford. The three of them climbed out of the car and walked down a flight of stairs to the boiler room. Toedoe knocked twice and when the door opened they stepped inside and adjusted their eyes to the dim light in the small musty room. Kimbue, who was the highest ranking member of the six comrades present, walked over to Sonovia and said: "Good morning, Commander, did you sleep well?"

"I did, thank you, Kimbue." Sonovia looked at the person seated behind the desk and asked: "Is that the reporter?"

Kimbue nodded and said, "Yes, Commander."

As Sonovia approached the desk, she sensed the young reporter was nervous as she started to stand and greet her. Sonovia reached out and touched her lightly on the shoulder and said, "Please be seated, Ms. Guadalupe. And relax. You're among friends."

The atmosphere in the room was suddenly less tense.

"Ms. Guadalupe," Sonovia said, "we've followed your stories on us over the years and felt they were both honest and objective. That's why we choose to have this interview with you. My name is Sonovia Oden-Muhammad and I'm Commander of the New African Revolu-

356

tionary Army, which is dedicated to an independent socialist Republic of New Africa. For the last 20 years NARA has waged war against u.s. imperialism. As of March 2, year 2003, that war was formally terminated with an announcement of public recognition by President Webster to recognize the RNA as an independent sovereign nation no longer under the jurisdiction of the u.s. government." She then looked at her watch and said: "For the next 20 minutes I'll answer as many of your questions as possible." The reporter nodded and produced a tape recorder from her purse. She turned it on and placed it in front of the Commander and began the interview.

"Commander, is it true that NARA has used and continues to use torture to further its aims?"

"Yes, this is quite true. We have done this. We torture lack of imagination without pity and we shoot down boredom without a trace of pity. We do this proudly and forthrightly."

The young reporter opened her mouth to protest this diversion, but then smiled and decided to move on to the next question.

"Commander, would you please tell me a little about Malik Shabazz, the person you were once rumored to have replaced as Minister of Defense?"

"Comrade Malik is a good revolutionary. I think his sensitivity makes him that. He has a singular capacity for amazement. Everything surprises him: the air, a dark sky, a bright face, the tracks of ants, the inevitable rising of the sun, the sounds of the sea. As Minister of Defense, comrade Malik's problem was that his background as a lawyer tended to hamper his initiative to push the struggle forward. In other words, he became too legalistic. One of the oddities of law compared to other areas of social science is that law has to be applied within the system. We have comrades who study economics, history, political science, sociology, but we take what we learn from these disciplines and use it to build a political movement which exists outside the system. It's very difficult, if not impossible, to do the same with law. Comrade Malik is of course still with us and continues to play an important role in the struggle, but in another capacity."

"Commander is it true that you were the leader of a faction within NARA that bitterly opposed Malik Shabazz's position on electoral politics?"

"Well, I wouldn't characterize my difference with my comrade as you did; but yes, I did take exception with his view that electoral politics could be used to push the struggle forward. My view, along with other comrades, was that to participate in elections was a violation of principle and not a tactical question as comrade Malik saw it. You see, our view was that under colonialism elections are used to divide our people and our leaders into opposing camps fighting for the right to control the colonial budget to administer our own domination. This divide and conquer tactic implemented by means of electoral politics gave u.s. imperialism absolute control over the political life of the New African nation. We felt that one of the conditions of independence was that we must place ourselves on the most favorable terrain where we, and not the imperialists, determine the rules of the game. We saw it as necessary to take the struggle for an independent RNA out of the enemy's electoral territory and into the streets, our territory, where we choose the forum in which to struggle, the how, when and where of the battle."

Sonovia paused, looked at her watch and said, "I have time for two more questions."

"You once took a position against seeking international support for the RNA. How do you reconcile this with your statement yesterday praising the international community for its support of the RNA?"

"Let me put that in context. When I became a member of NARO, a lot of time and resources went into trips abroad to develop support for our struggle as an oppressed nation. Gradually I began to disagree with this since we weren't gaining support and the resources used for these trips drained us to the extent where we couldn't put out a paper consistently. Given the vengeful nature of imperialism, I also felt that as revolutionaries we had no right to ask fraternal progressive nations to support a movement which at that time was not capable of supporting itself. My view was that our priorities should be toward developing a revolutionary mass movement which could project itself based on its strength—and then even imperialist nations in Western Europe could not deny our

358

existence. This way, when comrades went abroad to develop internatonal support they wouldn't be reduced to an intellectual discourse. Instead, their presence would reflect a concrete movement which had a voice people could hear."

"Last question, Commander. How do you envision a socialist RNA dealing with vices like drugs, crime, prostitution, etcetera?"

"People cannot behave according to truly human standards until they live under truly human conditions. The aim of socialism is to put the rule of reasoning back into all human activity. The supreme aim of socialism is humanistic in the highest and deepest sense. It is nothing less than the remaking of human beings in a thoroughly conscious and scientific manner. The prehistory of humanity will end and its development on a truly human basis will begin when wealth of all kinds flows as freely as water and is as abundant as air, and compulsory labor is supplanted by free time. Then free time enjoyed by all will be the measure of wealth, the guarantee of equality and harmony, the source of unrestricted progress and the annihilator of alienation. This is the goal of a socialist RNA, the promise of communism."

Sonovia stood and thanked the reporter for meeting with her, and asked that she wait five minutes after they left before leaving herself.

As the comrades began to walk toward the door, the reporter said, "Commander, the Mexican people inside Mexico and in the Southwest are happy over your victory. Imperialism has not erased our historical memory that the Southwest once belonged to us. But for Mexicans like myself who are colonized in the Southwest, we felt that this theft of our land was permanent. Your struggle has helped us see how a people determined to be free can create possibilities."

Sonovia smiled and said, "Thank you. It warms our heart to hear this."

As they emerged from the basement Sonovia bade Kimbue and the other two comrades farewell. She drove off in the Mercedes with Toedoe and Kiswana, and they began to discuss the latest reports from the national territory.

"Commander," Kiswana said, "it appears that comrade Cynthia miscalculated the numbers of New Africans who would migrate at once to the national territory. She didn't mean . . ."

Sonovia interrupted. "You never apologize for a comrade, you criticize them. Now give me some details. How far were our calculations off?"

"Yes, Commander. I have some figures here. The co-ops which have been built throughout the five states can house up to 3.8 million people. However, the number of New Africans migrating to the Republic of New Africa is three times that. Also, our medical provisions and food supplies have been devastated. Uh . . . and Commander . . . there are other problems that have been turning up."

"Go on, speak! What are they?" Toedoe barked.

"Well, a lot of New Africans in their seventies have been turning up throughout the five states with their grandchildren, producing deeds to land given to them by their parents. The problem is that these New Africans are driving whites off the land at gun point, insisting on the land back. In certain areas where the army is stronger, these incidents occur more frequently." Kiswana reached for the car phone and said, "Commander, I can get more information if you like."

"No, that's okay," Sonovia said. "Let's head for the national territory." She looked at her watch. "It's two o'clock now; with luck we can make Mississippi by dark."

Sonovia could tell from the flurry of activity ahead that they were approaching the border of the Republic of New Africa. Soldiers with K-9 dogs patrolled the border while helicopters hovered on the lookout for KKK infiltration. As the Mercedes came to a halt, a New African woman dressed in fatigues with an M-16 emerged from a booth to approach the car. One of the strengths of NARA was that it had attracted so many New African women. Over 47 percent of the guerrillas who made up NARA were women. Sonovia watched the young soldier approach the car and guessed she couldn't have been much more than sixteen.

"May I see . . ." was all she said before she recognized the commander and snapped to attention. "I'm sorry, Commander. I didn't know it was you."

"That's okay," Sonovia said.

The Mercedes moved slowly toward the soldier at the other end of the border crossing motioning them forward. Directly above the soldier's head was a sign which read

YOU ARE NOW ENTERING THE REPUBLIC OF NEW AFRICA— WELCOME.

Sonovia and her comrades breathed easier as they crossed the border, happy to be back in the national territory. The Mercedes slowed as it exited the highway to one of the major cities affectionately named Cush by New Africans. The city was crowded with late evening shoppers and a heavy concentration of military personnel could be seen among these pedestrians. But unlike under colonialism, New Africans who now wore uniforms were viewed as patriots and freedom fighters for the RNA.

As the Mercedes turned the corner to climb the hill to the capitol, Kiswana slowed down and watched in amazement the long line of New Africans who stood at attention saluting the car as it passed by. In a choked, cracked voice, Kiswana said, "Commander, they're standing at attention for you."

Sonovia looked into the faces of New Africans who ranged from age ten to eighty. Women stood at attention with babies in their arms while New Africans who were maimed by the war stood in salute on crutches.

The Mercedes pulled into the parking lot and the three of them emerged to walk toward the front entrance of the capitol. Just as Sonovia was about to climb the steps she noticed from the periphery of her vision a little girl who couldn't have been more than six, dressed in a pair of fatigues and tennis shoes. She wore tinted glasses and her hair was in dreadlocks. Like everyone else, she stood at attention with her right hand to her forehead in a salute. Sonovia approached the little girl, stopped and asked, "What's your name?"

"Sonovia," the little girl replied. But the little boy next to her said, "Stop lying, Genny, you name ain't no Sonovia."

"It is too," she pouted. "Mind you business."

Sonovia smiled and kissed them both on the cheek. Just as she rose to leave, the little girl said, "Commander, do I look like you?"

361

Sonovia looked at the little girl who stared up at her expectantly, and said: "You sure do!" She watched the child's face melt into a smile, then turned to climb the steps to the capitol.

Many difficulties lay ahead for the Republic of New Africa. Much of its economy had been destroyed by more than twenty years of war. Forecasts of doom for the future of the RNA could be heard from much of the imperialist world. But for the first time in over three hundred years, New Africans had the ability to shape their destiny in their own image, and they danced to the occasion with prayers to the God to protect the little nation and its people in the South.

Thomas Manning

Linda Evans

Linda, my sister,
sister of all
who long for
or fight for
real justice
and freedom.
My spirit
will always
vibrate so much stronger,
so much deeper,
having been touched
by you —
to feel your love,
strength, joy
and anger—
your beautiful
hate
of the enemy,
your eagerness
to sit and comfort a comrade
or stand with balled fists
to confront the oppressors.

Tom Manning
South Africa Will Be Free, 1989
ink on paper, 6 ½ ″ x 8″

Our fight will be that much stronger
our laughter that much louder
in liberation—
Because you are here
with us, in struggle
for as long as it takes.

Thomas Manning

(Note scrawled on a leaflet sent outside)

Sunday
Dear Maggie:
They seize these things
from our homes as evidence
then they supply us with copies
stamped with their numbers
and call it discovery
indeed
they only thing they really
discovered
is that we are for real
and it scares the shit
out of them
Love
Tommy

Chim Trang

from
The Rising Song

*Four verses by a revolutionary freed from a Saigon jail and
returned to Loc Ninh liberated area, February, 1973*

From the enemy jail a returnee,
I am singing now under a free sky.
The Loc Ninh forest is listening in deep silence
to the song which goes straight into man's heart . . .

The song now rises as high as the flames of hatred,
now whispers softly, kind and tender,
Now glows like the sun and glitters like the lodestar
Now thunders down the prisons . . .

The prison's wall could not
Cut us off from the land,
Nor fill my sleep with nightmares
And I dreamed of more and more greenery in my native village . . .

In the forest, patches of sunlight quiver.
The fighters listen, eyes red with crying,
No one cares about another day's decline,
And see only a perennial dawn ahead.

*From ELEVEN POEMS OF POLITICAL PRISONERS, Union of
Vietnamese in the U.S.: Berkeley, California. 1973.*

"It's this way:
being captured is beside the point,
the point is not to surrender."

— NAZIM HIKMET

Contributors

Mumia Abu-Jamal is a prisoner on Pennsylvania's Death Row. He is a writer with roots in the Ministry of Information of the Philadelphia, New York and National offices of the Black Panther Party, and a MOVE supporter. He is the past President of the Philadelphia Association of Black Journalists and his work as a radio journalist has been aired on the Mutual Black Network and National Public Radio. As a reporter he covered the 1978 police attack on MOVE, and as a result of his sympathetic coverage was himself targeted: he was shot and beaten, and a cop was shot and killed, on the streets of Philadelphia in September 1981. The prosecutor emphasized Mumia's Black Panther background ("of which I am in no way ashamed") in arguing for the death penalty. From his Death Row cell, Mumia Abu-Jamal continues to work tirelessly in support of others and writes for *Workers Vanguard, Big Red News, Revolutionary Worker, Jacobin Books,* and the *Journal of Prisoners on Prison (Journal des Prisonniers aux Prisons)* of Canada.

Sundiata Acoli, a New Afrikan political prisoner of war, mathematician and computer analyst, was born Jan. 14, 1937, in Decatur, Texas, and raised in Vernon, Texas. He graduated Prairie View A & M College in 1956 with a B.S. in Math and for the next 13 years worked for various computer-oriented firms, mostly in the New York area. During the summer of 1964 he did voter registration work in Mississippi. In 1968 he joined the Harlem Black Panther Party and did community work around issues of schools, jobs, housing, childcare, drugs and police brutality. In 1969 he and 13 others were arrested in the "Panther 21" conspiracy case. He was held in jail without bail for two years before being acquitted, along with all other defendants, by a jury deliberating less than two hours. Upon his release, FBI intimidation of potential employers shut off all employment possibilities in the computer profession, and stepped-up COINTELPRO harassment, surveillance and provocations soon drove him underground. In May 1973 while driving on the New Jersey Turnpike, he and his comrades were ambushed by NJ state troopers. One companion, Zayd Shakur, was killed, another companion, Assata Shakur, was wounded and captured, one state trooper was killed and another wounded; and Sundiata was captured days later. After a highly sensationalized and prejudicial trial he was convicted for the death of the state trooper and sentenced to Trenton State Prison (TSP) for life, plus 30 years consecutive. Upon entering TSP, he was confined to a newly created Management Control Unit (MCU) solely because of his politics. His stripped cell was smaller than the SPCA space requirement for a German Shepherd dog. He was only let out of the cell 10 minutes a day for showers and two hours twice a week for recreation and was subjected to constant harassment and attacks by guards. During one period he was not let out of the cell for six continuous months. In September 1979, *International Jurist* interviewed Sundiata and subsequently declared him a political prisoner. A few days later prison officials secretly transferred him in the middle of the night to the federal concentration camp at Marion, Illinois, although he had no federal charges or sentences. An entrance physical examination by federal medical personnel disclosed that he had been heavily exposed to tuberculosis while at Trenton State Prison. Marion is the highest security prison in the U.S., also one of the harshest, and there Sundiata was locked down 23 hours a day in a strip cell containing only a stone bed, toilet, wash bowl and a few personal items. Brutal conditions and violence are epidemic at Marion, where murders and assaults by guards and prisoners alike are common occurrences. During one turbulent period beginning in October 1983, all prisoners were confined to their cell blocks 24 hours a day for nine continuous months as wolf packs of guards roamed the complex beating prisoners at random. Sundiata spent eight years at Marion, longer than almost any other prisoner. In July 1987, he was transferred to the federal penitentiary at Leavenworth, Kansas, where he's presently confined.

Salvador Agron became known in the 1950s as the "Cape Man" after he was convicted of killing a white youth in a New York City gang fight. In his many years in prison he became politicized. He died in 1986 at the age of 43.

Hakim Al-Jamil was a New Afrikan political prisoner at Leavenworth at the time this poem was written.

Dalou Asahi, an Attica Brother, survived the massacre only to be killed in a shoot-out with police in Brooklyn in 1977. He wrote this bio at age 22:

Mariano Gonzalez, Born 1951 into family of eight, in a four room apartment in the ghetto of Spanish Harlem. Childhood Background: 3 or 4 J.D. cards in the 23rd and 25th precinct, never sent to a Youth Penal Camp, but been a victim of about 13 beatings (but between the ages of 9 and 15) supervised by law enforcers. Dalou possesses the normal scars of the average ghetto street Lumpen child, i.e., stitches, gun shot wounds and lacerations. *Educational and Social Background:* Elementary school graduate, J.H.S.

graduate, moderate drug user . . . certified poor . . . welfare recipient . . . 3rd world member and father of two out-of-wedlock children and community activist via Young Lords Party . . . skills: 6 years experience in tae-kwon-do . . . work: weeknights at community center P.S. 108 as tae-kwon-do instructor. *Dalou on Liberation:* "Only by re-educating the People and creating the atmosphere for constant mobilization (via armed struggle) can we move towards the inevitable phases of the Peoples' Revolution."

Kuwasi Balagoon defined himself as both a New Afrikan and an Anarchist. He was raised in a warm and loving DC-area family that he later expanded to include all of humanity. Originally one of the "Panther 21," and later an armed fighter with the Black Liberation Army, he escaped from prison several times, was captured after "Brink's" and sentenced to three consecutive life terms. A steadfast friend and a dangerous enemy, beloved for his fighting spirit and his irrepressible humor, he died of AIDS in 1985.

Alan Berkman is a northamerican revolutionary whose commitment to human rights and anti-imperialist struggle dates back to the early 1960s. Those commitments shaped his life as both a political activist and as a physician. He is currently imprisoned for activities related to the anti-imperialist armed clandestine resistance that developed in 1982-85.

Hanif Shabazz Bey and four other Virgin Islanders are serving eight (8) consecutive life sentences for the 1972 attack on the Rockefeller-owned Fountain Valley golf course in St. Croix, Virgin Islands. For more background, see *Crossroad*, Vol. 1, No. 1. For more information, write to Hanif (s/n B. Gereau) #96544-131, P.O. Box 1000, Marion, IL 62959, or contact Brother Al Saladin, Blisschords Communications Network, P.O. Box 53435, Chicago, IL 60653.

Terry Bisson served several months in a federal prison in 1985 along with five others who refused to collaborate with a Grand Jury investigating anti-imperialist bombings in DC. He is a writer and the editor of Jacobin Books.

Tim Blunk was born on May 21, 1957. Grew up in New Jersey. Mother is a teacher/musician; father, a Presbyterian minister. Graduated Hampshire College. Student activist in Western Massachusetts during the late 70s, working in solidarity with Southern African, Palestinian and Black liberation movements and campus human rights struggles. 1979— traveled to Cuba and Central America. Organized resistance to Ku Klux Klan and white supremacist violence in the Northeast. In New York City, employed as a daycare teacher; worked in solidarity with Puerto Rican independence movement. 1981— arrested and beaten by police in anti-apartheid direct action against South African Springbok rugby team's U.S. tour. Served one year at Riker's Island, New York City. 1984— arrested with Susan Rosenberg. Both took political position of captured members of anti-imperialist clandestine resistance, using "necessity defense" based upon international law; convicted of possession of weapons, explosives and false identification. Both received sentences of 58 years. Began serving sentence at USP Leavenworth. 1986— sent to maximum security federal penitentiary at Marion when accused by FBI of escape conspiracy with Puerto Rican POW Oscar Lopez Rivera and New Afrikan POW Kojo Bomani Sababu. 1988— charged with 5 other anti-imperialists in "Resistance Conspiracy Case." Accused of membership in revolutionary armed resistance and four bombings in Washington DC, including the 1983 bombing of the U.S. Capitol following the invasion of Grenada. A revolutionary artist and poet, Tim got Honorable Mention for his poetry in the 1990 Larry Neal Writer's Competition.

Kathy Boudin was born on May 19, 1943. May 19 is a very special day because it is also the birthday of Ho Chi Minh, Malcolm X, Augusto Sandino, and Lorraine Hansbury. It is the day that Jose Marti died. Kathy's father was a noted civil liberties lawyer and her mother is a poet. Their involvement and commitment to social causes was and continues to be an important part of Kathy's development. She graduated from Bryn Mawr College in 1965, after spending her senior year at Moscow University studying Russian language and literature. Coming back to the United States, she rejoined an SDS (Students for a Democratic Society) community organizing project in Cleveland, Ohio, where she lived for the next 3 years. From 1970 through 1981 Kathy was underground— until her arrest in Rockland County on October 20, 1981. After spending two years in isolation with her co-defendants and being moved to a variety of jails, she was finally placed in general population and is now at Bedford Hills Correctional Facility, New York State's maximum security prison for women. She has been teaching basic literacy and has completed a master's degree in education/adult literacy. She is also active in building a peer counseling and education program around AIDS and is a founding member of A.C.E.— AIDS Counseling and Education Organization. She has a wonderful son who is a member of a family of close friends, and a best friend and husband, David Gilbert, who was arrested at the same time she was. Her son has been the source of enormous joy and inspiration for her despite the pain of separation, and one of the things Kathy most enjoys doing is writing children's stories for her son and his brothers.

Marilyn Buck is a northamerican anti-imperialist. She is a long-time activist since supporting the Vietnamese people and the NLF against the U.S. war, the emerging Black liberation movement and women's liberation. Because of her consistent support for national liberation struggles worldwide and particularly her support for the Black struggle, she was targeted by COINTELPRO. In 1973 she received a 10-year sentence for buying two boxes of ammunition with false ID. She spent more than four years as a political prisoner and was denied bail. However, she got a furlough. She did not return. Although she was a fugitive she continued to support the Black liberation struggle as well as Puerto Rican independence and other international struggles. In 1985 she was captured after a concerted hunt by the Joint Terrorist Task Force. She was tried and convicted for participating in liberating Assata Shakur and in several bank expropriations. She is serving a 70-year sentence but is facing 45 years more since being indicted along with six other northamerican anti-imperialists for conspiracy to protest and alter U.S. government policies through violence against U.S. military institutions and the Capital. Marilyn believes that peace, social justice, and women's liberation can be realized only through victories of national liberation and socialism.

Judith Clark, a former member of SDS and the Weather Underground, was tried with David Gilbert and Kuwasi Balagoon in connection with the attempted "Brink's" armored car expropriation of 1981. She is serving 75-to-life in New York State prisons.

Edwin Cortés was born in Chicago, Illinois, on March 27, 1955. He is one of 15 children. He is married to his *compañera* Alva and together they have two children, Noemi, 10, and Carlos Alberto who is 8. As a student leader, he participated in struggles in support of the Iranian and Palestinian people. Edwin was one of the founders of the Union for Puerto Rican Students, an organization that defended student rights, promoted the history and culture of Puerto Rico and organized support for Puerto Rican independence. In 1978, he graduated from the University of Illinois, Chicago Circle Campus, receiving a B.A. in political science. Edwin was also active in several community struggles, particularly on the south side of Chicago, where he was born and raised. He helped found the Pedro Albizu Campos Collective, a group of independence activists who organized community and youth programs. He later helped establish the Latino Cultural Center. On June 29, 1983, Edwin was captured along with two other comrades and charged with seditious conspiracy. He is currently serving a 35-year sentence in federal prison. His biography was published in *The Indispensables* (bilingual publication, 1984). Address: Edwin Cortes, #92153-024, P.O. Box 1000, Lewisburg, PA 17837.

Barbara Curzi-Lamaan I was born in 1957 and am the mother of two daughters, 14 and 15 years old, and a six-year-old son, who I share with my comrade-husband, Jaan Karl Laaman. The youngest of four children, I was raised in an ethnic neighborhood in Boston where my grandparents settled after immigrating to the U.S. from Italy in the early 1920s. My parents worked in factories most of their lives. They taught us that everyone has a right and responsibility to their community and to themselves to develop to their fullest potential. As a working-class woman and mother, the struggles for decent health care and housing and against racism and pollution have always been part of my life. I saw that good health and education resources are available only to the privileged few. I saw that racism, sexism and class divide poor and working-class communities. They fight among themselves for the crumbs, too worn down to go after the real cause of the problem. In the mid-'70s, as Boston exploded with racist violence, I joined the Anti-racist Committee. From the community level, my view expanded to include international struggles against all kinds of suffering caused by imperialism. I have been in prison for four and a half years after living clandestinely with my husband and children for two and a half years. The government has threatened me with 265 years of sentences for being part of the underground anti-imperialist movement. After one trial, I received a 15-year sentence for conspiracy and for actions carried out by the United Freedom Front opposing U.S. government support for apartheid in South Africa and their war on the people of Central America. I became and will remain committed to building a just society in this country, free of racial and economic oppression. Whatever my conditions, I'll keep bright my vision and never stop working until we've built that better day.

Liz Davidson For the past several years I've lived in Vermont and worked with a coalition doing direct actions and education against the GE "gatling gun," favorite weapon of the Salvadoran military. I do support work around the DC Resistance Conspiracy case also. As I've become friends with some of the Resistance Conspiracy defendants, I've learned a lot about real hope and fighting to win. I want to see a common understanding of the need for Resistance bringing together people from the Sanctuary, Plowshares, Anti-Imperialist, and other movement communities. As an artist I'm equally involved with pen and spraypaint.

Joseph Doherty was born on January 20, 1955, and grew up in a working-class, republican ghetto in North Belfast. Unmarried, he is the eldest of five children; his parents and three of his sisters still live in Belfast. Joe joined the youth branch of the Republican MOVEment, a proscribed organization, when he was 15. When he turned 17, he was seized by the British Army and interned (no charges, no trial) for five months, first on the prison ship *Maidstone* and later in Long Kesh. His oldest sister and numerous relatives were seized as well. Upon release from internment, Joe joined the Irish Republican Army. In 1973 he was sentenced to one year for possession of firearms; in 1974 he was sentenced to ten years for possession of explosives. In 1981 he was sentenced to life for the shooting death of a British soldier resulting from a gun battle in Belfast between Doherty's IRA active service unit and British Army soldiers attached to the elite Secret Air Service (SAS). While awaiting conviction and sentencing on the charges resulting from this incident, Joe and seven other IRA volunteers escaped from jail. He fled to the Republic of Ireland and later, following the capture of several of his fellow escapees, made his way to the U.S. He lived quietly and peacefully until June 18, 1983, when he was seized in New York City by federal officials for having entered the country illegally. He was subsequently arrested pursuant to a request for extradition lodged by the United Kingdom. He has been held without bail since that date, in spite of the fact that a U.S. District Court has ruled that the acts for which his extradition is sought are not common crimes but rather offenses of a political character.

Bill Dunne is a prisoner of the state currently confined to the U.S. dungeon at Marion, IL. He was sentenced to 90 years for participation in the attempted armed extraction of a comrade from a Seattle jail in 1979, an operation allegedly financed by bank expropriation and materially facilitated by illegal acquisition of weapons, explosives, vehicles, ID, etc. He was given another 15 years as the result of an effort at self-emancipation from the U.S. Prison at Lewisburg, PA, in further pursuit of the first duty of the prisoner of war in 1983. There is no group or particular theoretical system to which Bill can subscribe completely or of which he claims to be an adherent. Radical left revolutionary collectivist synthesism strikes him as the most appropriate present course. The social organization to which humanity will eventually evolve is anarcho-socialist and it is toward that end the revolution for and in which Bill struggles is directed.

Elizam Escobar was born in Ponce, Puerto Rico, on May 24, 1948. His parents reside in Puerto Rico and are members of the Special Committee in Support and Defense of Puerto Rican Prisoners of War. His son Elizer is 11 years old and lives in New York. Elizam received a bachelor's degree in visual arts from the University of Puerto Rico and later continued his studies at City College, *Museo del Barrio* and the Art Students League in New York City. From 1979-80, Elizam taught at the *Museo del Barrio's* School of the Arts. He is considered one of our most illustrious Puerto Rican revolutionaries, poets and painters. His paintings have been exhibited in New York, Chicago, Philadelphia and in more than 10 Puerto Rican cities. The paintings he created in jail are currently being exhibited throughout the United States.

377

His works have been published in several magazines including *Beginnings* and *Currents*. He published a series in *De Pie y En Lucha* and soon will finish a collection entitled *The Onthological War Against the Art Market: An Act of Liberation*. His works have also appeared in the *Anthology of Latino Poets* in New York. Some of his more recent illustrations can be found in *Cuadernos de Poetica*, published in the Dominican Republic. *Quimera Editors* published his book, *Speech in the Night* and *Sonia Semenovena*, while another article appeared in the art magazine, *Left Curve*. Since April 4, 1980, Elizam has been serving a 68-year prison sentence, accused of seditious conspiracy. He was later accused of being a member of the Armed Forces of Puerto Rican National Liberation (FALN). Friends of Elizam, c/o Puerto Rican Cultural Center, 1671 North Claremont Avenue, Chicago, IL 60647. Elizam Escobar #88969-024, Box 1500, Colorado Unit, El Reno, OK 73036.

Linda Evans Born May 11, 1947, in Fort Dodge, Iowa. Revolutionary and anti-imperialist since 1967. SDS regional organizer against U.S. involvement in Vietnam and to support the Black liberation movement. Participated in 1969 delegation to North Vietnam to receive POWs released by the Vietnam-ese. Political/cultural worker in guerrilla street theater troupe, all-women's band, and women's printing/graphics collective in Texas. A lesbian, and active in the women's liberation movement and in the lesbian community. Organized support for struggles led by Black and Chicano/Mexicano grassroots organizations against the Ku Klux Klan, forced sterilization and killer cops. Fought racism, white supremacy, and zionism as a member of the John Brown Anti-Klan Committee. Worked with Southern Africa, Palestinian, and Central American solidarity organizations to raise material aid for national liberation movements and to oppose apartheid and U.S. intervention. Built support for Black/New Afrikan, Puerto Rican, and Native American POWs and political prisoners, and for the right of these nations to independence and self-determination. Began working to develop clandestine resistance movement capable of struggle on every front. Arrested May 11, 1985; convicted of harboring a fugitive and using a false name to buy four guns; serving a total sentence of 45 years.

Herman Ferguson is a Black educator and former NY school principal who worked closely with Malcolm X in his Organization of African Unity. A leader in the Ocean Hill-Brownsville struggle for community control of schools, Ferguson was targeted and framed under the FBI's COINTELPRO program and spent 19 years in political exile in Guyana. He returned to the U.S. to clear his name in 1989, at the age of 68, and is now a political prisoner in the NY State system.

Russell F. Ford Jimmy Carter did me one favor, at least. Being faced with draft registration brought a lot of us into the movement in a hurry. These days I live in a cabin in Vermont and correspond and visit with political prisoners. I'm also involved with Central America solidarity work, one local focus being the aircraft-mounted General Electric "gatling gun" built and tested in Vermont, and heavily used in the air war against the Salvadoran people. I recently spent a month working with the popular movement in El Salvador. In the long run, true "solidarity" means building a revolutionary movement here at home—what we bring back from Central America is as important as what we send down.

Larry W. Giddings Born October 6, 1952, in Rosstal, Germany. His mother is Silesian/German and his father is of various European and North American extractions. Larry spent his early years and some teens in Germany; with approximately eight years attending school and living in Glen Burnie, Maryland, until dropping out of high school. Wounded during a shoot-out and arms expropriation on August 21, 1971 (with four others, in Los Angeles, California), he was arrested at the scene. His trial focused on the need for armed struggle against the U.S. government and judicial system and the liberation of prisoners. Upon conviction, he received a 20 years-to-life sentence. New laws, and his status as a "first-time-felon" resulted in his parole after seven years. Larry spent more than a year on parole, working and living with a multi-cultural political, food and prison-support collective that was involved in progressive work in the San Francisco Bay Area. He then began clandestine activities. On October 14, 1979, Larry was again wounded and captured, this time during the liberation of a comrade from a Seattle, Washington, jail. Convicted on Escape (aiding), the shooting of a policeman, bank expropriations (used for funding the activities), and conspiracy, he received multiple sentences of life in prison and 75 years, all consecutive. He has no known parole opportunities. Larry's anti-authoritarian commitment, and non-nationalist political analysis, has played a key role in police repression of himself and friends, their trials, and later, his transfer from Walla Walla State Prison to the federal prison at Leavenworth, Kansas. Larry and his comrade William Dunne were transferred in August of 1982. Dunne has spent the majority of his federal time in Marion, Illinois, and Larry has spent the entire time in Leavenworth. From 1983-1988, Larry completed B.A. degrees in sociology and psychology with the University of Kansas. He is presently working toward completion of the M.A. degree in sociology, in the area of social movements. In Giddings' view, anti-colonialism and anti-imperialism are integral to an anti-authoritarian analysis and practice. In Larry's own words:

379

"I seek a world where people live without cultural, racial or national oppression. This can only happen in a non-nation-state world, a world without borders. My most inspirational historical example is that of the Seminole struggles of the 1800s, in Northern Florida, Oklahoma and finally in Northern Mexico and Texas. Indigenous People of various nations, Afrikans (both free-born and escaped from slavery), 'renegade' Europeans, and Maroons (ship-wrecked sailors and rebels from around the world) united under the banner of the Seminole and resisted the imperial slavocracy of the U.S. for decades. Some of these Seminole People continue to struggle to this day. These 'Seminole Wars,' as they are called, are filled with examples of non-authoritarian structures, multi-cultural developments and autonomy between a number of cultures united in struggle. It is from these roots that I believe a truly dynamic and successful movement for a socially and ecologically sound world will arise. A respect for the Indigenous People of the world and the environment is a primary step in creating this world."

David Gilbert, a longtime anti-imperialist, spent 10 years in the underground resistence before his 1981 capture in connection with the attempted "Brink's" expropriation in Nyack, NY. He was sentenced to 75 years to life in New York State and is currently being held at Attica. He's an AIDS activist and advocate for prisoners.

Pat Gros-Levasseur was arrested in 1984 while living underground with her husband Ray and their three children. Tried as one of the "Ohio 7," she won acquittal and was released after several years in prison.

Imam Hakim was born in North Carolina in 1942. He was raised in Philadelphia where he was almost beaten to death by police before his 18th birthday for violating curfew— an introduction to racism which was to shape his life of rebellion. In 1972 he and four other Black activists were charged with various anti-establishment bank robberies. In prison he became an Islamic spokesman and activist. Since filing a 1980 class action suit with other Muslims demanding religious freedom, he has been subjected to increasing harassment from the Bureau of Prisons. Address: POW Imam Hakim Abdul Hamid Ali (aka Charles Perry 41334-133), USP Marion, Box 1000, Marion, IL 12929.

Bashir Hameed I was born in Elizabeth, New Jersey, in December of 1940, the second oldest in a family of six children. I grew up in a little town just southwest of Elizabeth and north of Rahway, home of the infamous Rahway State Prison. My father was a butcher, and though he wasn't an educated man, he stressed education to all of his children. He constantly used the newspapers to show me examples of racism in America. He also told me about the various achievements of Blacks and refused to allow us to act in deferring ways to whites. Both my parents made great sacrifices to try to provide a decent life under the circumstances; for that I shall be forever grateful to them. I attended a racially mixed high school and experienced the subtle forms of racism prevailing in the North during that period. After graduating in 1958 I went to Delaware State College in Dover on an athletic scholarship. Though just three hours away from New York City by car, Delaware was like going back in time. Food service and hotel/motel accommodations were denied Blacks throughout the area. Students were refused service at the local Howard Johnson. While traveling to play other Black colleges in the area (Howard, Maryland State, Hampton, etc.) our stops and accommodations all had to be arranged at Black hotels and restaurants. All of this, mind you, while we were being taught that America was the land of opportunity, equal rights, and fair play. Totally disgusted with these glaring contradictions and the obsequious posture taken by school administrators toward the local white establishment, I returned to New Jersey the following year and attended Seton Hall University for a year. Tiring of that, I decided to see the world and joined the U.S. Army in early '61. After numerous run-ins with the military's racism, I parted with the Army in the summer of '61 with a general discharge, to both my relief and theirs. Still undecided about my goals, I returned to Delaware State that fall and completed another year. By now the student sit-in movement was hot and heavy on Black campuses across the South. I did not participate because of a low level of political consciousness— and sense enough not to buy the nonviolent philosophy which was the theme of the movement. I had also during this period been exposed to Malcolm, having seen him at rallies in New York City. I attended the Nation of Islam's Sunday services, though never embracing its philosophy. In January '63 I got married and moved to Jersey City, New Jersey. I became the father of a son that year and resided in that area, moving from job to job for the next few years. After the marriage failed in early '68, I moved to Berkeley, California. While working and living in the Bay Area, I began to follow the happenings with the Black Panther Party. Huey Newton's trial was taking place during this time and I followed it in the local papers. Toward the end of '68 I started going by the party's headquarters. After attending classes and participating in the party's new free breakfast program at St. Augustine Church, I fell in love with the party, its philosophy and its people. In early '69 I was sent back to New Jersey to try and help restructure the remnants of the New Jersey Chapter of the BPP, which had already come under attack by the U.S. Government and local police. The leadership of the Jersey City branch had been jailed for allegedly machine-gunning a local police precinct. The Newark branch office had been bombed and both branches were in shambles. The local police immediately started to harass me and my family. I was arrested numerous times while selling the party's paper, driving, and participating in community issues. In spite of this, we were able to reestablish the Jersey City branch and developed several free breakfast programs, free clothing drives, political education classes, etc., in the community. The attacks and frame-ups on various charges continued against party members. By the fall of '70 I was due to go to trial for several arrests, all for doing daily party work. Facing over twenty years, I left. I was arrested a year later and sentenced to Trenton State Prison, where I ended up doing four years. While there, Sundiata Acoli, John "Andaliwa" Clark, Kuwasi Balagoon, myself and others developed a study group. In September '75 I was released. In January '76 there was an attempted prison break in which Andaliwa was murdered and a prison captain shot. Having just been released I was a prime suspect as an outside source. Not having much faith in the criminal justice system, I left the area. In April '81 a van was stopped by two New York City cops in St. Albans, Queens. Two Black men exited the van, advanced on the police car, and fired into it 27 times. One cop died, the other was wounded. Another BPP member, Abdul Majid/Anthony La Borde, and I were suspects. I was arrested in Sumter, SC, four months later, Abdul the following year. Our first trial in '82 ended in a hung jury on the murder charge, two not-guilty charges for assault, and a guilty charge of 2nd degree attempted murder. The second trial was hung again after being declared a mistrial with the jury 8 to 4 for not guilty. The state, realizing its plight, instituted a reign of terror in '86 against family and friends. Three people—none of whom had been in the state of NY at the time of incident—were brought in as witnesses to state that we had admitted while in their company months later having been participants or in the area during the time of this act. We were sentenced to 30 years-to-life with the recommendation that we never be paroled.

Shaheem Malik Jabbar, a former pro football player and an activist in Harlem, served 17 months in federal prison rather than collaborate with a political Grand Jury investigating the Black liberation movement.

Jamal Josephs's poetry has been published in *Essence* magazine, the *New Life Journal* and the *New Afrikan Poetry* anthology. His articles have appeared in *Karate Illustrated* magazine, the Vanguard Press and The Liberation News Service. He is a co-author of *Look for Me in the Whirlwind*, published by Random House. The steel of Jamal's artistic sword was forged in the political fires of the sixties and seventies. As a teenager he joined the ranks of the Black Panther Party. He soon moved into the circles of Panther leadership, becoming a spokesman and program coordinator. He helped to

382

implement and run the Free Breakfast Program, the Free Health Clinic, the People's Legal Clinic, the Black Student Union and several tenants and welfare rights organizations. He also traveled and lectured extensively on behalf of the Panthers. Jamal was destined to spend close to ten years in prison as a direct result of his involvement in the Party.

Sekou Cinque T. M. Kambui, a veteran civil rights activist and a conscious New Afrikan, is a political prisoner in Alabama.

Vincent Kay My most significant "stint" in prison was for my participation in the 1982 "Trident Nein" action at the Electric Boat shipyard in Groton, Connecticut. Nine of us damaged, with sledge hammers, the missile hatches of the Trident submarine, the USS Florida. I did a year for that one. At present I'm the director of the Phoenix Poetry Series in Connecticut.

Katya Komisaruk. I am a Jewish anarcho-feminist, with considerable confidence in nonviolence as a tool of social change. I was born in 1959, in Detroit, MI. I became politicized in 1982, while getting an M.B.A. at U.C. Berkeley. It was there that I woke up to the role of the defense industry in escalating the arms race. I am affiliated with the Plowshares Movement. My particular group is named in honor of (and is in contact with) an earlier White Rose Group which resisted Hitler— and was mostly executed by the Gestapo. In June of 1987, I hiked onto Vandenberg Air Force Base and destroyed a NAVSTAR computer, designed to guide nuclear missiles during a U.S. first strike. On the remains of the machinery, I listed the treaties our country has signed, in which we promised never to initiate a war of aggression or genocide— like a nuclear first strike. My trial was brief. I was not allowed to mention the treaties precluding nuclear war. The judge forbade me to say the very words "nuclear missile," "first strike" or "international law" in the courtroom. Upon conviction, I was sentenced to serve five years in federal prison.

Jaan Karl Lamaan Born in 1948, grew up as a working class youth during the Vietnam War in upstate New York. Served a five-year sentence as a youth offender; sent to Attica in 1970, after becoming an activist, for violating parole. Spent seven years in prison after a 1972 conviction for bombing a Nixon re-election headquarters and a police station in New Hampshire. Moved to Boston in 1979, went underground in 1981. He was captured 1984 along with his wife Barbara and others of the "Ohio 7."

Raymond Luc Levasseur. Born October 10, 1946. Convicted in 1985 for bombing u.s. military facilities and multi-national corporations. Sentenced to 45 years imprisonment. Presently on trial with comrades known as the

"Ohio 7" for seditious conspiracy and RICO charges. I have 3 daughters: Carmen, 13, Simone 11, and Rosa, 9.

Oscar Lopez-Rivera was born in San Sebastian, Puerto Rico, on January 6, 1943. At the age of 12, he moved to Chicago with his family. He was a well-respected community activist and a prominent independence leader for many years prior to his arrest. Oscar was one of the founders of the Rafael Cancel Miranda High School, now known as the Dr. Pedro Albizu Campos High School and the Juan Antonio Corretjer Puerto Rican Cultural Center. He was a community organizer for the Northwest Community Organization (NCO), ASSPA, ASPIRA and the First Congregational Church of Chicago. He helped to found FREE (a half-way house for convicted drug addicts) and ALAS (an educational program for Latino prisoners at State Prison in Illinois). He was active in various community struggles, mainly in the area of health care, employment and police brutality. He also participated in the development of the Committee to Free the Five Puerto Rican Nationalists. In 1975, he was forced underground, along with other comrades. He was captured on May 29, 1981, after 5 years of being persecuted by the FBI as one of the most feared fugitives from U.S. "justice." Oscar, who has a 17-year-old daughter named Clarissa, is currently serving a 55-year sentence for seditious conspiracy and other charges. He was recently convicted of conspiracy to escape along with Jaime Delgado (a veteran independence leader), Dora García (a prominent community activist), and Kojo Bomani-Sababu, a New Afrikan political prisoner. During his incarceration, he has written many short stories and articles for *Libertad*. He also writes for the pro-independence publication *Patria Libre*. Oscar is considered one of the most brilliant political thinkers in Puerto Rico. (Oscar López-Rivera #87651-024, P.O. Box 1000, Marion, IL 62959)

Paul Magno, Jr. is a peace activist in Washington, DC. He has been a member of the Catholic Worker movement there since 1981 and lives at the Olive Branch Catholic Worker house with his wife, activist Marcia Timmel, and their daughter, Sarah. Working with the Plowshares direct disarmament movement since the early 1980s, he served 20 months in Federal Prison as a result of his participation in the Easter 1984 Pershing Plowshares action in Orlando, Florida. Paul was born in Boston on November 26, 1956, and graduated from Georgetown University in 1978 with a degree in sociology.

Tom Manning
· A Boston native from a large, Irish, working class family.
· Joined the military in the fall of '63, doing tours of duty in Guantanamo Bay, Cuba, and Quang Tri province, Vietnam; discharged in August, 1966.

384

· Sentenced to 5 years, Walpole State Prison, armed robbery, assault & battery. Discharged, May 1971.

· In the early 1970s he and his comrade wife, Carol Saucier Manning, worked with an organization of prisoners, ex-prisoners and their loved ones ("SCAR") serving many parts of the community finding jobs and housing for people coming out of prison, trying to stay out. Moral support and welfare advocacy for families, transportation to the jails and prison for visitors, childcare, organizing youth, a bail fund, a bookstore with a free books-to-prisoners program coast to coast ("Red Star North") and a newspaper that covered local, national and international struggles, the "SCAR'd Times."

· Went underground in the mid 1970s to continue work of a progressive/clandestine nature in support of those struggles— local, national, international. Captured in April 1985, charged with being members of the "Sam Melville, Jonathan Jackson Unit" that carried out armed actions in the 1970s and the "United Freedom Front" that carried out similar actions in the 1980s. Charged with seditious conspiracy he recently was severed from the "Ohio 7" trial at Springfield, MA, to begin a life sentence in NJ for the 1981, self-defense killing of a state trooper and 53 years federal time for the United Freedom Front bombings.

· He and Carol are the parents of a girl, Tamara, and two boys, Jeremy and Jonathan.

Mike McCoy is a "social prisoner" in the federal system. He is active in the NAACP and writes for a number of progressive journals. He hails from the DC area.

MOVE (A collective biography of the imprisoned MOVE members written by Mumia Jamal):

The MOVE evokes shadowy imagery, resistance, surely, but "Who?" and "Why?" echo like continuing drops of rain on the mind's windowpane. We attempt here to address the questions, as regards imprisoned MOVE members, at least. Members of MOVE come to the naturalistic clan from all walks of life, some for widely different reasons. Some, like Chuck, entered as a youth. Others, like Delbert, joined as an adult. All exhibit a militancy, a tight sense of cohesion, and an *esprit de corps* that can only be called remarkable in the face of the repression that MOVE has had to endure in its relatively short but intense, eventful history. To quote MOVE founder, John Africa: "A REVOLUTIONARY MUST BE OF ONE MIND, DRIVEN BY ONE FORCE, IN ONE DIRECTION, A REVOLUTIONARY MUST UNDERSTAND THE ADVANTAGE OF ONE MIND, ONE FORCE, ONE DIRECTION, A REVOLUTIONARY MUST THEN BE WILLING TO APPLY THIS PRINCIPLE SO THAT THE MIND CAN BE SET TO ONE AIM, THE AIM OF REVOLUTION, FOR IT IS THIS SINGLE AIM

385

THAT WILL THRUST YOU ONWARD WHEN ALL ELSE FAILS . . . ." (from *Strategic Revolution* by John Africa, unpublished) Long Live John Africa! MOVE, in an age of the dismantling of "revolutionary" socialist states, as in Eastern Europe's Warsaw Pact nations, retains a militant sense of resistance to the re-form World system, and is still of one mind pointed toward revolution . . .

Ramona Africa (07564, P.O. Box 100, Muncy, PA 17756) Probably one of the best-known MOVE members, 'Mona is serving a seven-year sentence for daring to survive the fiery holocaust of May 13, 1985, when police forces, following several months of planning, rained deadly incendiary bombs on MOVE's Cobby Creek area home and headquarters, from which a badly burned, permanently scarred 'Mona emerged, the sole adult survivor. Calls for Ramona's freedom have come from around the world, notably the London-based Ramona Africa Support Group (2318 Lambeth Rd., London SEI 7JY, U.K.) 'Mona, a Temple University graduate, came to MOVE via the revelations she witnessed at MOVE trials during the late 70's in Philadelphia. As a paralegal for a center city-based tenants' support group, she was attracted to the notion of going back to school, to net a law degree. What happened? MOVE happened. "When I *heard* the undisputable wisdom of *John Africa* that MOVE people put out durin' the trials I knew that *John Africa* had *completely* nullified the *entire* legal system and I had to decide whether or not I was gonna *try to ignore* what John Africa have *proven* about the legal system and arrogantly proceed with a career in legal law *knowin* the legal system *ain't just, ain't rite,*" 'Mona wrote.* Her own persecution (so-called "prosecution") proved beyond the shadow of a doubt the injustice, and unrighteousness, in the legal system. For her part, her survival, she was punished severely. The cops who bombed her, the FBI/AFT agents who suppled the deadly explosives, the politicians who gave the nod, the firemen who stood by watching sky-high flames consume people, who offered jokes instead of water, have never, ever been charged with any crime, state or federal. That 'Mona had to do even a day in jail, when at least 11 members of her family were incinerated in their own homes, is itself a crime.

Chuck Africa (3901 Klein Blvd., Lompoc, CA 93438) Chuck entered MOVE, as a barefaced preteen, one of the youngest and most militant of Africas. Like many MOVE folks, he is laconic when it comes to speaking of himself, but stirring and lucid when writing about the evils of this system. Of his background, he "lived the typical slave existence; hunger, pain, family break-up."* Chuck was one of the MOVE 9 framed in the notorious cop assault on MOVE of August 8, 1978, in University City, West Philadelphia. During the siege, he was shot by police, but the healthy youth recovered. The October 1989 riots which rocked Pennsylvania prisons touched Chuck's life, as he was housed in the hole of the infamous Camp Hill prison, and there became the victim of a premeditated assault by guards imported from nearby Dallas (Pa.) prison, to assist in quelling the rebellion. Fortunately, due to his remarkable strength, he protected himself from his armed, armored assailants. Shortly thereafter, Chuck found himself moved from prison to prison, day by day, until he was housed in the Federal Correctional Institution at Lompoc, in Southern California. He remains a motivated, upbeat, fit, MOVE soldier.

Eddie Africa (P.O. Box 1000, Leavenworth, KS 66048) Minister of Education. Ed came to MOVE from the streets of West Philly, and a religious background that he describes as "racist." In his own words Ed describes his life, pre-MOVE: "When I first came in contact with MOVE I was a follower of Elijah Muhammad, known as the Black Muslims. I was an 'avid' drug user and sickened with epilepsy also. I was attending school thinking to help *Black* people thru education, *Black education*, because i was a *racist* who thought *all whites* were *devils*. Upon coming into MOVE which has *all* races, *Black, White, Spanish* or whatever, it was shown to me that *racism* is a disease that sickens all those infected with it; since coming to MOVE I have come to realize that the *only* consideration is that you work to be *right*, work to get close to *God*, to *life*, work to understand that *all* life is the *same*, all created by *God*. The prejudice, confusion that separates life, man from woman, parent from child, black from white, Spanish from Indian, that creates class, levels, superiority, inferiority, all these problems come from man's education, man's reference, this system, and until people understand what our *Coordinator, John Africa*, teaches, that the only *true law* is the *law of God*, life, people will continue to be plagued by man's system of confusion." Ed, like Chuck, was also at Camp Hill during the wave of destruction. He was transferred to the federal facility at Leavenworth, Kansas.

Phil Africa (P.O. Box 1000, Leavenworth, KS 66048) The loquacious Phil is widely remembered for his retort to MOVE's infamous sentencing/trial judge, Edwin S. Malmed, at the conclusion of the 1981 trial of himself and 7 others MOVE codefendants for the trumped up murder charge stemming from the death of a cop during the August 8, 1978, siege of MOVE HQ. After being told that he was sentenced to 30-to-100 years, the organization's Defense Minister reacted in righteous indignation, telling the biased jurist, "John Africa was *right* about y'all! You ain't nothin' butta pawn for politicians, an errand boy of big business and the trash man of industry to clean up their filth, just like *John Africa* say! You ain't just, you ain't clean, you ain't true!" Phil bellowed, citing an excerpt from the *Judge's Letter* (written by *John Africa*). Phil, like Ed, was also transferred to the federal system in the aftermath of the October 1989 rebellion at Camp Hill, and as of this writing is being held in Leavenworth.

Mike Africa (AM 8335, Drawer R, Huntingdon, PA 16652) Mike came to MOVE via the U.S. Marines and the Muslims, and was attracted by MOVE's street and courthouse demonstrations against judicial injustice. He participated in MOVE demonstrations at the Philadelphia Zoo protesting the caging of animal life as an injustice way back in the 1970s, long before the "animal liberation" movement of the 1980s. MOVE's position— the caging of any life was an act of criminal exploitation. Their loud but nonviolent protests against the legal evil of animal incarceration merited MOVE numerous arrests, beatings and jailings.

Delbert Africa (AM 4985, Drawer K, Dallas, PA 18612) The face and form of Delbert is known internationally as the unarmed, unshirted Black man who was beaten on TV at the bloody conclusion of the August 8, 1978, police assault on MOVE's Powelton Village headquarters and home. In another stark instance of injustice, stemming from anti-MOVE bias, the cops who rifle-butted, helmet-slapped, jack-booted, stomped and pummeled Delbert's prone figure, were all acquitted in a sham of a trial, despite indisputable videotape evidence of an unprovoked naked assault. Delbert, in the aftermath of the August 8th war, was called by one prominent Philadelphia Black official, "The greatest Black man who ever lived." Delbert would disagree. [The remark was made by Phildelphia City Councilman Lucien Blackwell in a broadcast interview with this reporter.— MJ] Delbert, a quiet, articulate MOVE member, has been held in the "dungeon" at Dallas prison for several years now, on the pretext that he will not cut his hair. His powerful, insightful oratory reminds one of his southern roots, where spirited preachers have touched hearts and minds for centuries. But Delbert's message, the *Teachings of John Africa* is neither religion, nor reform, but revolution, and revolt against this reform world system's way of death. A former Black Panther, Delbert credits his health and strength to the specific teachings of *John Africa*, which healed crippled, painful legs that he was told would never run again. Today he runs miles with ease.

Merle Africa (O-6306, P.O. Box 180, Muncy, PA 17756) Despite the "injustice; inequality, and murder" that MOVE folks have suffered at the hands of this system, Merle, a member since 1973, calls her life in MOVE "the most satisfying and happiest I have ever experienced." She adds: "Before joining MOVE, I had relatively the same type of existence as everybody else . . . school, a job, plenty of problems and no hope of finding solutions to my problems. My only outlet was intoxication. I was an alcoholic from the age of 8 and a drug addict since 15. My father was a heavy drinker, along with other relatives, as a young child they would let me take a drink from their glasses— 'taking a sip' until I acquired the taste for liquor and as I got older I started sneaking drinks until I turned into a drunk." Her childhood, she says, was "far from happy," and she describes herself then as "fat and mentally unstable." This chronic unhappiness led to severe bouts of depression, until it led to abuse of diet pills, speed, cocaine, heroin— in her own words, "I took any drug from angel dust to acid because I wanted to escape the confusion and pain I was experiencing." The drugs, the violent behavior, the depression led to the brink of psychiatric hospitalization. To escape, and find a new situation, the Germantown-reared young woman fled to West Philly— where she met MOVE. First curious, then intrigued, she attended study sessions where MOVE members explained to community folk the teaching of *John Africa*, and Merle says: "John Africa's teaching opened my eyes for the first time to what was *really* causing my frustration and confusion— this system. I realized that I didn't have to be a floormat for this government any more— take what they dish out and not being able or capable of speaking out and being heard. *John Africa* teach that I *do* have a reason for living and the reason is *so* simple— to live in *harmony* with *life*, *Mama Nature* without suffering, and this was something that psychiatrists and ministers could never answer when I asked them to tell me *truthfully* why was I here when I was suffering so badly. *John Africa* have taught me that I *do* have something. *Very* reliable, *very* effective and *very powerful* to fight this system with and win! *Long Live John Africa Forever!*"

Sue Africa (O-6325, P.O. Box 180, Muncy, PA 17756) Sue came from the most unlikely of backgrounds— white, well-to-do, upper-middle class, academically oriented, with a heavy scientific bent— to meet and merge with the predominantly Black, money-poor, lower-class, anti-technology, radical, MOVE organization. Also, her background was one of sickness, nervousness and serious kidney problems beginning at the age of 7, which demanded "constant hospitalization, treatment, operations and medication all [her] life until [she] came into MOVE." Her mother, diagnosed as manic depressive at 30, remains so some 46 years later, and that neurotic influence had its impression upon her; she was similarly diagnosed in her 17th year as manic depressive. Her father, an engineer and inventor, developed the ejection catapult seat for the Frankfort Arsenal, and later died from a brain tumor. It was mother, however, who provided psychic influence over young Sue, who grew into a younger mirror-image— sickly, headachey, drugged by Darvons and other pain killers. She sought all the classic roads to relief— college, travel, various religions, politics, psychiatrists, and drugs— but relief did not come, until 1973 when she met MOVE folks, and was introduced to the teachings of *John Africa.* "Now," she explains, "At 40 years of age thanks to the powerful profoundly wise teachings of *John Africa* I am cured of being a manic depressive. I don't even *get* depressed anymore thanks to my strong belief which has made me strong of mind as well as strong of limb. I can and have run as long as 40 miles, and run 5 miles every morning here at Muncy Prison. I don't get headaches anymore, haven't even had an aspirin tablet in 16 years. I don't have a kidney condition anymore as it was *cured* by John Africa. I don't even catch cold anymore and wear a size 12 instead of a size 18. I gave natural birth to my son Tomasso in my own house, *aided only by the principle of motherhood taught to me by John Africa! Long Live John Africa Forever!* There were no doctors, no nurses, no midwife, there was no medical treatment assisting me in *any* way, not even my husband was needed by me. I suffered *no* labor pain, ran 5 miles the morning *of* my delivery and did 50 situps the morning *after* delivery and this is due only to the powerful coordination of *John Africa!*" This remarkable tale is all the more remarkable as it is true. The *Philadelphia Tribune,* in fact, published a piece on it shortly after her son's birth. Tomasso was one of the child martyrs of the May 13th, 1985, bombing of the Africa house by city police. Prison officials rushed to Sue's cell with news of his murder, not to console a mother gripped in grief, but to torment a revolutionary woman with "news" of her son's torture. Sue remains a strong MOVE soldier, committed to *John Africa's* Revolution.

Janine Africa (O 6309, P.O. Box 180, Muncy, PA 17756) The memory of Janine is one of those things that marks time for me as a man and as a journalist. Over 15 years ago, the MOVE mother sat on a tree stump, crying a river; her body shook in waves of grief. I had the unpleasant duty to report on the death of a MOVE child, following a late nite raid on MOVE's house on 33rd Street, a death that police denied arrogantly, saying, "no such kid lived cuz there ain't no birth certificate." It *was* a dead MOVE baby— her baby— Life Africa, knocked from her arms by club-swinging cops, crushed under police jackboots buffed to a severe spit-shine, left lifeless, his light brown naked body crushed and broken. The bane of a reporter's existence— how do you interview a young Black mother whose child was trampled to death by cops who act as if they stepped on roach? Do you ask, "how do you feel?" Do you dare? You set up your tape recorder and wait— no rush. You sit with her, you feel for her, and see beyond the crazy hairstyle, to *your* sister, *your* daughter, your kin caught in the hellish throes of countless Black mothers since Africans touched these shores, their babies targets marked from birth. You listen. You look away to allow hot tears to fall for a beautiful wild child who will no longer feel the sun on his brown skin— in anger— no— hatred at the forces which bind and crush our souls in the name of the "law." "I was a very unhappy person before joinin' MOVE. I was unhappy because I was very disappointed and I was disappointed because I did everything this system said to do to be happy and I wasn't happy. I went to school and got A's but I wasn't happy. I started experimentin' with alcohol and parties because I was taught that that was fun and exciting— that didn't make me happy. I got a job, that didn't make me happy. I started usin' drugs because that was supposed to make me feel good and forget my troubles, that didn't make me happy. I got married, had a child, that didn't make me happy— all me and my husband did was argue and fight and I took my frustration out on my child. All of this, the alcohol, the parties, the drugs, the job, the arguments and disappointment had turned me into an emotional wreck; my nerves was so bad that my throat would close up, cuttin' off my breath. I went from doctor to doctor and none of them could do anything for me, I couldn't get no relief nowhere I turned. It was so bad that I was contemplating *suicide* to get relief. I would have committed suicide too if I hadn't found *John Africa! John Africa* brought me into the MOVE Organization, took me off of cigarettes, alcohol, drugs and cured the problem with my throat! *Long Live John Africa Forever!*" Her son Phil was a child martyr who was murdered in the May 13th police bombing. She remains strong and committed to MOVE.

Carlos Africa (AM 7400, Drawer K, Dallas, PA 18612) Carlos, of Puerto Rican origin, has been a dedicated MOVE member for many years who has suffered and sacrificed to uphold his belief. Like Delbert, the outspoken Carlos has spent years in the holes of Dallas for refusing to violate his faith, the teaching of *John Africa*, and cut his hair. As with Carlos and other MOVE men, this is used as a pretext to justify locking Africans down, to blunt their influence among prisoners, through isolation. Carlos used to virtually *preach* MOVE *law* in both Spanish and English from the barricades of West Philadelphia MOVE Hqs. Carlos met MOVE members in jail while doing time, and was attracted to the clarity and power in *John Africa's* teaching. Since joining he has been a loyal, dedicated MOVE member, widely respected among Puerto Rican and African prisoners, and all folks who know him.

Debbie Africa (O-6307, P.O. Box 180, Muncy, PA 17756) When MOVE folks speak of miracles, the remarkable example of Debbie Africa is never far from mind. In a letter to a supporter, she detailed her life before MOVE, and in MOVE, by describing herself as an "insecure, unsatisfied" young woman: "When I was 14 years old I got pregnant and my mother influenced me to get an abortion. After I had an abortion it completely messed up my productivity and caused me to be sterile. I couldn't have children before I came into MOVE because of that, and it wasn't until I was in MOVE after 3 years that I was able to have babies, after our *Coordinator* worked with me and my husband for those 3 years (for example coordinating my diet and giving us information from the teaching of *John Africa* to correct what this system did to me). I was 21 years old when I had my first baby. I had a healthy strong baby girl *naturally* at home, with *no* medicine, no *midwife*, no IV drugs, pills, nothing but me and my baby aided *only* by the principle of motherhood. I had my 2nd child 2 years later naturally also. I was in prison [the so-called House of 'Correction,' N.E. Philadelphia. -MJ] for the case I'm serving time for now *unjustly*; I had my 2nd child in my jail *cell* and had a strong healthy son the same way I had my daughter and *all* MOVE women have our babies. *Long Live John Africa the Coordinator!* Now that I am in MOVE I do have happiness, security, true satisfaction because true satisfaction comes from doing right . . . thanks to *John Africa* I got a strong loyal husband, children, a *true family* yet MOVE is a money poor organization, we don't believe in fashion and cosmetics or material things, we believe in *life*, we live simple, we don't drive fancy cars or wear fancy clothes and we're *happy, healthy*, strong, *secure*, truly satisfied, because when you do right you *feel* right, you feel *content*, satisfied, truly happy. Thanks to *John Africa*'s teaching I have all I want all I need and all I'm interested in . . . . *Long Live John Africa!*"

Janet Africa (0-6309, P.O. Box 180, Muncy, PA 17756) Short, intense, Janet is a veteran of both the August 8, 1978, and the May 20, 1977, confrontations between MOVE and the system. Her daughter, Delisha, was martyred in the May 13, 1985, mass murder police bombing of MOVE folks. This militant MOVE mother remains committed to John Africa's family, telling one publication that "these have been the best years of my life despite all the injustice, prejudice, persecution spit on MOVE by this system. I wouldn't give up my belief for nothing this system has got to offer."*

Alfonso Africa (AY-5522, Drawer K, Dallas, PA 18612) Tall, lanky "Mo" Africa has experienced first hand the bitter injustices of this system when it comes to MOVE people. Although his manner is quiet, his mien thoughtful, he too has been the butt of the most outrageous of "legal" shenanigans by the judiciary widely regarded as America's most corrupt—Philadelphia's. Attacked by gun-wielding cops in June 1984 on bogus traffic infractions, Mo, unarmed, defended himself against his aggressors, and was shot, whipped and jailed, on charges of aggravated assault on a cop. As he left home on the way to court, he was again set upon, and brutally attacked by blue-shirted nazi cops, and later wrote of this encounter: "When I got to court, my blood-soaked clothes was disordered and in disarray, while cuts and knots was swollen on my head and body."* Attacked, dazed, beaten by cops with the clear intent to intimidate, Mo continued to trial, and defended himself with the teachings of *John Africa*. Remarkably, the jury acquitted Mo of the assault charges, but the racist prosecution did not end there. In his closing arguments to the jury, Mo explained that based upon history in Philadelphia, a MOVE defendant could expect no justice in a court of law, and that if the jurors did not reject this clearly biased frame-up, he would pursue civil litigation in defense against them, the judge, the DA and the cops. For this expression of his presumed "constitutional right of free access to the courts," Mo was charged with terroristic threats, and, incredibly, battery— a crime stemming from colonial and Civil War days to discourage people from filing suits in court. In a catch-22, Mo, though acquitted of aggravated assault, was convicted of threats! No one, it needs noting, who assaulted Mo was ever even charged with a crime! He was sentenced in 1985 to 7 years in prison.

Consuewella Africa (O-6434, P.O. Box 180, Muncy, PA 17756) Consuewella, a veteran of both the May 20, 1977, and August 8th, 1978, confrontations between MOVE and the system, has another deep link in the chain of racist injustice. May 13, 1985, the Mayor Goode-approved bombing of MOVE's home meant murder for two of her girls, Tree and Netta Africa, both in their early teens, both child martyrs to American infamy. The deeply committed MOVE mother is frank and open about her searing pain: "It is very painful and upsetting to think about. But I will not give into this corrupt rotten system of double standards, paradoxy, lawlessness. I will continue to fight it. I'm grateful that I'm a member of the MOVE organization. My life in MOVE is everything I was looking for in the system, a family, home, love, security, confidence."* Consuewella is a shining example of the depth of commitment in MOVE, inspired by *John Africa*'s teaching. On the eve of the "prosecution" (persecution) of MOVE veterans of the August 8, 1978, police assault and confrontation, prosecutors approached her with a deal: Denounce John Africa, quit MOVE, and we won't charge you— you'll go free. The dedicated, principled revolutionary mother refused the offer and was charged and convicted of conspiracy— the "crime" of being a MOVE member— and sent to prison for a decade. She remains a strong, deeply dedicated naturalist revolutionary, despite being a victim of America's most blatant act of state terrorism in modern-day history.

Conclusion Facing beatings of startling brutality, unjust imprisonment, judicial vengeance, legalized police terrorism culminating in a government bombing, MOVE has every reason not to exist today. That they do, is testament not only to their gritty determination, which is utterly remarkable, but offers poignant proof of the power of a belief— the teaching of *John Africa*— the power of an idea. Many would have succumbed to far less repression, with good reason. That MOVE remains active, engaged, militant, united in spirit despite a dispersal across the nation, and in death, across the very cosmos, forces us to come to grips with their central motivating theme: the teachings of *John Africa*. For it is for this, that MOVE has shed their tears, their years, their blood, their brood— to energize the world with a way of life singularly at odds with accepted, everyday life; to bring this teaching to the fore. In an age of Marxist retreat and capitalist advance, where greed goes global, and need goes grievously unrequited, where multi-billion-dollar multinational corporations span continents in search of profit, while millions of refugees, from war, from want, both within and without the empire, continue their fruitless search for help and home, the teaching of *John Africa* has a place. There must be room for a teaching that bridges Black and white, that submerges rank and class into the sea of common, that exalts the natural world as an integral part of ourselves, that regards all life as one all, and that makes health not a mystery, but a reality. For a world, split into rich and poor, is a world breeding war. For a world, severed by race, is a pretty dangerous place. For a world, choking on pollution, is deeply in need of solution. MOVE points to *John Africa*'s teaching. There are lessons for us all to learn here.

(by Mumia Abu-Jamal with the permission and cooperation of MOVE; all starred quotes are from *Class Struggle Defense Notes*, PDC, Box 99, Canal St. Sta., New York, NY 10013)

Sekou Odinga I was raised in a family of nine, with three brothers and three sisters. My schooling ended in the 10th grade when I was kicked out for defending myself against an attack by a teacher. At the age of 16 I was busted for robbery and sentenced to three years as a "Youthful Offender." I spent 32 months at Comstock (Great Meadows Correctional Institution) in upstate New York. In 1961-63, Comstock was very racist. No blacks worked in any capacity at the prison. One of the sergeants working at Comstock was the head of the local KKK. My first Political Education came at Comstock. In 1963 I was caught in a serious race riot. The teachings of Malcolm X, who was then with the Nation of Islam, became a big influence on me at this time. After my release, I became involved in Black political activity in New York, especially revolutionary nationalist politics. In 1964 I also became involved in the Cultural Nationalist movement. By 1965 I had joined Malcolm X and the Organization of African American Unity. I began to move with and among many young African Nationalists. My political consciousness was growing daily. I was reading and listening to many Afrikan Nationalists from Africa and the U.S. and became convinced that only after a successful armed struggle would New Afrikans gain freedom and self-determination. I also became convinced that integration would never solve the problems faced by New Afrikans. After Malcolm's death the OAU never seemed to me to be going

394

in the direction I desired. By late '65 or early '66 I hooked up with other Revolutionary Nationalists to organize ourselves for the purpose of implementing what we felt was Malcolm's program. We organized the Grassroots Advisory Council in South Jamaica, New York. We were all very young and inexperienced and got caught up in a local anti-poverty program. By 1967 I was thoroughly disillusioned with "anti-poverty" work, when I heard about the Black Panther Party in Oakland, California. Some of my closest comrades and I decided that this was the type of organization we wanted to be part of. We decided that some of us would go to California, investigate, and join the Black Panther Party if it was what it claimed to be. A few brothers who were prepared to leave did so immediately; those who remained behind began working together in New York. By the spring of 1968, we heard that representatives from the BPP were coming to New York and that there was a possibility of organizing a New York chapter. I attended the meeting and decided to join and help build the Black Panther Party in New York. I became the section leader of the Bronx section, sharing an office with the Harlem section, in Harlem. In the late summer of '68 I married a sister who was pregnant with my second daughter. In November '68 I was busted on trumped up charges of attempted bank robbery. I was bailed out on January 10, 1969, the day my daughter was born. One week later, on January 17, the day Bunchy and John were murdered, I went underground. I was told that Joan Bird, a sister in the Party, had been busted and severely brutalized by the police; furthermore, that the police were looking for me in connection with a police shooting. On April 2, 1969, I was awakened at 5:30 AM by the sound of wood splitting around my door. When I investigated, I found that my house was completely surrounded, with pigs on my roof, fire escape, in the halls, on the street, etc. I was fortunate enough to evade them and go deeper into hiding. I was eventually asked to go to Algeria to help set up the International section of the BPP, which I did. After the split in the Party, caused by COINTELPRO (the FBI's Counter Intelligence Program), I decided to come back to the U.S. to continue the struggle. I continued to work until my capture in October 1981. I was charged with six counts of attempted murder of police, for shooting over my shoulder while being chased and shot at by police. I was also charged with nine predicate acts of a RICO indictment. I was convicted of attempted murder and given 25 years-to-life for that, and I was convicted on two counts of the RICO indictment— the liberation of Assata Shakur and expropriation of an armored truck. I was given 20 years and $25,000 fine for each RICO charge, all sentences to run consecutively. Directly from court, I was sent to the Federal Penitentiary at Marion, Illinois. After 3 years at Marion, I was sent to Leavenworth, where I am now being held. The pig judge recommended that I never be given parole.

Dylcia Pagan To understand why people like myself get involved in national liberation movements, it is of great importance that the observer understand that the evolvement and involvement of a revolutionary is a process that encompasses one's lifetime. I was born on Oct. 15, 1946, in New York City and was raised in El Barrio (East Harlem). Having two loving parents, Delia y Sebastian, who emphasized my "*Puertoriquenes,*" enabled me at an early age to feel secure as to who I was in relationship to overall urban life. Being an only child of a working class family— my father was a plumber— provided certain privileges that most Puertorican children in my neighborhood did not experience. I attended Catholic grammar and high school and was provided with many creative outlets in music, drama and dance. At the early age of 15 I was involved in my community teaching ballet classes to younger children. With the advent of the civil rights movement I became involved in community activism by participating in voter registration drives and other civil rights activities. The early '60s provided me the opportunity to engage in a variety of community projects which were a direct result of anti-poverty legislation. I was a community organizer by age 19, working in housing, health and educational programs which were supposed to be the answer to the disparity of economics and social programs which were lacking in our community. Rent strikes, demonstrations, and takeovers became everyday things for me. At this time I sincerely thought that the jargon "maximum feasible participation of the poor" was the means by which our communities would become self-sufficient and in turn acquire the power to bring about change. In 1969 I had the opportunity to work directly at CDA (Community Development Agency) as an evaluation assistant. I was responsible for assessing all the poverty programs in NYC's five boroughs. As part of a team I went out to see what services were being rendered to the people. It was my first awakening, because the unintended result of a major study clearly pointed out that the recipients of services were not becoming self-sufficient. On the contrary, what was developing was an inter-dependence between the agencies and the people. The mechanisms created by the City of New York were merely paying lip service to the real problems facing our communities. Simultaneously, those of us who perceived ourselves as leaders also became involved in electoral politics. We formed independent parties and created liberal coalitions to see if we could get our own legitimate locals elected. Our financial backing was limited yet we forged ahead to challenge the system and we did get certain candidates on the ballot. Awakening number two: electoral politics was so corrupt and controlled by the regular machine that unless you were prepared to join their bandwagon it was literally impossible to establish and successfully elect independent candidates. By this time I felt the need to further my education and decided to attend college on a full-time basis. I attended Brooklyn College, majored in political science and psychology, and became very active in student activities. While at BC I helped organize the Puertorican Student Union, which was a conglomeration of all the PR student organizations throughout the CUNY system. The end result of this effort was the formation of the Puerto Rican Studies Department controlled by the students. College for me represented a means to survive. I had lost both of my parents and realized I needed some form of credentials to enable me to cope in society. I taught in the educational system at the grammar school level and did a variety of consulting work in community development and the arts. During the late 1960s, NYC experienced the resurgence of organizing around the issue of Puertorican Independence. I became actively involved and participated in demonstrations and study groups. At the community level the Young Lords Party brought to the limelight *"Soy Boricua."* Many community concerns were exposed and of course "Puerto Rican Independence and Socialism" was an issue to organize around, as well as the release of the Five Nationalists. By the early '70s I began my career as a TV producer and writer in an attempt to create positive images of our people. My field of endeavor centered around investigative documentaries and children's programming at NBC, ABC, CBS and PBS. To attain access to the media The Puerto Rican Media and Education Council filed a series of law suits against the major television stations which facilitated the local public affairs programming we have today. My journalistic capacities were also utilized as the English Editor of a bilingual daily, *El Tiempo*. Throughout my life I have strived for qualitative change. My work experience served as the means through which I confronted the contradictions that exist in our communities and society at large. It has been the praxis that has confirmed the necessity for socialism and revolutionary principles. In light of my many observations, I decided to join the clandestine forces for the liberation of my homeland, Puerto Rico. I have borne a son, Guillermo, who has been in clandestinity since my capture April 4, 1980. Presently I am at FCI Pleasanton, Dublin, California, serving my federal sentence of 55 years for the inconceivable charge of "seditious conspiracy." I am a Puertorican Prisoner of War. The biggest sacrifice I have had to make is the separation of my loving son, Guillermo. Yet I am certain that my incarceration has not been in vain because I believe in our struggle and know that Puerto Rico will one day be free and socialist. My son and all our children will be able to participate in a more humane society free from all the vestiges of Yankee Imperialism.

Leonard Peltier A national leader of the American Indian Movement, artist/ activist Leonard Peltier has spent the last 14 years in federal prison as the subject of one of the most controversial law cases in this country's history.

Born on the Turtle Mountain Ojibwa Reservation in North Dakota in 1944, Mr. Peltier is rapidly emerging as a master of Native American art. His passionate self-taught portrait style is an outgrowth of drawing and carving lessons he received as a child from tribal elders. Mr. Peltier was convicted on circumstantial evidence for the shooting of two FBI agents during a day-long siege in 1975 on the Pine Ridge Reservation in South Dakota. As a result of the ambiguity of the evidence against him, Leonard Peltier's case has been the subject of three books. World religious leaders, 60 Democratic and Republican Congressmen, as well as the National Association of Defense Lawyers and over 20 million petitioning private citizens have asked the White House for a new trial for Leonard Peltier.

Prince Cuba This is the only creative, inspirational writing I've done in the 7 years of my imprisonment. The mixed metaphors are a synthesis of theology and politics: my dialectical materialist poetry. And of course, the irony that is my sense of humor. Orphaned at an early age, raised by an authoritarian state bureaucracy of incompetent functionaries, I learned and yearned for personal independence and self-determination. This was to be further enlarged in perspective as my world grew larger, and my identity grew beyond the individual self (ego), the tribal, the national, the international, to the Universal (collective) self. My father came from Cuba with the first wave of anti-imperialist Martís. My mother came from Borinquen, from the same family as Don Pedro Albizu Campos. He, one of the lumpen-bourgeoisie in Exile, reviled Anglo-Saxon culture, while she, taught in English on her native island, attended Tuskegee. I received my primary education in private schools (my education "in Pharaoh's house"). Raised in areas where no Latinos had yet gone, I was raised in the New Afrikan culture and milieu. It was only later that I familiarized myself with the culture, language, and histories of my parents' nations. Having been schooled by the Euro-Americans, and socialized by New Afrikans, with all the contradictions that entail thereto, I think I was afforded, through happenstance, or destiny, a unique opportunity to synthesize the best of all those worlds. Without a doubt, I credit the nature of my upbringing with the world perspective I now hold, which is a Universal perspective. I am not a tribalist, a nationalist, an internationalist, or of the First World, the Second World, or the Third World. I am Universal, and of this One World. I am not relegated to a partial world view, or a sectist, divisionist world strategy. Oppression and capitalist world domination and enslavement is not a tribal, national, international accident of history; but is, itself, a pragmatic world view, predicated upon its own versatility to constantly change and revolutionize and improve its own means of production. Surely, in all honesty, we can recognize that reality and objective historical materialism is not a world view that comes into existence

398

solely through the power of idealistic faith? I hold a world view, a Universal view toward revolution. I believe in and work toward that goal; and having been born within the "belly of the beast," I know full well his nature and his dietary habits. My struggle is here and now.

Alberto Rodríguez I was born in Bronx, New York, on April 14, 1953. My parents, Manuel Rodríguez and Carmen Santana, had been forced to leave their beloved Puerto Rico due to the depressed colonial economy and the widespread repression against workers and displaced peasants during the early 1950s. At the age of 15 I committed my first political act by participating with New African students in a walk-out of high school classes in protest of the assassination of Dr. Martin Luther King, Jr. A year later school was boycotted in protest of the assassinations of Fred Hampton and Mark Clark. These two experiences along with reading Young Lords literature began a process of radicalization for me. I attended the University of Illinois-Chicago Campus receiving a B.A. in political science. During my four years at the university I became active in the student movement protesting the racist and elitist practices of its administration and in support of national liberation. It was at the university that I became profoundly impacted by the history of struggle of the Puerto Rican both in the island and in the diaspora, impelling me to make a commitment to the independence movement. Upon graduation I worked for the Borinqueña Campus, an alternative college program in the community and later at Northeastern Illinois University. During this time I was enrolled at Governor's State University in their graduate program, completing all my requirements for a Master's Degree in Cultural Studies. My arrest in 1983 stopped me from actually receiving my degree. In the seven years that I was active in the community, before being arrested on June 29, 1983, I worked with many organizations and committees. I was active at various points with the Workers Rights Center, National Committee to End Grand Jury Repression, Committee to Free the 5 Puerto Rican Nationalists, *Comité Pro-Orientación Comunal*, National Committee to Free Puerto Rican Prisoners of War, Puerto Rican Cultural Center, Latino Cultural Center, and *Teatro Guanín*. It was this work in the community which demonstrated to me the need for radical political organizing which challenges the political-economic system and raises revolutionary consciousness. I was arrested, along with three *compañeros*, Alejandrina Torres, Edwin Cortés and José Luis Rodríguez, accused of being members of the FALN-PR (*Fuerzas Armadas de Liberación Nacional-Puertorriqueño*), and charged with the impossible crime of "seditious conspiracy." I have assumed before the colonial courts and my people the position of Prisoner of War. I did this to reaffirm the right of Puerto Rican people in defense of their human rights of self-determination and national freedom to wage armed struggle against their oppressor, the United States Government. My claim to POW status is based on international law, which recognizes the right of colonial peoples to use whatever means necessary to achieve freedom, including the use of arms; on the historical reality that the U.S. invaded our island and has maintained control through military power whenever its authority has been threatened; and on the political-moral need of our struggle to clearly challenge imperial hegemony in all its spheres. My imprisonment today is a continuation of the struggle to destroy imperialism and colonialism, which the world has condemned as a crime against humanity, and to contribute to the establishment of a free, democratic and socialist Puerto Rico. (Alberto Rodríguez #92150-024 Unit B-3, P.O. Box 1000, Lewisburg, PA 17837)

Alicia Rodríguez was born October 21, 1954, in Chicago, Illinois. She attended the University of Illinois in Chicago where she studied for three years for her bachelors' degree in biology. Alicia was captured April 4, 1980, along with her sister Ida Luz and other comrades. She is serving a 30-year state charge and has a 55-year federal sentence awaiting her on charges of seditious conspiracy. Since her capture she has artistically contributed to the Juan Antonio Corretjer Puerto Rican Cultural Center in Chicago and she teaches a photography class in prison. Her biography was published in the book: *Puerto Rican Women: A History of Oppression and Resistance*, and John Langston Gwaltney, the famous author and anthropologist reveals part of her life in his book *The Dissenters: Voices From Contemporary America.* (Alicia Rodríguez #NO7157, Box 5007, Dwight, IL 60420)

Ethel Rosenberg and her husband Julius were executed in 1953, allegedly for "stealing atomic secrets," actually for being communists. To the very end, both refused to collaborate with the Cold War inquisition that took their lives.

Susan Rosenberg was born in New York City in 1955. She is a revolutionary, an anti-imperialist, a doctor of Chinese medicine and acupuncture, and a political prisoner. While in high school she joined the High School Students Union, the youth branch of Students for a Democratic Society (SDS). Through that work she was greatly influenced by the Black Panther Party and Young Lords Party. She was active in the anti-war and women's liberation movements. Throughout the '70s she worked in building solidarity with national liberation struggles and Black Liberation and Puerto Rican Independence movements. She was a member of the New York Women's School—a community-based organizing project. She was in a women's singing group that was part of the radical movement's efforts to create an alternative culture. In 1976 she traveled to Cuba to help build a daycare center as part of the Venceremos Brigade in solidarity with Cuban revolution. Susan trained with the Black Acupuncturists Association of North America

(BAANA), a community health center in Harlem dedicated to fighting the drug plague and providing health care through acupuncture and Chinese medicine. Susan was a member of the May 19th Communist Organization. Stemming from the 1979 prison liberation of Black liberation leader Assata Shakur, a massive FBI Joint Terrorist Task Force investigation culminated in 1982 with the targeting of 37 activists in the Black struggle and their supporters. Susan was targeted and later indicted on federal conspiracy charges. She went underground into the clandestine movement. These charges were later dropped. In November 1984 she and Timothy Blunk were arrested, charged and convicted of possessing weapons, explosives, and false identification. They both took the position at trial that they were part of the clandestine anti-imperialist resistance, and that the U.S. is guilty of crimes and international law violations. They were given the longest sentences for weapons possession in U.S. history: 58 years. Susan was one of three women political prisoners imprisoned in the small group isolation basement unit at Lexington, KY— the first explicitly political prison in the U.S. Susan, Puerto Rican POW Alejandrina Torres, and Silvia Baraldini, Italian national anti-imperialist political prisoner, were targeted by the Bureau of Prisons for this experiment. Its goal: the psychological destruction of women political prisoners. After two years of exposure and protest the unit was shut down. After 20 months in this unit, Susan was indicted along with six others in the Washington, DC, "Resistance Conspiracy Case." The seven are charged with "seeking to change, influence, and protest U.S. foreign and domestic policies through violent and illegal means" and with four bombings of U.S. military and government buildings, including the 1983 bombing of the Capitol after the U.S. invasion of Grenada. There were no casualties in these bombings. Susan faces another 40-year prison sentence and is awaiting trial in Washington, DC.

Kojo Bomani Sababu My Afrikan name means "unconquerable warrior, one who takes the struggle of his people to heart." I am a New Afrikan political prisoner. My political persuasion is Communism, and i am actively engaged in the New Afrikan liberation movement. I was in the Black Liberation Army, immersed in the struggle for our land and independence. I sincerely believe our national independence struggle has to culminate in the formation of a state called the Republic of New Afrika, since the problems of oppression for New Afrikans cannot be resolved primarily through multinational class conflict. I was born Grailing Brown, May 27, 1953, to Clarence and Edna Brown, who had nine children. Both were good parents until their deaths. My father was a diligent worker whose only indulgence was loyalty to the bosses. His life was cut short while he was returning home from work during a flood and hurricane. Two years later my mother was brutally murdered, stabbed at least 35 times. It was after my mother's tragic death that i began to acquire New Afrikan consciousness. That was 1964, in Atlantic City, New Jersey. The National of Islam was strong in my community, and as it did for many other Brothers and Sisters, it attracted my interest. It was the Nation of Islam that provided me with my first lesson in nation-building. The NOI placed much emphasis on studying history, which, ironically, later in my life influenced my departure from that organization. The NOI lacked the ability to evolve into a nation— an incredible history lesson. The Black Panther Party had a chapter in Atlantic City in 1968, and i attended a few of their political education sessions. But cultural and religious nationalism continued to dominate my perspective. In 1972 i was sent to New Jersey State Prison. While there i met two people who helped me develop a revolutionary nationalist perspective— Kuwasi Balagoon and Andaliwa Clark. Both these comrades forced me to reread history and to reinterpret it. They showed me how history was made through the actions of the masses, and not through passive rhetoric. Even the civil rights movement, which is presented to us as "nonviolent," was actually characterized by violent confrontations. My only regret in that period was that we had no cohesive ideological upbringing: our politics were eclectic. In 1975 i was released from prison; i returned to the community, and to the Black Liberation Army. In December of that year our unit was destroyed and i and two others were captured during a shoot-out following a bank expropriation. I was charged with attempted murder against two colonial pigs; later, additional charges of liquidating drug dealers in New Afrikan communities were lodged against me. The colonial media tagged me as "leader of a Third World death squad." In 1981 i was transferred to Leavenworth, where i met Comrade Oscar Lopez-Rivera, the Puerto Rican patriot. He taught me much about the history, culture, and contemporary struggle of Puerto Rico, and much about colonialism through the Puerto Rican experience. While at Leavenworth i was charged, along with Oscar Lopez and others, with conspiring to escape using firearms, explosives, and a helicopter. The plot was manufactured by the u.s. government, using prison turncoats, primarily to repress the aboveground Puerto Rican political movement, political attorneys, and New Afrikan and North American anti-imperialist groupings. In this, the government's scheme was mostly a failure. Comrade Oscar and i were held in Chicago for nearly two years while the proceedings and trial around the escape charges went forward. During that time i was married in the Chicago MCC to my childhood sweetheart, Shirley Miller of Atlantic City. My lovely wife struggles with my colonial imprisonment; she is a beacon of inspiration requisite to survival. We have no children. I received 5 years on the escape charges; two Puerto Rican comrades from the public movement, Dora Garcia and Jaime Delgado, received 3 and 4 years respectively. Comrade Oscar, already serving multiple decades for his commitment to Puerto Rican liberation, got a much longer sentence. Currently (1988) i've been incarcerated 13 consecutive years on the various charges lodged by the state. The earlier convictions led to multiple life terms and consecutive years. At each colonial inquest i represent myself, and condemn the bizarre treatment of New Afrikans in North America. Presently i'm at Marion federal penitentiary.

Obafemi Senghor I am in prison for endeavoring to expose this government's complicity in Ku Klux Klan activities by State Prison Guards. I am extremely to the left of the political spectrum. I've never been politically involved within any organizational context. I absolutely hold the philosophical position that only an uncompromising revolutionary violence can bring about a progressive world order. I am extremely anti-religion. Only the establishment of a progressive communist world order can save the world.

Atiba Shanna is a pseudonym used by a member of the BLA-CC. He's imprisoned in Illinois; a Conscious Citizen of the Republic of New Afrika; a communist. He can be contacted c/o Spear & Shield, 1340 W. Irving Park, Suite 108, Chicago, IL 60613.

Standing Deer (*aka* Robert H. Wilson) In 1978 Standing Deer, an Oneida-Choctaw, exposed a government plot to assassinate his compatriot Leonard Peltier in Marion Prison. In 1984 he, Peltier and Albert Garza conducted a 42-day religious fast that brought worldwide attention to the denial of religious and human rights at the Marion political prison. The government retaliated by holding them for 15 months in solitary confinement cages, barren but for a steel bunk and toilet. In 1985 Standing Deer was moved to the deadlocked Oklahoma State Prison which is another state clone of the Marion Control Unit. In spite of the deadlock he remains strong and In Total Resistance. His prophetic piece in this anthology was written about a year before the Marion lockdown of October 27, 1983. (Standing Deer, *aka* Robert Wilson 83947, McAlester State Prison, P.O. Box 97, McAlester, OK 74502)

Mtayari Shabaka Sundiata, a citizen of the Republic of New Afrika and a soldier in the Black Liberation Army, was shot down in cold blood after a gunfight with New York City police, October 23, 1981.

Carlos Alberto Torres was born in Ponce, Puerto Rico, on September 19, 1952. His parents moved to New York, finally settling in Chicago. He studied in the University of Illinois in Carbondale and Chicago. Carlos was one of the founders of the Rafael Cancel Miranda Puerto Rican High School now known as the Dr. Pedro Albizu Campos Puerto Rican High School and participated in the Committee to Free the Five Nationalists. In 1976, Carlos was forced

403

HAULING UP THE MORNING

to go underground and was on the FBI's 10 most wanted list. He was captured along with other comrades and sentenced to 88 years on charges of seditious conspiracy, among other charges. Carlos Alberto is a regular writer for *Libertad*, and his short stories have been published in *Cuentos para la Libertad*. (Carlos Alberto Torres #88976-024, 902 Renfroe Road, Talledaga, AL 35160)

Kazi Ajagun Toure I am a New Afrikan political prisoner who has been held in captivity my entire life. Ever since the mid 60s when i learned about Nat Turner, Denmark Vesey, slave revolts and the history of resistence, i've been of one mind and spirit with Afrikan peoples' struggle for self-determination and freedom. The u.s. government was founded on the genocide of Native people, the enslavement and colonization of Afrikan people, and the robbing of Mexican peoples' land. Our only means of survival is building our New Afrikan nation, fortified by stiff resistence. We must organize our communities and build alternative institutions to meet that communities particular needs, and also be able to defend ourselves and our communities. No people have ever gotten their freedom without a fight. In 1982 i was convicted on federal charges of possession of firearms and sentenced to six years. Later i was convicted of the same charges under state law and sentenced to a consecutive four to five years. I am currently serving a sentence of seven years for the conviction of Seditious Conspiracy— conspiring to overthrow, put down, destroy by force and violence the u.s. government. I am one of the few, if any, New Afrikans to be charged of this act. I will be eligible for parole in October, 1991. Stand Firm . . . Amandla

Dhoruba Bin Wahad, formerly known as Richard Dhoruba Moore, is a former Black Panther and a victim of COINTELPRO unjustly imprisoned for 19 years in New York State.

Albert Nuh Washington has been a political prisoner for the past 18 years. A former member of the Black Panther Party and a BLA combatant, Nuh has been confined under the tightest security in New York State prisons. In spite of the hardships, his spirit remains strong.

Laura Whitehorn I grew up during the era of the rise and victory of national liberation struggles, so my own hatred of oppression, injustice, racism and sexism could be channeled into a productive direction: revolutionary anti-imperialism. I've been in struggles for human rights for a little more than 20 years— from the Civil Rights movement, and the New Afrikan Independence movement, to fighting the KKK and organized white supremacy, supporting the struggle for independence for Puerto Rico, to struggling for the liberation of women and full democratic rights for gay people. In Boston,

404

I helped Black families to defend their homes against racist attack during the "anti-busing" offensive, and I helped to found the Boston/Cambridge Women's School. In New York, I worked to expose illegal FBI counterintelligence (COINTELPRO) and was a member of the John Brown Anti-Klan Committee and the Madame Binh Graphics Collective. A visit to Vietnam in 1975, in an anti-imperialist women's delegation, confirmed my belief that socialist revolution lays the basis to fulfill human needs and creativity— including achieving peace and justice. Over the past 20 years, the intransigence, corruption and aggression of the u.s. government has made sustained militant resistance necessary. I've struggled to be part of that, because justice is worth fighting for and the real terrorism of u.s. imperialism needs to be defeated. I've been involved in the clandestine resistance because the government uses the full force of repression to destroy developing opposition. Since my arrest in Baltimore in 1985, I've experienced this first-hand as a political prisoner: held in "preventive detention" without bail, kept in solitary confinement for much of the time, classified as a "special handling" prisoner, because of my political ideals and because I'm determined to live by them and fight for them. I currently face a five-count indictment (for making and using false I.D., assault on a federal officer, and weapons possession) in Baltimore, in addition to the "Resistance Conspiracy" case in DC. I have been held in preventive detention since May 1985, except for one year during which I served the sentence on the NY conviction (got parole after 1 year).

Richard Williams I have three beautiful children ages, 18, 11, and 8, and am not married. I was born in 1947 in Beverly, Massachusetts, a small coastal city 25 miles north of Boston. My mother was a factory worker and seamstress and my father was a machine operator. I have one sister younger than me by six years. Just when the draft was getting heavy for Vietnam I turned 18 years old and promptly received my notice. Like most working class kids, white or Black, there was no easy way out of it. Either get drafted, join, or hide. I chose not to go. At 20 years old I was arrested for having marijuana, which in Massachusetts was a felony. Given the choice of six months in jail or joining the army, I went to jail in 1967 and became ineligible for the draft. I continued to have brushes with the law *and* in 1971 was arrested for robbery in New Hampshire and received a seven to 15-year sentence. I was 23 and faced five solid years in jail, at the least. I realized at that time that I was going nowhere fast, that I needed to change something— so I started with myself. I became involved with trying to better the prison conditions I was in, which were deplorable. It was 1971, the year George Jackson was murdered, the year of the Attica Rebellion. There was unrest in most prisons, because overall the prisons were brutal and inhumane. I was elected chairperson of the New England Prisoner Association. Inside, I met with legislators, and participated in food and work strikes and protests for better conditions. I read a lot of history and worked in political study groups. I was locked up, beaten and shipped out for my activities. I learned through study and my efforts that the struggle was much larger than my then-present surroundings. I became a communist. Upon my release I worked briefly with the Prairie Fire Organizing Committee. I went to work for the New England Free Press—a radical print collective—for almost two years. Along with Barbara, Jaan, and Kazi, I was part of The Amandla Concert in Harvard Stadium in 1979. Featuring Bob Marley, Amandla was a benefit concert to provide aid to liberation forces in Southern Africa. My role was as part of a People's Security Force which provided security for the concert. We also did security work for the community—such as house sitting with people who were under attack by racists. We went to Greensboro, North Carolina, in 1979 to protest the killings of CWP members by the KKK. I went underground to join the armed clandestine movement in 1981 and was captured in Cleveland in 1984. *Venceremos!*

Resources

Bulldozer P.O. Box 5052, Station A, Toronto, Ontario, Canada M5W 1W4

Friends of Kathy Boudin P.O. Box 020003, Brooklyn NY 11202-0001

Center for Constitutional Rights 666 Broadway, New York NY 10012

Comité Contra la Represión P.O. Box 61066, Hartford CT 06106

Committee to End the Marion Lockdown 343 S. Dearborn, Suite 1607, Chicago IL 60604

Spear & Shield 1340 W. Irving Park Road, Suite 108, Chicago IL 60613

Freedom for Herman Ferguson Committee P.O. Box Box 393, Brooklyn NY 11238

Freedom Now The National Campaign for Amnesty and Human Rights for Political Prisoners: 59 E. Van Buren, #1400, Chicago IL 60605

MOVE Defense Committee 1630 S. 56 St., Philadelphia PA 19143

National Committee to Free Puerto Rican Prisoners of War P.O. Box 476698, Chicago IL 60647

New Afrikan Network in Defense of Political Prisoners and Prisoners of War P.O. Box 90604, Washington DC 20090

New Afrikan People's Organization P.O. Box 11464, Atlanta GA 30310

Nuclear Resister P.O. Box 43383, Tucson AZ 85733

Nuke Watch P.O. Box 2658, Madison WI 53701

Partisan Defense Committee P.O. Box 99, Canal St. Station, New York NY 10013

Leonard Peltier Defense Committee P.O. Box 583, Lawrence KS 66044

Prairie Fire Organizing Committee P.O. Box 14422, San Francisco CA 94114

Prisoners of Conscience Project—Racial Justice Working Group, Division of Church and Society National Council of the Churches of Christ, U.S.A., 607 Lake St., Evanston IL 60201

Queens Two Community Support Coalition P.O. Box 1354, Brooklyn NY 11247

Research Committee on International Law and Black Freedom Fighters in the U.S. P.O. Box 2085, Manhattanville Station, New York NY 10027

Sedition Committee P.O. Box 4690, Springfield MA 01101

Washington Area Committee for Political Prisoners' Rights P.O. Box 28191, Washington DC 20038